£ 4.95

Sorry, Vessa

VANESSA PERKINS
with MAUREEN OWEN

Sorry, Vessa

CHAPMANS

1991

Chapmans Publishers Ltd
141–143 Drury Lane
London WC2B 5TB

A CIP catalogue record for this book is available from the British Library

ISBN 1-85592-513-3

First published by Chapmans 1991

Photoset by Rowland Phototypesetting Ltd
Bury St Edmunds, Suffolk

Printed and bound in Great Britain by
Clays Ltd, St Ives plc

Picture Credits

Vanessa Perkins (Vanessa Perkins)
Philip returned to work (Peter Wilson, *Harrow Observer*)
Officially Philip's girlfriend (Associated Newspapers plc)
Philip received a High Commendation for Bravery (Metropolitan Police)
Philip's future in the police force was uncertain (Associated Newspapers plc)
Tests at Wright State University (Graham Wood, Associated Newspapers plc)
With lab technicians Brad and Don (Graham Wood, Associated Newspapers plc)
Philip's thirty-first birthday (Graham Wood, Associated Newspapers plc)
At Buckingham Palace (Vanessa Perkins)
On the exercise bike (Graham Wood, Associated Newspapers plc)
Connected to trailing wires (Graham Wood, Associated Newspapers plc)
Philip on night patrol (Graham Wood, Associated Newspapers plc)
Philip wearing the combined system (Graham Wood, Associated Newspapers plc)
Philip posed in uniform (Graham Wood, Associated Newspapers plc)
On a Mississippi river boat (Graham Wood, Associated Newspapers plc)
Philip with Roy Douglas (Vanessa Perkins)

Vanessa with Simon (Vanessa Perkins)
With Donny and Woody (Martin Emerson)
Godparents to 'Little Philip' (Vanessa Perkins)
Christmas 1983 in America (Graham Wood, Associated Newspapers plc)

Introduction

On Christmas Eve 1980, I heard the news that a policeman on duty had been shot and seriously injured. Philip Olds, the name that caught the public imagination and was later to dominate my life, didn't register at the time.

In the section house at Tottenham where I was stationed, someone was planning a party. I was on duty that Christmas and wouldn't be going home. But with a hundred young policemen and women, all in their first years of service, under the same roof, there was no chance to feel lonely.

I had been in the police force for five years and knew violence could happen, but the shooting of a policeman, even if we didn't know him, was a reminder that there was a darker side to the job. One which you deliberately didn't think about, because if you did, you would never be able to go out on the streets.

For us Christmas meant two very different things: the festive spirit, which we were determined to enjoy like anyone else the minute we were out of uniform; and the knowledge that for the police, this is always a busy time. Crimes of violence, especially domestic violence, usually escalate at Christmas.

I was 24 and busy being a young person: working hard and playing hard. I hadn't given a lot of thought to what it would be like to be on the receiving end of an armed attack, or to be with another police officer who was. All I knew was that if it happened, you stayed by your colleague and radioed for help.

That is exactly what PC Laurie Howarth did when Philip Olds, armed only with a truncheon, was shot by a masked raider on 23 December at around ten o'clock at night. Philip and Laurie, both traffic policemen, were patrolling in their car, expecting to return to their garage at Alperton at eleven. Afterwards, Philip was to continue on overtime for an hour or more, driving an Inspector on crime patrol. If anything was going to happen that evening you would have expected it to happen then, while visiting some known trouble spots, rather than when it did.

In need of some extra energy for the hours stretching ahead, Philip decided to buy some sweets and a packet of cigarettes at a shop they were passing in Hayes, Middlesex. The shop, which was also an off-licence, was well lit and stood at the junction of two lanes – Yeading and Willowtree. It looked an innocent enough place. Philip had got out on the pavement, leaving Laurie to turn the car round, when he saw two men about to run out of the shop. Both were dressed in the classic robber's disguise of balaclava masks with slits cut out for eyes.

Seeing what was happening, Philip took his cap off with his left hand to stop it falling over his eyes and drew his truncheon from his right trouser pocket. Having fired a shot in the ceiling and come out empty-handed, one of the raiders was holding a silver-coloured gun, probably a revolver, while the other was clutching what later turned out to be an imitation gun. In an act of almost suicidal bravery, Philip, holding his truncheon in front of him, moved slowly towards what he rightly thought to be the more dangerous of the two. The man, who was about the same height as Philip, raised the gun above his head and slowly brought it down into aiming position just like, his accomplice was to say later, a character out of *The Professionals*. Philip cautioned the man, and, realizing that the dramatic gesture was about to become the reality of a shot fired at point-blank range, turned sideways. When the shot hit him in the left shoulder, puncturing a lung, Philip collapsed on the pavement. At that moment he thought he was going to die. Then one of the men – Philip thought it was the second one – kicked him with a hard boot or shoe in the left eye. Unable to get up or use his legs, Philip remembered saying: 'Police – stand still . . .', and to the man with the gun still standing over him: 'If you kill me there will be twenty-five thousand coppers out to get you.'

He also remembered seeing a dark brown mark on the gunman's hand, something like a tattoo which had at one time been removed. It was bird-shaped, like a swallow, and was on the side of his hand, going to the back of his palm under the little finger. As he felt his lungs filling with blood, Philip remembered thinking he had seen something like that mark before, on a friend.

Hearing the men run off down Willowtree Lane, Philip knew he was paralysed. He was in considerable pain yet felt totally at peace. As he swam into unconsciousness, he remembered that the pavement felt soft and that the stars were twinkling with an incredible brightness. By the time PC Howarth arrived and radioed at once for help, Philip was unconscious.

From the time he stepped out of the police car on his own two legs, to the moment when he found himself lying paralysed on the ground, less than five minutes had gone by. His spinal cord had been severed and he was never to walk unaided again.

This was the shooting of a policeman. A factual account, which Philip was to present in his official statement when the case came to court in June 1981. After I met him, few weeks were to go by without Philip recounting every detail of those moments over and over and over again. The scene became etched into his mind like a video that he would wind backwards and forwards, as though he was never fully going to believe what had happened in such a short space of time.

The man who shot Philip, twenty-six-year-old Stuart Blackstock, was cleared of attempted murder but convicted of wounding with intent to resist arrest. His accomplice, twenty-one-year-old Leslie Cooke, was also acquitted of attempted murder. Both of them were Hell's Angels. Blackstock, who had a lengthy criminal record, was jailed for life. Cooke got seventeen years for unlawful wounding. With remission, both could now be out of gaol.

When Philip died in 1986 from the combined effects of pain-killing drugs and alcohol, he had known that the man who shot him might one day walk free from prison. Once someone has been brought to justice, the police officer has played his part and that's usually that. But to be both police officer and victim, to have given evidence in court and to hear that the man who deliberately pointed a gun at you and fired was not attempting to murder you, is an experience that can never be forgotten. Not for a day, not for a week. Not for the rest of your life. In Philip's case, I never found the words to switch off the memory of those brief minutes outside an off-licence that were to end his freedom as a man.

Now that Philip is dead and nothing can bring him back, I know only that I loved him. The pain, rage and bitterness he felt for the five and a half years left to him, went far beyond the two petty criminals who attacked him. There was something deeply disturbing about the burning frustration he showed at being imprisoned in a wheelchair. Philip felt cheated of a clean and – to his mind – honourable death. He thought his life would have had more meaning if it had ended on the pavement outside the shop at Willowtree Lane. Philip hated being dependent. He hated everything that reminded him of his dependency. Spreading like a poisonous chemical over our love for each other, the volatile emotions of a man who wanted to die yet found so much to love in life, frightened and bewildered me.

Since Philip's death there has hardly been a day when I haven't thought that perhaps if I'd been able to handle things differently, I could have prevented his death. A cruel and unnecessary death, as I have always seen it.

Thinking about the 'if onlys . . .' has not helped. It has taken me five years to come to the understanding that whatever I did or did not do, I could never have healed Philip's damaged soul. Any more than the research he pioneered to help paralysed people to walk again could bring about the complete cure he craved.

Philip was seldom out of the headlines for long during the last years of his life. His bravery in tackling armed gunmen carrying nothing more than a twelve-inch piece of wood earned him the Queen's Gallantry Medal and made him into a public hero. But it was courage of another kind that caused him to remain a household name long after the shooting. Despite obvious physical pain and the less evident psychological suffering, he became a figurehead for seriously disabled people while knowing that the treatment he underwent in America was to be of little avail in his own case.

Philip never pretended to be a saint, nor did he suffer in silence.

A BBC television series about his fight to walk again left three impressions: his courage, his good looks and his anger.

This explosive mixture was Philip's attraction. At parties he had usually been the man who would leave with the best-looking woman. Handsome and charismatic, Philip was also vain. Confined to a wheelchair, the pleasures of the chase were ones he could not easily give up.

Sharing Philip's last years was both a nightmare and an experience of great happiness. During that time he hurt and abused me – mentally and sometimes physically. He wrote love poems and was a tender and perceptive lover. He was well read with an analytical intelligence that would never let any subject rest on face value. He was sociable, a magnet to friends. He was unfaithful yet honest. He was considerate and he was cruel. He was a complex man strung out on a rack of mental and physical suffering.

Philip wasn't everyone's idea of the traditional copper. But how much do most people know of the ordinary policeman? What is a hero made of? If he has weaknesses, don't these make him more human? These were questions people thought about when they saw him on television or read about him in the press. Sometimes, when asked a tactless or silly question, Philip would explode and his replies were unprintable. On TV, he made Desmond Wilcox shudder when he referred to himself as a 'pig-ignorant bloody bobby'. His direct, unaffected emotions and refusal to resign himself to a wheelchair shocked, yet aroused public admiration.

Philip never played for sympathy. But he got it in abundance. Letters, donations and messages of goodwill flowed in from the public. As time wore on and Philip became almost a public figure, many people requested his help and he was able to give as well as receive. While never wanting to act as a symbol, Philip inspired courage and hope in many disabled people.

Through Philip I learned that there is a more acceptable way of life for the paralysed, the disabled whose human emotions are often forgotten. With forethought and imagination, their lives can be made less of a struggle, less humiliating than they are, unfortunately, in Britain today.

Both before and after the shooting of PC Olds, there have been many policemen and women injured and sometimes killed on duty.

At the time, Philip seemed to stand for a certain kind of policeman. The kind whose concern for what is right and commitment to duty would lead him to risk his own life. I am part of the same service and know that this commitment is still the same. But sadly, in the short time since Philip's death, a more hostile attitude towards the police has appeared to emerge.

The following account is a love story rather than a police story. About two 'English bobbies' as they always called us in America, whose relationship was not to run the usual course of true love given to most ordinary couples.

When Philip was found dead at home on that terrible afternoon he had left a message. The words 'Sorry, Vessa' were scribbled on his bedsheets in felt pen. Vessa was his pet name for me when feeling particularly loving or contrite. Sorry – sorry for what? Sorry for the raging anger that had once more exploded round my head as I left the house the night before? Or sorry for taking his own tortured life? I'll never be completely sure.

It is ten years since Philip was shot. It has taken me all this time to make sense of the events that led to so much pain. By writing this book, I hope to free myself of the tormented image of Philip's love and live again. But I can never forget. The only way I can come to terms with what happened to Philip is by remembering what he represented at the time: his courage, his honesty and his humanity. For all his faults and imperfections, people liked and admired Philip as a man. As a policeman, they knew what he stood for. As a figure determined to live with dignity, Philip made disablement more acceptable to society.

The world may forget that policemen are human. That every time they go out on patrol, respond to an emergency or simply stop off at a shop dressed in uniform, what happened to Philip could happen again.

Philip needs remembering.

Chapter 1

The road to Harrow, where I live today, is dominated by the gaunt concrete shell of Wembley Stadium, built between the wars as a monument to the great days of English soccer. Policing it, from FA Cup finals to pop concerts, is the work of the Metropolitan Police division to which I belong. Half a mile away is the Police Traffic Garage in Alperton where Philip was stationed; Kingsbury, where he was born, is further out from central London.

Fifty-seven Eastcote Road, the terraced house where I first met Philip in 1981, is near to Pinner in north-west London and set on a noisy main road.

No longer able to climb the stairs, Philip occupied only the ground floor. The two first-floor bedrooms were unused, piled high with unwanted furniture. He and his wife, Rhona, had separated before the shooting and were soon to be divorced. Philip lived on his own with a constant flow of visitors streaming in and out of the front door.

Tottenham, where I was based at the time, is in the north London borough of Haringey, where the Broadwater Farm riots took place in 1985. It's about ten miles from Pinner, about half an hour's drive, depending on traffic.

Although we were both part of the Metropolitan Police Service, I might never have met Philip had it not been for two American police officers.

Over here on a visit from New York were Joe Millier of the New

York City Transit Police and Chuck Bennett from the Diplomatic Protection department. They had come to see the royal wedding and as many of the London sights as they could fit in. Hearing what had happened to a brother at arms, Chuck had written to Philip, arranging to meet.

Philip had recently been discharged – 'paroled' as he put it – from Stoke Mandeville Hospital and Chuck and Joe were staying at the Tottenham section house where visiting policemen were put up from time to time. When you're abroad, it's natural to pay the local police a visit. And as people everywhere turn to crime for the same reasons, so every police force faces the same problems. Policemen – and women – are much of a breed. They have a special rapport, sharing internationally the copper's sense of humour – often bizarre and sometimes considered in poor taste, but a necessary antidote to some of the more gruesome tasks we all have to deal with.

As usual when there were visitors, we did our best to entertain Chuck and Joe; suggesting places they might like to see and introducing them to people they were likely to find interesting.

As a gesture, I arranged to take them on a real English picnic. Together with Nick Clark, a boyfriend of mine also in the police, we went to Berkhamsted Castle, a few miles out of London. After looking round we took the picnic to a trout lake set in a landscape of trees and lush green fields. On the menu were pâté, salads, home-made fruit salad and ice-cream, fresh bread and cheeses. Nick brought beer and wine. It was a gorgeous summer's day, and the outing a welcome break from the city and its problems. Chuck still talks about the day of his English picnic, all laid out on a special tablecloth – grey with a red trim and 'MP', standing for Metropolitan Police, in large letters in the middle. Chuck mentioned Philip Olds – 'a great guy' – and his plans to invite him over to New York.

About a week later, I had a phone call from Chuck, who was seeing the sights in town. He had been invited to attend the Ceremony of the Keys at the Tower of London and as this was an opportunity no American would willingly miss, asked me to ring Philip, whom he had previously arranged to see, explain the situation and maybe take him out for a drink instead.

Introducing myself to Philip on the phone, I asked him if Nick and I could take him for a drink. As it happened, we already had plans: there was almost always something going on and that night we had arranged to go to a pub in the East End for the farewell party of a friend who was leaving the force and transferring to the States. He hoped eventually to join the California Highway Patrol, which, as it turned out, had also been one of Philip's dreams, having applied for info shortly before he was shot.

Getting out of the car at Eastcote Road, I saw that a wooden ramp had been built over the front doorstep and, for the first time, had a feeling of apprehension. I remembered reading that Philip Olds had been very severely injured. How difficult would it be to deal with someone badly disabled: getting him out of the house and transporting him to the other end of London and back?

At the front door, a security phone had been installed so that Philip could press the buzzer and let visitors in without going to the door. As I said my name, the door was released and I stepped inside, I noticed the inky smell of chemicals in the background. Sunshine streamed through from the kitchen at the rear. There was a dry scrape of metal on wood as Philip came into the hall in his wheelchair.

Neither the wheelchair nor his freshly turned-out appearance made as remarkable an impression as the radiant Colgate smile, the strong masculine jaw and the most intense pair of blue eyes I'd ever seen. He had a wonderful smile, one of those that really work. Raven hair crowned this wondrous creation. This was Philip Olds: twice, three times as handsome as the picture I had seen of him in the paper. Nick hovered in the background as I listened at a distance, it seemed, to my own voice doing the introductions.

If one word was always used to describe Philip throughout his life, it was charm. Apart from his looks, this had much to do with a natural quality of making people feel good about themselves. It wasn't anything put on. He was interested in people and gave out a strong impression of friendliness.

As I talked brightly – perhaps rather too brightly – my heart was doing an impersonation of a roentgenometer on a nuclear testing site. I was thinking: You're *gorgeous*. My legs felt light, weak, as if they couldn't be relied upon to do their usual job of keeping my backside off the ground. I was totally hooked – gobsmacked, or would have been if the word had been invented in 1981. He was

9

heartstopping. It was – to prevent any more inadequate clichés – love at first sight.

At the pub, there was no question of monopolizing Philip. He was the star attraction. This was my first experience of the way people tend to swarm round a celebrity and, of course, Philip was a police hero and this was a police party. Apart from buying rounds of drinks, the bloke who was leaving hardly got a look in. We stayed for a long time. The party went like a bomb. Friends later told me I ignored them, but I remember it as a wonderful evening. The pub overlooked a river and as a full-blooded sunset gradually splattered out into the water, I was slowly drowning in two beautiful blue pools – Philip's eyes across a crowded room. I was as slushily romantic as that. But that's the point about falling in love – there's no being clever about it.

There had been no particular problems about the wheelchair. Philip was quite capable of getting himself out of the chair and into the driving seat of his car which had been fitted with hand controls. It was evident that he enjoyed driving it, feeling at least on even terms with other road users, if not a little superior, having mastered the police system of driving. The wheelchair was then folded up and Nick put it in the back of the car. The reverse procedure on the way back. No problems.

Before leaving Philip at his house that night, Nick asked him to a barbecue a friend was giving in a few days' time. When Nick offered to pick him up, I immediately jumped in and told him not to worry. Afterwards Nick told me I nearly bit his head off. I said that as I happened to have some business in the district that day, it would make sense if I picked Philip up, and swiftly fixed a time.

I had set racing a stable of emotions. As we drove home that night, I knew that although I had no business near Philip's house on the appointed day, I was definitely going to make some business. And after a day on duty, how was I going to get changed in time to collect Philip? Then there was the question of what I was going to wear. I wasn't the sort of girl who'd ever done much about clothes, jeans, jumper and trainers being the norm. I obviously needed some time off to buy something. Perhaps I needed the whole day off. Re-arranging my shifts was the first priority the following day.

The big date started very differently from the way I'd imagined.

Somehow I'd thought that Philip's disability – being paralysed from the chest down, being able to use his arms though not his legs – being a paraplegic in medical terms – was something he had miraculously overcome. That except for the inconvenience of being in a wheelchair, which, a bit like a pair of glasses could be downed and donned as required, he was no different from anyone else.

As I pressed the buzzer, Philip's voice told me to come in, but this time he wasn't in the hallway to greet me. He called out, 'Hang on a minute, I'm in the front room.' After a moment or two, I went in and to my right was a bed with Philip lying on it. He turned round and I saw his beautiful eyes had darkened like storm clouds. He said, 'My plumbing's gone wrong.' There was a wet patch on his trousers and he was fed up and angry. I thought: what am I supposed to do?

The room contained a bed, a TV, a standing frame, some chairs, a commode smelling of chemicals, and, in the rear part of the through-lounge, a dining unit, where I later learned he kept his clothes. Trousers and jackets were on hangers round the room and folded over chairs.

I said, 'Well, you tell me what to do and I'll do it.'

He suggested making some coffee, so I went into the kitchen which obviously doubled as a bathroom as there was a toothbrush and a bottle of shampoo on the draining board. I boiled a kettle on an old and dangerous-looking gas stove. When I returned, he was still struggling away, looking even more fed up. So I took off my jacket and said, 'Here, I'll take the trousers,' cleaned them with soap and water and hung them up to dry. I brought him a bowl of hot water, soap, a flannel and towel and left him to wash. He told me where to find clean pairs of underpants, trousers and socks and, as he got dressed, I saw the leg bag for the first time: what he referred to as his plumbing.

Being paralysed in the lower part of his body meant that Philip had no bladder control and the urine had to be drained into a bag round his leg from a contraption attached to his penis. While I was clearing away the soap and water, he said, 'I bet this is the first time you've ever seen anyone with one two-foot long with a green stopper on the end.'

The joke defused any embarrassment either of us might have felt.

By the time we left, the clouds had cleared and the windows of this man's soul were magnificent again. Losing control of your body, he had said, was the most hateful thing that could happen.

This was the first reference Philip made to his loss of dignity, something I was to discover had a crucial bearing on his state of mental well-being. He had spent many months in hospital undergoing operations, physiotherapy; even psychotherapy, which he had spurned, to help him come to terms with the stark truth told him at Stoke Mandeville: 'You will never walk again.'

He had been only too glad to get out of the place and was now concentrating on coping on his own. He had the assistance of a district nurse, a daily home help and an occupational therapist. But he preferred to rely on friends. They had helped to reorganize the house and if the presence of a commode in the sitting-room was a little prison-like and socially undesirable, to him it was better than enduring the humiliations of hospital. The one big advantage of being home, if only to live in turmoil on the ground floor of his house, was seeing friends and going out with them – freedom from hospital routine. Philip hated to be alone and the nights of pain were the longest and loneliest.

Usually Philip's car was parked on the next-door neighbour's hard standing, at the front of the house, but this time it had been left on the road outside, up a slope. He obviously needed some help to reach it, and having had no experience at all of pushing a wheelchair I thought it might be like a loaded supermarket trolley and gave it an energetic push. I had clearly been overenthusiastic, because, instead of going straight up, the wheelchair, with Philip in it, turned a complete circle and came down again with me still hanging on to it trying to prevent it from demolishing the neighbour's wall.

I found this little exercise quite unnerving – the whole wheelchair might easily have tipped over – but Philip hooted with laughter and explained you had to get 'the damn thing' absolutely straight, otherwise it followed a will of its own.

The second attempt went smoothly and in folding up the wheelchair to stow in the back of the car, I had my first experience of just how heavy one can be. This was a National Health issue and later Philip chose to buy lighter models but the hated wheelchair was always referred to as 'the pram', 'the cage' or 'the prison'. He never talked about it without cursing and I have to admit that later I cursed it as well. Why did it always choose to bucket with rain while we were transferring from home to car, and why did the wheels always choose to spit mud over anything new I was wearing?

At the party I spent the warm summer evening sitting by Philip's side. He might not have had a care in the world. He was entertaining – wonderful company with a fund of funny stories. Once again, I felt as though I had been hit over the head with a cricket bat, thrilled out of my mind to be with him.

'You didn't have to stay by my side all evening,' he said, when we got back to his house.

'No, I wanted to,' I said.

He was lying propped up on the bed. 'I thought that because you'd come over and picked me up, you felt you had to.'

'No, I wanted to stay by your side.'

'Oh,' he said, 'you did . . . ?'

The implications of this cautious little exchange were, in fact, that I wanted to stay by his side forever. Philip always said that I arrived on his doorstep and never left. From that moment, I never made any secret of how I felt about him and I think it was also the moment when we both knew what was going to happen.

For me, Philip's attraction came in three powerfully overlapping waves: the strength of his personality, the masculinity of his looks and the questioning honesty of his conversation. Questions: his talk was laced with them. Why did I say that? What made me think this? My opinion was sounded out in a way that was intense and flattering. His view of the world was fascinatingly different from any I'd heard before. Philip seemed to outshine anyone I'd previously met. Spellbound, I raised any subject that came to mind, just to stay there with him, listening to a power of reasoning that could almost convince you black was white. How easy it was to make false assumptions. He had a way of sharpening the issues which made me realize that with Philip you had to be able to back up your convictions.

We drank coffee and talked into the early hours of the morning. I left with the arrival of the dawn. Then I had to go back to the drab surroundings of Tottenham and to work. Our parting was made with a kiss.

As I got to know Philip, I was eager to hear about his background. What sort of little boy had he been? I learnt it wasn't a particularly happy story.

Once, he showed me a poem he had written for the school magazine when he was at Kingsbury County Grammar School:

Wait pretty bird, I would talk with you.
Yes, I too have known freedom,
Yes, I once played in meadow and forest, brown and green.
There have also been colours in my world.
These stand for my love and life.
But there is black among your feathers.
This stands for my inevitable silence.

I thought it was an extrordinary poem for a thirteen-year-old boy to have written, almost as if he'd foreseen his loss of freedom. Philip wrote poetry throughout his life. At school his best subjects were English language and English literature. He was never a sporty rugby-playing type. When he was sixteen, he was accepted into the Metropolitan Police Cadet Corps at Hendon, a couple of miles from Kingsbury where his family lived. It was the first step in his ambition to follow his father into the police force. Philip Olds senior had been a lifelong officer in the Met, a Sergeant and, in latter years, an instructor at the driving school at Hendon.

They were a police family all through. Philip's grandfather had been an officer and I don't think Philip ever had any ambition other than to join the force. He saw it as a high calling. His brother, Christopher, joined, and when his sister Jennifer was old enough, she joined the Cadets, so at one point all three Olds children were in the police force together. Jennifer dropped out to train as a nurse, then married a police officer in Wales. Now only Chris is still with the Met, an officer with the Traffic Division.

Philip's father had died from a heart attack at the age of fifty-seven, only a few months before Philip was shot. Philip had been devastated. He thought the world of his father. He would say that the only lie his father had ever told him was: 'They don't shoot at

14

the silver buttons, son.' He was glad he never had to tell his father he'd been wrong.

Philip thought his father was the only person who would have truly understood how he felt about being paralysed. He was the person he always wanted in his darkest moods of pain and distress. Philip's parents Audrey and Philip snr., divorced when the children were older. Philip's father remarried to someone much younger than himself and his mother had married again as well.

According to Philip, the effects of his parents' failing marriage had stretched back into his childhood. When he was little, Philip had been the type of kid who went out on the streets to play in the morning and usually finished up round at a friend's house by the evening. According to Philip, as far back as he could remember, there had never been a close relationship between his mother and himself.

In every community there is always some little boy or girl who attaches themselves to someone else's family. This was Philip; the type of friendly, adaptable child who fitted easily into other people's households – was asked to stay to tea and go on outings. If not, he was capable of inviting himself. By all accounts a good-looking and attractive child, he won the affections of various Mums in the neighbourhood. He learned how to flatter and entertain; to understand women and enjoy their company. He was remembered as the local housewives' pet.

According to his teacher, who I went to see after Philip died, he was the sort of bright boy at school who only achieves half his potential. At Kingsbury, he got a satisfactory number of GCE O-level and CSE passes and later in the Cadets, an A-level in English. 'Could have done better,' said his teacher. But Philip was too busy socializing. Even at school, he found it easy to attract female admirers. The discovery of girls and motorbikes more or less took care of his spare-time interests, and his father, also something of a Don Juan on wheels, encouraged him. After that, serious work more or less went out of the window.

He joined the Cadet Corps to get away from home. The vast police estate at Hendon also houses the Police Training College. The cadets receive a course that aims at achievement while trying to provide a well-rounded education. The place is run on the lines of a fairly spartan boarding school but the cadets are not entirely closeted; they go out on a variety of projects in the community, visiting hospitals and working with the disabled and elderly. Philip got full marks in this area. He was good at building up a rapport with people. Only later did he look back at this experience, realizing he had seen the disabled as a race apart.

Moving from the junior part of the training system into the big boys' department at Hendon presented no problems. It was like a home from home and Philip completed the sixteen-week training course without any hiccups. After all, he had been virtually born into the police.

When his parents' marriage ended in divorce and the Olds family dispersed, Philip found almost without realizing it that the police force had become his job, his home and his family. Posted to Vine Street Police Station in central London, he lived at Trenchard House in Soho, a police section house providing accommodation for single male officers.

An area that has long been a centre for every type of vice from prostitution to pornography, Soho can come as a bit of a culture shock to a young policeman fresh from training college. It is a district where close teamwork pays off. As often happens when working closely with someone, Philip struck up a firm friendship with a fellow PC, Michael Williams, whom he called Gus. On the long stretches of night duty that alternate between stupefying boredom and sudden danger, they kept alert by discussing everything from politics to girlfriends. They had their own jokes and got on so well they were almost telepathic. Much of the night-shift was spent in the unrewarding task of handling drunks; often violent and frequently messy – seeing people at their worst. Without a sense of humour and a mate to share it with, you'd go mad.

Once they were called to the rescue of a potential suicide ninety feet up on a ledge outside a Piccadilly store, Swan & Edgar. They got the man back inside, but in the process Gus nearly slipped and was only saved when Philip, precariously balanced himself, grabbed him by the tie. Good thing the ties weren't clip-on like ours today. They got rid of the traditional variety because people in the process of being arrested sometimes tried to strangle the policeman with his tie. It happened often enough to make it worthwhile re-kitting the entire force – 28,000 in the Met alone today. For this rescue operation, Philip was given the Bow Street Award for Bravery, plus £200. Gus and another officer at the scene also received the award. The man they rescued turned out to be deranged and after the case, naturally, they never saw him again or heard if he made another suicide attempt.

Much police work where lives are risked, sometimes pointlessly it seems, is recognized by a system of awards. In all, Philip received five commendations for bravery before he was given the Queen's Gallantry Medal in 1981 after the shooting. He was in hospital when he was presented with the fifth commendation for 'the courage, determination and devotion to duty' he showed on the previous occasion when he chased and arrested a burglar who threatened him with a brick. The burglar got a £100 fine, or in default, three months in prison. He chose to pay the fine.

When Gus got married to his girlfriend and moved to a cosy house in Blackheath, Philip began to see the virtues of domesticity and the happiness it had brought to his friend. A short while later, Philip married Rhona. They had been going out together for some time but were both very young. First of all they had a flat in Edgware, where Rhona was a hairdresser; then they moved to the house in Eastcote Road. The marriage lasted four years.

After a few years on the beat in central London, Philip decided to try the CID. This was a department whose glamorous image and reputation for hard work was matched at the time with hard play and hard drinking. You had to be prepared for endless hours of duty, followed by equally long hours in the pub, sometimes followed by no sleep at all before returning to the enquiry in hand or the next one in line.

When Philip managed to throw up in the Detective Superintendent's car at the end of a tough day, he put the seal of fate on his future with the CID. I also spent some time in the Crime Squad attached to the CID and although the work was motivating, I ended up legless after the first week and look back on the course as an interesting experience if nothing else. Things have changed in the drink department. Younger officers are now more health conscious and the older ones more aware of possible consequences. But in those days, if you joined a bunch of detectives in the pub after a case and asked for a bitter lemon, they'd send you home to Mummy and Daddy.

Philip's father and brother had both specialized in the Traffic Division, and with his acceptance into the department Philip had found his role. The Traffic Division is rather different from other police departments in that their base is 'a garage' rather than an operational police station which has public access, and their duties cover a wider area. It also opens up the freedom of the road, which Philip, with his love of speed and motorbikes, appreciated in full. A traffic cop in his dark blue jodhpurs, shiny boots, white crash helmet and goggles, cuts quite a dash. Philip undeniably liked this aspect of the job. His appearance was always immaculate and colleagues took to nicknaming him Mekon after the cartoon strip. As he flashes gracefully past, 'Black Rat', as a traffic officer is known to other more earthbound members of the service, often appears to lead a charmed life.

To the motorist, traffic policemen are often the most dreaded members of the force. Philip soon found that the hardest thing for any member of the public to accept is any kind of criticism of his or her driving. Traffic officers become accustomed to handling delicate encounters with motorists. 'Why aren't you out arresting criminals?' is the usual cry.

Philip's colleague, Mick Rawson, has been known to produce a chilling answer to this standard question. In fact, if you ever meet up with Mick, now a Sergeant, you will find him extremely ready to explain how, if you happen to be a traffic officer, never a day goes by without a number of accidents to be dealt with. And how, when someone is as dead as if he had been stabbed with a knife, it is of little comfort to the relatives to be told that the victim has been killed by another sort of lethal weapon – a car in the hands of a speed maniac. Motorists are notorious for lengthy arguments where their driving abilities are concerned and Philip once said, 'You can insult a man's wife or kick his dog, but if you criticize his driving, it's as though you're challenging his manhood.'

Contrary to popular belief, by no means all traffic police time is taken up pinching motorists for doing 40 m.p.h. in a 30 m.p.h. area. Often, they will be the first to arrive on the scene of a break-in or any other kind of disturbance because they are mobile and can get there fast. In addition, with 36,000,000 vehicles using our roads, some are liable to be driven by criminals moving stolen property around. London is the centre for many criminal trades and traffic police, always in contact with the main radio channels, may suddenly be diverted to chase armed robbers, follow a stolen car or escort an ambulance at high speed in a life-saving dash across London. After an accident, they attend to victims, inform relatives, direct the traffic and sort out the mess, and are highly trained in technical skills to discover the cause. Giving evidence in court, traffic police-men, with their comprehensive training, are considered 'expert witnesses'.

Given the adrenalin-fuelled life he was enjoying, an early mar-riage, though traditional with policemen, didn't altogether fit the picture for someone like Philip who had all the instincts of a bachelor on the loose.

After a couple of years of marriage, Philip was just spreading his wings. Fatherhood, the one thing that might have diverted his flight, was not to be.

Philip enjoyed the twin pleasures of the chase: crime and women. Like many a young man, he was driven by a need to prove himself. But it had long been obvious that his need was greater than most. Whether demonstrating his courage in the Metropolitan Police or his success with women, Philip was out to make an impression. With his dark good looks, he felt the eyes of women following him as he cruised by on the big white police bike. It mattered to him that they found him attractive.

Philip was frankly vain, but he could also laugh at himself. One of the first stories he told me was self-derogatory.

Posted to a motorcycle patrol one morning, he found his machine out of order. As the only other roadworthy bike available was allocated to the Sergeant, Philip went to plead his case for borrowing it. Philip had already had several mishaps with police motor-cycles – which on one occasion had resulted in a broken leg – and the Sergeant had a strong desire to keep his own vehicle in good working order. If Philip had temporarily run through the fleet, the Sergeant felt that his time would be well occupied with some desk work. It says much for Philip's charm and persuasion that he eventually got his way, and with the proviso that he returned the bike in one piece on pain of death, the Sergeant gave reluctant permission for PC Olds to ride off into the bright sunny day. Having gone about his business, Philip decided to call in at Wembley Police Station to write up his reports and have a cup of tea. The journey along Wembley High Road was uneventful with little traffic around and few pedestrians as the shops were closed. Cruising sedately, he couldn't help noticing his reflection in the shop windows and admiring what he saw: an immaculately dressed officer on a gleaming machine, highly polished boots and silver buttons glinting in the sunlight. What, unfortunately, he failed to notice, was a council sand truck, dead ahead. Colliding with the truck as astonished council workers looked on, Philip somersaulted into a heap of sand which, as he scrambled out, covered his dark blue uniform like bread crumbs stuck to a Wiener schnitzel. The bike, damaged and twisted, lay at his feet.

Needless to say, he suffered for his sins at the hands of the Sergeant whose verbal version of the threatened death sentence was long remembered at Alperton Police Garage as an all-time classic.

Philip had many a tale to tell from his active policing days, which amounted, it seemed to me, to more than the average record of escapades. The stories were always recounted with humour, as though being threatened with a brick was the height of farce, but it became obvious that, a mixture of courage, vanity and youthful high spirits apart, Philip had the knack of all too frequently being in the wrong place at the wrong time.

Philip was twenty-seven when he parted from Rhona. He had just thirteen months in which to enjoy the world, to live the life of Jack the Lad, to be lucky or unlucky as he was the night he jumped out of the patrol car to buy some sweets and a packet of fags.

Philip had been twenty-three when he got married. By the time the bust-up came, there had been a series of girlfriends including a spectacular Greek beauty who was to remain in his life for several more years. Up to this point, Philip had always confided in Gus. The two had a good relationship, talked over problems and vetted each other's girlfriends. Like Crockett and Tubbs they had stuck together, keeping their minds alert on the long night stretches by arguing and getting a rise out of each other. When Philip no longer confided in him about his increasingly complicated love affairs, and he knew that Gus was at odds with him over the rights and wrongs of his infidelities, they were both hurt by the rift. For the time being, their friendship came to a halt.

The close relationship between two people in a police team is something that matters – an irreplaceable friendship. To Philip, Gus had been a stabilizing influence. When Gus went back to the county in which he was born and joined the Norfolk Constabulary, Philip's private life went out of control. His short-lived marriage had been a failure, but his overdeveloped machismo began to attract attention. Always seen to leave a party with the best-looking girl, one fellow policeman described his life at the time as a revolving bedroom door. Despite his disability, this aspect of Philip's character was to be the last to change.

Chapter 2

Surname: Perkins. First name: Vanessa. Date of birth: 7. 10. 55.
Joining: 13. 10. 75. Rank WPS.

The annual report made out on all serving police officers looks
much like a school report, only shorter. Fitted into just one page
are the twelve categories apparently of the most importance to
the Metropolitan Police. There are six grades of assessment,
marked by a system of Xs. In each category a short comment
is typed in the right-hand corner. The report is marked 'In
Confidence'.

Vanessa has four Xs under 'Very good. Consistently above
average': 1. 'Appearance, dress, bearing, personal appearance'
The comment reads, 'Above average in appearance at all times.'
2. 'Temperament, self-control, stability, reactions' – 'Very
calm and stable at all times.' 3. Judgment, assessment of people
and guidance of others' – 'A shrewd judge of character.' 4.
'Reliability' – '100% – can be relied upon to complete any task
competently.'

She also gets six more Xs under the column marked 'A good
standard', including one described as 'Personal relationships,
work with others, social adjustment'. Here the comment
reads: 'Well liked, fits in well, enjoys good working relationships.'

The report is dated 1987, less than a year after Philip died.

After an illness Vanessa had been on what is called 'restricted duties'. Showing that the police have a human face, the Inspector's report concludes: 'Since last year this young lady has been faced with an extremely emotional time in her private life . . . She continues to put a very brave face on her situation and is bearing up extremely well . . . She has a very cheerful personality and I hope that when her problems are resolved she is able to return to full duty – where she has proved herself in the past to be a very capable supervisory officer in every respect.'

Soon afterwards, Vanessa returned to full-time duty, once again proving herself to be the capable supervisory officer so caringly described in the Inspector's report. To go back to what happened in the meantime, is to see a girl from a stable background whose not unusual fate was to fall in love with a police colleague but who was to meet a series of extraordinary and heartbreaking challenges. The simple love story that was to bring with it an avalanche of sorrows began with a choice of career – a career in which a group of ordinary people are asked to do extraordinary things in the name of public service.

I had the best start in life any child can be given. I was one of three much-loved children of parents who have always been devoted to each other and their family. Born in Paddington in 1955, I was in the middle of an older brother and younger sister.

My father, John Perkins, was a lifelong policeman and my mother, Georgina, had been a nurse at Westminster Hospital before becoming a full-time Mum.

I didn't have a burning ambition to be a policewoman. I could just as easily have wanted to be a nurse, or a doctor. I enjoyed science at school, but the real thing was, I hadn't the patience to spend years qualifying. I wanted to get out in the world. I wanted variety and, in a way, the police does give you that. No two days are ever the same.

My brother, Chris, is a teacher, following at one remove from a grandfather who had been a headmaster. Chris is diabetic and always needs insulin injections. My mother showed me, as a child, how to inject a syringe by practising on an orange – I suppose in case Chris ever needed a jab when we were at school together. Anyway, it never happened. Chris would have run a mile if he'd seen me coming at him with a needle. Being a nurse, Mum was wonderful if any of us were ill. Chris sometimes had to go to hospital and Mum would take me along. It can be quite disturbing for a child to walk into a paediatric ward and see other children who are seriously ill, with drips and so on. But Mum always explained very carefully what was wrong and what was being done to make them better, so I grew up hearing quite a lot about the medical matters and was not at all frightened of sick people. Mum had an instinctively reassuring approach. Fear of illness and disability makes people uncomfortable, so they tend to avoid the disabled. Learning from my mother that there was a way to cope and care was later helpful in the job; at least I never fainted at the sight of blood! It also played a part in my relationship with Philip.

Dad has a wonderful sense of fairness. He'd always put both sides of any argument and never tried to make up our minds for us. Bringing up children to stand on their own two feet, making them independent, means letting them come to their own conclusions, making their own mistakes if need be, but always letting them know that advice and, above all, interest, is on hand.

When I first joined the police force, I was green enough to think that everyone had more or less the same outlook. Some may be richer or poorer or perhaps had divorced parents but I didn't think it made any great difference. I thought that if there were any strains or problems, everyone did the same as Chris, my younger sister, Tracey, and I always did at our house in Eastcote, near Pinner – just sat down with Mum and Dad and talked things over.

The first big lesson I had to learn was that the majority of people who are in trouble with the law for one reason or another don't have what seemed to be this very ordinary background. I thought people got into trouble through some big mistake, a slip-up of some sort, which could obviously be put right after a chat or something. Well, it can happen that way sometimes. For instance, when an old age pensioner on a low income sees a tin of salmon on a supermarket shelf and can't resist the temptation. It's a luxury to her, an extravagance she can't afford, and in a couple of seconds she falls for it, pops it into her handbag. If she's caught and there's a fuss, she'll probably never do it again. The disgrace is terrible.

Obviously, it's quite different from a life of organized crime. I think the main difference is that to most people, getting caught up in any sort of crime is a nightmare. If I'd slipped up over something, I'd have been ashamed for my parents to know about it, but a child whose parents are otherwise occupied or don't care too much what he's up to may decide to take risks.

Not that I was exactly a goody-goody. Out of the three of us, I was the most adventurous – always climbing trees or playing with the boys; the despair of my mother who sent me off to school clean and neat with plaited hair and snow-white socks and saw me come home a wreck with hair ribbons lost, my knees smothered in mud.

I learned that I would be no good as a criminal at the age of about ten. I sometimes went to stay with my best friend, Mandy Smith, who lived only a few streets away, and as an occasional treat we were allowed to have a midnight feast. Both mothers were in on it, in fact, Mum had made a cake and Mandy's mother provided crisps and lemonade.

Perhaps these kindly gestures took the edge off the excitement. What was wanted was some element of a forbidden feast: chewing gum – horrible and naughty, disapproved of by one's parents – seemed a brilliant idea. Moreover, I'd heard from schoolfriends about a trick whereby they'd been getting it for free. They simply went to a machine outside a local shop, pretended to put money in the slot, pulled at the empty drawer then went inside and told the shopkeeper they'd lost their tuppence or whatever it was. He then handed over a packet of chewing gum. It always worked. Criminal that I was, I decided to try it. I didn't even have tuppence with me, but after rattling the machine I went into the shop and reeled off the patter: 'Excuse me, I put tuppence in your machine and didn't get any chewing gum back.'

The shopkeeper looked at me with intense interest. 'Oh really?' he said. 'Would you like to come outside and show me exactly what happened!'

This wasn't supposed to happen. Cheeks reddening, I had no alternative but to follow him. He took me over to the machine. It had a bar across the slot. You couldn't put any money into it. I took to my heels.

For a week afterwards I had nightmares, expecting a knock on the door and a uniformed policeman breaking the news to Dad that I was about to be arrested.

My life of crime was over.

Most of the time, I didn't think of my father as a policeman. He never, as they say, 'brought his work home with him'. Or at least, nothing that we got involved in. He went to work in plain clothes and changed at the police station. A lot of people do that, mainly, I suppose, because you fit in better with the neighbourhood. On the very few occasions I saw him in uniform I was very proud of him.

From the age of eleven, I was totally taken up with school, Northwood Secondary Modern. I was interested in just about everything. I did quite well in English, French, drama, science and art. Ended up with 14 GCE and CSE Grade I O-levels, an RSA diploma in Spoken English and became deputy head girl. It was co-ed. I enjoyed drama and games, flirted with the boys. I thought school life was brilliant. My only problem was what project to choose next. For a time I got involved with running the library. There were lots of other projects. Never a dull moment.

One of the things I enjoyed most was an Outward Bound course in Wales. Sometimes we went without tents and slept in the open with sleeping-bags covered in a sort of binliner called a Polybag. Both Philip and I did courses in Snowdonia and whereas Philip actually had a tent but hated the whole thing, I loved it. Once you've done your clamber round the rocks and got down again safely, there is a sense of achievement. I even enjoyed the reconstituted food we took with us in packs. In fact, mixed with water taken from a stream as transparent as a veil, then cooked over a campfire, it tasted like the world's most delicious dish. It was so good that when I came home, I served it up again, promising my parents a new gastronomic treat. It was quite a lesson in life to discover it never tasted the same as it had in Snowdonia.

I was enjoying myself so much at school, I didn't realize it had to end. An exaggeration, but after leaving in 1971, I went straight back next term to work as a lab technician. I was employed by the

Local Authority and felt very grand. But it was only a temporary job and I was faced with the usual questions about a career. At school I had been what is known as a good all-rounder, but had never specialized in anything: a jack of all trades. So unable to come up with anything much in the way of future plans, but wanting to get out into the big wide world, I took any job that sounded even faintly adventurous. I worked as a barmaid in Alderney (and can still pull a pint), then managed to convince a couple who had lived near us in Eastcote and were going to America that I would make the ideal nanny for their two small children.

The mother was an MA in maths and the father a professor of statistics. They were in Minnesota, the state of a thousand lakes and here it was I met my Waterloo. When I arrived the lakes were frozen. It was 57 degrees below freezing. The lakes were so solid that huge bonfires were lit on them for skating parties and there was absolutely no danger. I couldn't believe my eyes, but nothing could melt that ice. The chill factor sometimes made it seem even colder than it really was. While waiting for the bus on an excursion into town, it was so cold it was painful to breathe in. In the icy, swirling wind my ears ached and I found that every time I blinked it felt as though a couple of pieces of sandpaper were being scraped across my eyeballs.

Going out with the children meant you had to swaddle them up like a pair of papooses and after crunching through the ice to watch the skating parties, there was nothing much I could think of to do with them. You had to make special arrangements to go out anywhere and with the parents out at work most of the time, I was confined to the house with the children for days on end.

At seventeen and mainly concerned with enjoying myself, I was too immature to be left in sole charge of two tiny tots all day. I had little in common with the parents. After a few months, by mutual agreement, I left.

After this, I went to stay with distant relatives on the north shore of Lake Erie in Canada where the lifestyle promised to be less confining. It wasn't long before I found a challenge. Riding an extremely strong-minded horse, I took a nose dive and had to go to hospital. Then I ran out of money.

When Mum and Dad met me at London Airport, I had a broken nose, stitches in my face and a noticeable limp.

'She's been mugged!' shrieked my mother, as I limped through customs, empty-handed and penniless. This was an example of where Dad's advice had been weighed in the balance, then cast aside. He'd always thought I'd been too young for the job and the trip on my own and arriving back like this, I hadn't exactly proved him wrong.

When I was better, I painted the outside of the house to prove I could get something right. I also did it in lieu of keep. No one had asked me to, but one of the house rules I'd grown up with was that everyone did their bit. Without a job, the last thing I wanted to feel like was a freeloader. As children we'd been expected to clean our rooms and keep them tidy, rather than letting Mum wait on us, so even if the rooms weren't one hundred per cent, we kept each other up to the mark. The same applied to taking our turns at washing up and generally not being a strain round the house. It was a small semi in a quiet close where, as we got older, we could ride our bikes and play with the neighbours' children.

I joined the police force for no more compelling reason than it was the first thing to come up. I'd still been toying with the idea of nursing, in particular Queen Alexandra's Nursing Corps, or the WRAF or navy. I also enquired about Customs and Excise. I wanted something with a very definite career structure, not just a job. I sent off for application forms for both the navy and the police, and the police form came back first. The main thing I was looking for was diversity and in the police you're not stuck in one trade, as it were. If you get into a branch and it isn't what you want, you can come out of it while staying within the same sphere. There are dozens of branches in the police force and, like a starfish, they are always creating new ones while dropping others in the name of flexibility. From Crime Squad and Close Protection, which means guarding VIPs, to Dog Section, Mounted Branch, Drugs Squad and Special Branch, who collate information of a political nature, there is a huge choice of specialist fields. Uniform duty, while sounding the most prosaic, offered, I reckoned, the widest scope. At least you don't see the same people or types of people every day. Dad, as usual, didn't try to encourage or discourage me. He gave me the good and the bad news about policing, answered any questions I wanted to know and left me to make up my own mind.

First came an interview at Paddington with a rather awe-inspiring row of officers all of whom asked me questions. Mum had made me a bright yellow dress for the interview with a yellow tie to match and I sat there feeling rather like a banana. Apparently I got a chuckle out of them, which is reckoned to be an encouraging sign although, of course, you don't exactly sit there cracking jokes like Dave Allen. To be accepted you need five O-levels, including English and maths. The more intangible qualities such as character and perseverance are assessed later.

I spent the whole day there having medicals and eyesight tests. They like you to be fit, not overweight, and a prime factor is that you have to be – for want of a better word – honest. Since then, entry conditions and selection procedures have changed but references have always been required and your background looked into. It is easy for the police to check on criminal records.

Hendon in 1975 had, much as it has now, the bustling atmosphere common to all training establishments. My first impression was of high-rise buildings and spartan surroundings full of all types of people, the men all being over five feet eight, a requirement that no longer applies.

We were all allocated identical rooms, approximately nine feet by eight, which contained the bare essentials: one bed, top and bottom sheet and folded regulation blankets; a wash basin; cupboard and desk with three drawers and one chair. There you sleep and study. There are communal bathrooms and ironing rooms. The police are perpetually ironing. Male recruits are required to be clean-shaven with faces as smooth as a baby's bum and beards allowed only if fully grown and trimmed.

The unofficial endorsement of this rule led to one recruit, whose wispy attempts at a beard had not come to full fruition, being held down by the others who smothered his face in Immac. Clearly there were to be no half measures in the police: either someone grew a beard in his time off or his efforts were cut short.

At 6.30 in the morning we were roused from our cells and given a school-type breakfast, which didn't include toast. After this it was out on the parade ground to be inspected by a senior officer for turn-out and smartness.

The sixteen-week training course, now extended to twenty weeks, includes rigorous drilling. It was at this point that I begun to wonder what on earth I'd done. Our drill instructor, Sid Butcher, looked about ten feet tall, with a ramrod-straight back and flourishing a swagger stick. His voice travelled for miles as he barked out the commands. Every class had the inevitable recruit with a co-ordination problem. We had one who could only manage to swing his right arm together with his right leg, attracting the close concern of Sergeant Butcher, who marked his sleeve and trousers in chalk with left and right signs, causing a certain amount of entertainment for the rest of us.

There was also PT and swimming. Even if you didn't know how to swim when you arrived at Hendon, you learned by the time you left, just in case, presumably, you ever had to dive in and rescue somebody. Even if police only have to march on rare ceremonial occasions – the Queen's birthday for example – we all had to be able to march as though in the army. Then there are weekly exams. All the instructors have been police officers on the beat so are not just talking from text books. They tell you how things happen. You take it all in and write it all down but sadly, once out on the beat, you forget it. You have to learn from your own experience. Then what you've learned in training college, comes back to you.

Kitted out in our blue uniforms, nothing seemed to fit the new intake as well as it did the confident specimens I'd seen patrolling the streets.

The men had to learn how to wear their strange corked domes without looking as if they were precariously balancing coal scuttles on their heads. The women had to adapt to the flat and spinsterish-looking lace-ups, which when new feel as though you're paddling along in a pair of twin canoes. Later on, you're grateful for the comfort.

The phrase 'not a hair out of place' must have started with the police. Regulations state that for WPCs hair must be worn off the collar. You can wear your hair long or short, but with long hair like mine I had to learn how to twist it under my cap so that no stray locks escaped. This is for safety as much as smartness. Hair ripped out by the roots by someone in a fight can be extremely painful. A plait, which I sometimes wear off duty, is likewise an open invitation to having your hair pulled. You have to think of everything. The real problem about hair comes when you've had it short and are growing it so that it's too long round the collar and too short to tuck under your cap. No one has managed to solve this problem as far as I know.

I felt neither smart nor unsmart in my new uniform. I just hoped I wouldn't look stupid wearing it because walking round the streets in uniform you are immediately high profile. Compared to wearing the blue, you feel anonymous in plain clothes. The change which comes with uniform is more than just cosmetic. People react to you in a completely different way, yet you're the same person. The first time I sensed the reactions, I had mixed feelings. I felt like saying: 'Here I am, someone who will help you deal with your problems.' Then when I realized people just reacted to the uniform I wanted to say: 'Underneath this outfit there's a real person, you know. Don't just look at the uniform.'

Despite all the marching around and inspections – 'When did you last clean your shoes?', that sort of thing – the army atmosphere ends with the more democratic structure of the police. Everyone starts off equal and there is no officer class. Promotion is on merit and examinations. Many of our senior officers have come from working-class backgrounds and you respect them because they have worked their way through the ranks.

You are a police *officer* as soon as you pass out of Hendon and I departed with a brand new uniform and a certificate to prove it. Unfortunately, I missed both the passing-out parade where Sid Butcher's drilling techniques finally came to fruition and the full evening dress graduation party, a spirited affair where each group of recruits celebrates to the full while the authorities turn a blind eye. My grandfather had died and together with the rest of the family, I attended his funeral in Worcestershire where he had been a much-loved headmaster at a village school. I was to miss his wise counsels and regretted he would never see me in the uniform of a public service that to me at that stage had much in common with the ideals of the other family professions, teaching and nursing.

The uniform I was to be wearing for the rest of my career – give or take some exchanges as it wore out or was altered – had been selected with some care. You are shown into a storeroom with all the garments stacked according to size. You try everything on, making sure it fits properly rather than admiring yourself in the mirror. My first impression of the famous blue serge was that it felt extremely stiff – a bit like a cardboard cut-out. But I found the uniform became more comfortable with wear, rather like a pair of slippers. Not that it must ever resemble a pair of old slippers. It was impressed on us that we were always expected to look smart – no creases, sharply pressed pleats and, of course, no laddered tights. Nothing shows a hole or a ladder more than black tights, so from the first I always kept a spare pair in my locker.

The uniform comes free apart from the tights, which you buy yourself and for which you get a uniform allowance. Trying on the uniform, I found the sizes seemed to vary a bit. I am a normal size twelve but have wide shoulders so the top half of a garment doesn't always fit. You are unlucky if you are mid size because you have to choose it slightly too big or else too tight. Whatever size you choose, skirts must just cover the knee. The work of a WPC is not just seeing old ladies across the road and you have to bear in mind that when it comes to 'active policing' – that is, any sprints, scrambles or struggles – skirts that ride up or jackets that burst open under the strain can, at the very least, give an undignified impression. I had learned self-defence at Hendon, mainly a matter of official holds, a restraining technique rather than a method of attack, but this had been practised wearing tracksuits. Getting used to wearing the uniform – looking confident in it and not feeling restricted by it – was something to be sorted out in the two-year probationary period that lay ahead.

Part of the Hendon course had included a week in a real police station where you go out on the beat with a fully fledged bobby. It was good because you work with a team of chaps who will answer your questions on the spot and don't mind if some of them sound a bit dumb. I was sent to Edmonton in north London with another female recruit, and while we were there they had a leaving do for one of the chaps which went on till the small hours. As luck would have it, we were on the early shift which means 6 a.m. and of course we overslept and had to be dug out of bed. Oversleeping is one of the transgressions that can earn you a very black mark at Hendon, but if it didn't go on our reports at least it was an introduction to the hard work hard play social ethic of the police force. It takes time to get used to it. Every birthday, transfer or promotion is an occasion for a party, which is fine when you're young but you have to learn to be able to take it.

After Hendon, I was pronounced suitable material to be moulded and prodded into shape, hopefully to emerge as one of the 3,000 or so women police officers who are now on equal terms with the 23,000 or so police men who make up London's Metropolitan Police Service.

Although we had received the basics at Hendon during our sixteen-week course – how to patrol, how to investigate a case, how to prepare reports and the importance of writing everything down and in what order – it takes a little longer to learn the subtler arts. How to talk, act and even move in relation to the general public is not easily taught. As with a lot of other things, you only learn with experience and that experience has to be absorbed into your own personality.

You are often the bearer of unpleasant news. This includes having to tell relatives that someone close to them has been killed. If it's a child in a road accident, it's extremely distressing, one of the worst things you are called upon to do. While being of as much positive help as you can, the sympathy you feel has to come from your own personality. One of my first experiences was seeing a child flung across the bonnet of a car. A group of them had been playing 'last across' on a main road and I was dealing with the effects of that death on the motorist as well as the parents.

The first time I was told to break the news of a death I said, 'What am I going to say?' It's not something that can be rehearsed. Being the bearer of bad news is a job nobody likes.

When I first started it was usually a job that was passed down the ranks to a WPC on the grounds that women are better at these things. I don't know if it's true. In fact, I've often thought that the presence of an understanding family man can be of just as much comfort to bereaved relatives – a kind and solid shoulder to cry on. And people do cry on police shoulders. You're told you shouldn't get too involved, but if you're not involved you can't do the job as it should be done. You can't just stand back, tell someone the bad

33

news and that's it. You have to go in, prepare them for a shock, say there's been an accident and that someone close to them has been killed. You're bringing people the worst news they could possibly hear. It's horrible. Then you stay with them for as long as it takes. They often show you photographs. If you've seen the smashed-up body it's doubly difficult. I often had a lump in my throat but you're no use to anyone if you crack up as well. You have to be the one organizing everything. You can't just leave someone on their own so you try and find other relatives or friends to come in.

I used to long to be able to knock at someone's door and give them some really terrific news – tell them that they'd won the pools or something. But apart from occasionally returning stolen goods there wasn't much scope for being a little ray of sunshine.

A high proportion of people who come to the attention of the police are mentally not responsible for their actions. They have to be dealt with as well, and carefully because you can't always second guess their reactions.

After a few weeks in uniform I was beginning to believe that all the job was about was the dead and the deranged. I wondered how long I was going to last.

One of the first things to get used to is the shift system, known as a relief. Duty hours are usually composed of three shifts: early turn, 6 a.m. to 2 p.m.; late turn, 2 p.m. to 10 p.m.; and night duty from 10 p.m. to 6 a.m.

Probably the least popular shift is early turn, but once I got used to it I didn't mind because it means having the afternoon to yourself to do whatever you like. As I like to get to the station half an hour or so early to sort myself out and get an idea of what's been happening, I found that early turn meant getting up around 4.30 a.m. I also found it was no good having a sleep when you got home because you're liable to lose track of whether it's six o'clock in the evening or in the morning. It's better just to have an early night but I didn't take much account of that when I first started.

On night duty the busy time is after the pubs and clubs close and the fights have been settled one way or the other. This is followed by a quieter period and any calls that come in thereafter are usually serious. On a relief you can be on a walking patrol or driving, on communications, or any special posting required on that day.

You work nine days on duty, followed by two days off. It's hard luck if you are needed to appear in court on a day off because you don't often get a whole day off in lieu. An entire weekend off is a comparative rarity. The shifts are rotated weekly between the thirty officers on my relief and the worst time is when a night-shift ending at 6 a.m. is followed by the new shift which starts at 2 p.m. the same day allowing a bare six-hour rest. This is when the bags under the eyes really begin to show.

The problems of human beings don't always fit neatly into shifts and overtime is inescapable because you can't just sign off in the middle of an incident. As a result of the hours, relationships outside the force proved really difficult. This was no immediate problem when I was first posted to Tottenham. Living in the section house, males outnumbered females by about fifty to one.

I had boyfriends, but no serious boyfriend. I was very flighty. If someone annoyed me, I'd go out with someone else and if he got heavy or possessive, there was always someone else.

We were nearly all young, and were a very sociable group, game for a laugh and any fun that we could find. Off-duty time was a round of parties, nightclubs and sports. The attitude was that life was to be lived. All that made us different from any other group of young people was that we had an added responsibility. So trouble with a capital T had to be avoided at all costs because it would mean an end to our careers.

Although there were the short-lived flings with boyfriends, the longest lasting friendship I formed at Tottenham was with another woman officer, Elaine Smith.

As a change from the rough and tumble of communal police life, Elaine and I would sometimes go out together for a drink or a meal. We would decide beforehand what role we were going to play for the evening, so that if we met any chaps who weren't in the police, no one would picture us in the blue serge. The reaction to finding that we were uniformed policewomen had generally been irritatingly predictable. A bit of a turn-off, you could say. We'd pretend to be something ordinary like shop assistants or typists. Sometimes the magic wand would turn us into more glamorous figures in the advertising world. Or we were PAs, enabling us to be even more mysterious as nobody knows exactly what they do. We also had a go at being diamond dealers, law students or brokers in insurance and commodities.

Often, it would be quite a laugh just trying to sustain the image. We'd be sitting at a bar or in a restaurant and a couple of guys would chat us up and start asking awkward questions. Elaine and I would exchange glances over the table and try to keep straight faces as one of us launched into a terrible long tale. We couldn't always keep it up but it added an extra edge of fun to the evening.

When on occasion we revealed ourselves in our true colours, there was almost always the standard reaction. They'd duck and say, 'Ooh, are you going to arrest us?' Another form of unconscious abuse was to tell a story about some friend who was always unfairly accused of some offence or other – 'He was only doing this or that' – always a perfectly innocent chap. You'd find yourself being asked to act as judge or jury on a case about which you were only hearing a distorted version. It got dead boring.

Although women make up twelve per cent of the force and are accorded equal pay and respect, a lot of men have a problem about thinking of them as butch and unfeminine. A WPC can be a dream of feminine beauty in her off-duty clothes, but try telling a bloke you've just met at a party what it is you do for a living and the reaction is always the same: 'Ooh, are you going to arrest me? . . . Can you do judo? . . . Where are the bracelets?' and so on.

You get accustomed to this routine form of chauvinism. Best just to swallow the next cup of coffee and smile.

The public image of being a law enforcement officer is that we are seen as doing 'a man's job'. To say that it's a people's job is closer to the truth because people vary and that includes police officers – male and female. There are many occasions when the man's approach provokes instant hostility and it is felt it might help for someone to talk to a policewoman who can say, 'Come and sit down and tell me all about it'. But it also happens that some policemen come across as more sympathetic. So much depends on the individuals involved. The same as in any other walk of life really.

Women doctors and barristers might get a bit of the old chauvinism and I expect women bus drivers do as well, but I can't think of another role that provokes the chaps as much as that of a policewoman. Unlike a nurse, for instance, who is looked upon as sympathetic and caring but might well be an iron disciplinarian on the wards. To some men, the thought of being stopped by a woman and having their liberty taken away comes as a bit of a blow to the machismo.

All in all, it's not surprising that many women police officers tend to marry their male counterparts. At least they understand the unsocial hours and are not going to ask if you're going to arrest them. We really are on equal terms though, come to think of it, I've yet to hear of a male PC staying home to look after the family while the WPC goes back to work. But I'm sure it will happen eventually, particularly as women officers are achieving the higher ranks.

The first two years in any new recruit's service are spent on the beat. You're supposed to walk at about four miles an hour, though not with feet turned out at an angle of fifty-five degrees like they do in *The Bill*, I hope. The measured tread is aimed at a combination of looking as though you have a firm destination in view while seeming to be approachable. Your eyes are scanning all the things that wouldn't be noticed just going past in a panda car and you're using all your senses.

It is also a good idea to look upwards from time to time, because it's not unknown for bottles and other objects to descend without warning from windows high above your head.

One of the first things I learned when first going out in uniform on the streets was that although I considered I was there to help people, there were others who saw me in a different light.

I certainly didn't expect in my first week to be presented with an apple – dropped from the top of a high-rise block of flats. If you dropped a penny from the Empire State Building, it would crack a plate in half. As far as physics are concerned, I don't know how much an apple would weigh coming from twenty-four storeys up, but I was walking along one bright and sunny morning when this apple hit the ground in front of me, stinging my legs right up to the knees like shrapnel.

You realize that in uniform you have a fairly high profile, but I hadn't thought that I looked either frightening or aggressive – but then I certainly hadn't been expecting an unprovoked attack either.

You can hardly be prepared. It's extremely frustrating because you look up and there's absolutely no way you can see whether it was a child or an adult who did it. Okay, it was only an apple. But that's not all that has come out of a tower block: we've had three-piece suites, a television and milk bottles. All you're doing is wandering round on your beat or making enquiries, and you're a target.

Sooner or later, the day comes when you have to put all the paperwork you've learned since leaving training college into action. You've got your first case. You've taken your official notebooks with you everywhere and written things down, you've practised writing reports, but you've never actually charged anyone or appeared in court.

My first appearance in court was probably the most embarrassing in my career. Some young mothers had reported that, as they took their children over a crossing after leaving school each day, there was a young man at the window of a nearby building who masturbated in full sight of the little procession.

This was hardly a CID case so I was sent along: I had no trouble getting into the building and arresting the man in question. Most people do not take kindly to being arrested, but in this case there was little resistance. However obvious the crime (and this chap had been caught red-handed, so to speak), all details have to be clearly documented by the police because if there is anything incorrect about the procedure, a solicitor can have the case overturned in court. Accordingly, I knew that I must try to get a statement. When I took a statement under caution, a more straightforward admission of guilt in an indecent exposure case could hardly be imagined. The man said quite clearly, 'I enjoy wanking in front of women.' He was then charged according to the book and I wrote it all down as evidence. Mission accomplished.

Later it dawned that I would have to read this statement out in front of the court. As the moment drew nearer, I began to have extreme doubts about whether I was going to be able to repeat these words in the calm, factual tone of voice customary in court.

It being my first court appearance, the word had got about and I entered the room to see the place crowded with smirking uniformed colleagues, arms folded and eyes trained on the new recruit to see whether she was going to be able to get the necessary words out.

With knees knocking and butterflies in my stomach, I read out the wretched statement. By letting my mind go blank to the surroundings, I was able to get through without a blush. To prevent my voice cracking, I pretended the room was empty apart from the magistrates.

I soon learned it doesn't do to let embarrassment get the better of you. After that experience, it would have been hard for anyone to bring a blush to my cheek in court.

Chapter 3

The trial of Stuart Blackstock and Leslie Cooke, the two men responsible for the shooting of PC Philip Olds, took place on 14 June 1981. Giving evidence from his wheelchair, Philip saw them cleared of attempted murder. Sir David McNee, the Metropolitan Police Commissioner, later wrote to Philip:

Dear Philip,

I have followed carefully the recent trial, convictions and sentencing of those responsible for causing you such grievous and tragic injuries.

At the time of the trial you must have been under great personal strain but I thought you dealt with the media honestly and responsibly which reflected creditably on you and the Metropolitan Police. Too easily, an ill-chosen word or phrase can be misconstrued or misrepresented but with thoughtful care and sound judgment you successfully negotiated potential obstacles.

The Force can feel proud of the way you conducted yourself and the public re-assured of the professionalism of their officers.

When I first joined the Metropolitan Police in 1975, I thought that life was wonderful. I thought the world was wonderful; that all it needed was a bit of kindness and help and everyone would be all right. I thought that if you treated people decently, treated them with respect and had due regard to their property, it was enough to bring out the best in them.

I still firmly believe that as a basic philosophy it works in the case of bringing up children. But I was beginning to find out that it was not quite true in the grown-up world. Or not in the one I'd found myself in. A lot of the crime I saw seemed senseless and avoidable.

After a fair amount of disillusionment, I decided I wasn't about to change the human race, took things as they came, learned a sense of self-preservation and still had plentiful supplies of enthusiasm for other pursuits.

If there was a chance to try anything new I was always first in line. Water-skiing was one craze. We'd cram as many people as you can into a car and drive down to Southend at six in the morning, do some water-skiing, crowd into the pub and stay until it closed. Having showered and changed, we were at work again for the ten o'clock shift. Burning the candle at both ends was not just the name of the game – it was a way of testing yourself.

At the section house I organized discos, which took place in the gym. It was not unusual to have about three hundred people. In police work, you need a strong antidote to stress and having a ball at the policeman's ball was a way of letting off steam.

Afterwards we had to tidy up and clean the floor and while there were always plenty of helpers to set up the bar and bring in the beer barrels, you could count the number of clearers-up on half a hand. The worst part for me was doing the accounts.

With the amazing police social life, I made more friends in the force than outside. It's not just a question that we understand and share the same unsociable hours; we seem to get on very well as a group and because you have to rely on your fellow officer when there's trouble, we get a good indication of character. In the main we trust each other and are probably more honest and outspoken than most other people working together. All the same, to avoid becoming insular and boring, I found it essential to have friends outside the force.

One advantage of living with a group, though, was that there was always someone ready and willing to have a go at anything with you. Another sport I developed a passion for was parachuting, one of the most exhilarating experiences I've ever had. We went from

Lydd Airport in Kent. Sitting half in and half out of the aircraft, I couldn't wait for the moment when you jumped out on the static line. It's a fantastic sensation to drift through the air, waiting for the moment when the earth seems to come up to meet you. On one slightly off-target occasion, it looked as if I was heading for a herd of cows instead of the airstrip. But, narrowly avoiding some wire fencing and several cowpats, I landed a long walk away from the hangar. Too busy admiring a spectacular view, I'd forgotten I was supposed to be steering.

When I joined there were far fewer women in the police force than there are now. We were a new breed – younger and, we liked to think, rather more daring than the old-style WPCs who worked different shifts to the men and were a separate branch of the police force, rather than fully integrated with the men as we are now. Before, policewomen didn't do night-shifts and their main fields were missing persons, child protection, women and rape. They didn't do patrols like we do, or have the same opportunities for promotion as the men. We were the first to do the same job as the men and to have the same training, pay and equality of opportunity.

My first police station, however, had changed little from when it was first built around the turn of the century. With time-worn brickwork on the outside and the inside depressingly painted in cream and battleship grey, trepidation was the feeling as you passed inside.

Men who had joined after the war were still the backbone of the force. Old-guard policemen of the Dixon of Dock Green breed and Sergeants who believed in iron discipline were firmly in control. One inflexible rule was that if you met a senior officer outside the building and you were both in uniform, you were required to salute. I felt stupid doing this and used to try and spot the senior officer before he saw me and scuttle quickly for cover, occasionally getting caught in no man's land and having no choice but to chuck up a salute.

While conceding that women police had their place, the main fear among the old guard was that, faced with serious trouble, a WPC would be likely to turn and run in the opposite direction. To be fair, they also felt protective about us to a degree.

WPCs were so few and far between at that time that it was sometimes necessary to phone round several police stations to find a woman on duty who was free to go out on a case that required the female presence.

For obvious reasons, when it comes to searches WPCs search women and the PCs search men. I arrived one morning to find that I was to go on a drugs raid with the CID. The first thing that happens is that you're briefed. You're told why you are going there, what you're looking for and what you're expected to do. This was done going along in the car. I wasn't nervous, just rather excited. At last it seemed I was taking part in the sort of police work you see in the films.

An important part of briefing is knowing what powers you have. Such as whether you've got a warrant to search the place, because if you don't have a warrant you have to use a different power. What we had was a drugs warrant. I was taken along because there was no guarantee that there wouldn't be a woman at this rendezvous in a seedy part of north London. And lo and behold when we got there, there was one particular woman who had to be searched. I took her into the bathroom and found some drugs tucked in the back of her belt.

So there was this woman and there was me. No one else in the bathroom. She put her clothes together again and I handed the drugs over to the CID officer. She was duly arrested and taken along to the police station. Apart from having to give evidence, I thought that was the end of it. The next thing I knew, she made a statement accusing me of planting the drugs on her. Not only was it quite a serious allegation, but I had no way of disproving it: there had only been the two of us in that bathroom. I knew I hadn't planted those drugs on her – apart from anything else I wouldn't have had the foggiest idea where to get them. But I was really worried, because if she says I planted the drugs on her and I say, no I didn't, where do we go from there?

It was the first time I'd had a complaint made against me. It was investigated and later withdrawn, but in the meantime I felt it was hanging over my entire career. With my mates, I couldn't talk about anything else. Nowadays, complaints about police planting evidence on a suspect – anything from drugs to a stolen lorry – are not unusual. Sometimes you feel quite despairing when all you've done is no more than an honest job. But the procedures all have to be gone through and everything investigated.

One of the things you have to get used to assessing is whether or not someone is lying to you. Showing sympathy, showing understanding when taking a statement, is an art. Something you only learn from experience. You have to remember the ground rules. The sulky punk in the corner who is refusing to answer questions and looks like a prime suspect may be as clean as a whistle, while the articulate chap in the pinstripe, who threatens to report you for detaining him, could well know more than he is letting on. We don't use the lie detector here, but any officer worthy of the title can tell a lot from the way people sit, tilt their heads, look away and generally connect or otherwise. Body language – you learn to pick up a lot on that. But as far as the legal side is concerned, the only thing that matters is to be able to prise out and prove the truth.

And the only test of whether or not someone is lying is by means of question and answer: taking pages and pages of notes and going over the statement until all of a sudden you hit on a question the person concerned doesn't want to answer. You go over the story again. He says, 'Yes, I went into the shop. I did this and that,' and because he's having to think about lying, you notice that his mannerisms are unnatural. The other thing about lying is that you have to remember what you've said, and if you've told a porky pie, you have to remember that, too. Then, after a length of time, it could be weeks in some investigations, you have to say it all over again. So when a discrepancy pops up, I'll say, 'Are you sure? Can you tell me again what happened on 22 January?' I don't know that I'd remember what I'd done myself, going back weeks, so if you've told a lie in the first place, it's a hell of a lot to remember. Fortunately, the majority of interviews are now taped and security sealed. This has many advantages to all concerned, not least for people like myself who used to get writer's cramp. At the same time you had to make the notes legible, while learning how to give the impression that you had all the time in the world.

It's hardest to get to the truth when you come across someone who has put themselves in the position of living a lie so that they have almost forgotten what the real story is.

One of my first cases concerned a baby who had been stolen from a north London hospital. The baby was abducted from the nursery at night, her absence only discovered the following morning. No one had seen what had happened and as usual with a case of this kind, there was absolutely nothing to go on so we had to rely on information from the public. Intensive publicity in the media helps a lot. With other officers and a Detective Chief Inspector working on it, the case was a major enquiry.

Often in such events, the kidnapper has prepared the ground well in advance so that neighbours are not taken by surprise with the arrival of a baby. Our suspect had done exactly this. She had gone round with cushions strapped under a maternity dress and denied her boyfriend sexual contact so that even he thought she was really pregnant. She had equipped herself with a cot, nappies and baby food. A girl of only sixteen, it was doubtful she could support herself, let alone a baby, too. Neighbours became suspicious. Arriving at the flat, I talked to the girl who seemed quite calm and relaxed. Her story was that she had delivered the baby herself and had not yet got round to registering her. The beautiful baby girl looked perfectly contented and well cared for, sleeping in the cot. I could see that the girl really believed in her own story and regarded the baby as her own.

Further questions on the medical side yielded a less convincing account. If she had delivered the baby herself, what had she done with the afterbirth? Flushed it down the toilet, she said. Naturally, a medical examination would have revealed that the girl had not recently given birth to a baby. By this time we were almost a hundred per cent certain that this was the missing baby. All that was necessary was a brief examination of the child which showed that her umbilical cord had been cut and dressed with the professional expertise of a doctor or midwife. No girl of sixteen on her own and without medical training could have done this. We challenged her with it. She still wouldn't admit to stealing the baby. So as kindly as we could, we told her that it was necessary to have some further talks and, still holding the baby, she came with us in the car to the police station.

There, the worst part was when the child was removed for identification and subsequently returned to the mother. I had actually never seen the real mother, so it was only by picturing her anguish that I managed not to be overcome with pity for the girl. Over tea and floods of tears the whole sad story poured out. The girl had left her family for her boyfriend and to keep the situation going had pretended to be pregnant. She had been told by her doctor that she would not be able to have children of her own and in keeping up the fantasy, she had really begun to want a baby. Stealing one was the next logical step. She had blanked her mind out to the feelings of the real mother; by then the pretence had become so real that it was possible for her to forget the existence of any other 'mother' but herself.

The girl's parents turned out to be extremely nice, sensible people, horrified by what had happened, and mystified. Their daughter had simply wanted to take a job in another part of London and they thought she was living with friends. She was remanded in Holloway and given psychiatric help. I was fascinated by the way the girl had continued to live through her fantasy right up to the last minute. Her mother was distraught. I felt sorry for everyone concerned: the girl, her parents and, of course, the deprived mother in hospital. The only one who appeared not to have suffered was the baby.

I remember wishing that once it was all sorted out, the girl would manage to get on with her life and put it all behind her. It was certainly a lesson in how your feelings can become deeply involved in a case.

Another lesson that has to be learned at an early stage is the folly of running unnecessary risks. Despite training on the subject of self-protection, I forgot everything I'd learned when one day a message came through that there was a man armed with a shotgun on the seventeenth floor of a tower block. In my enthusiasm, I charged into the lift, taking another PC with me, and pressed the button, realizing too late that when the doors opened, we might well be looking into the barrel of a shotgun held by a mad-man. Not a brilliant thing to do under the circumstances. But I hastily pressed the button to go down and we got out on the floor below.

When we arrived he wasn't in possession of a shotgun but an air rifle – which would still have hurt if he'd used it. However, there were no offences disclosed and everyone left in one piece, a little wiser for the experience.

I'm not an authorized police shot and unarmed police officers are not advised to tackle men with guns like the Charge of the Light Brigade. What happened in Philip's case unfortunately proved the point.

In 1980 I failed my Sergeant's exam. I had been doing too much socializing and not enough studying. Promotion exams are largely a question of learning points of law. You have to know the procedures and how to apply them. What makes it difficult is that the whys and wherefores of charging people are couched in the sort of cumbersome language which doesn't exactly trip off the tongue. If you change the formula to sound more to the point – using less complicated everyday language – you risk changing the meaning. If you don't stick to the book, it's all too easy to finish up with the opposite effect: no charge when you are intending to charge somebody.

After a few years of communal life in the section house, where most of my salary went on enjoying myself, I decided it was time to get my foot on the first rung of the escalating property market and buy a modest flat. I'd saved the money for a down payment on a mortgage, but unfortunately I was gazumped and the agent ran off with the money. It took a year of negotiating through solicitors to get it back and then I was taken for another sort of ride.

My sister and I had always been mad about horses. Tracey was now working at a riding stables and whenever I could, I would go to Epping Forest and go out for a ride. I had no intention of buying a horse but in a moment of madness one day I fell in love with Simon after he had run away with me. He was a spirited animal, but he had such a good nature I instantly forgave him. I wanted him for myself so that I could ride him whenever I had a free moment, so there and then I paid for him with the money I'd got back on the flat.

I now had a horse but no flat. The sensible thing would have been to move in with Simon and share his rather splendid accommodation. Visiting him now took over all my spare time. The few months I had left to devote to him were well spent. Cantering

47

through Epping Forest on Simon, I was in another world and any cares or worries I had would fall into perspective.

Meeting Philip was like meeting no other boyfriend. Compared to former boyfriends, he was like a legendary figure who belonged to a different environment. Although I felt ordinary beside him, he had the gift of making me feel very special. I admired his honest, outgoing personality. In particular, the sophisticated way in which he handled the press. While guarding his words, he managed to give the impression of conducting a philosophical chat. In effect, the press were encouraging him to say that the gunmen were bastards and that he wished he could have had the opportunity of shooting them before they shot him. Without rising to the bait, Philip let it be known that although he and his colleagues weren't overjoyed at the verdict, he accepted that there was nothing further to be done. It struck me, that with his lively intelligence and mental agility, Philip enjoyed the challenge of a press inquisition. He regarded it as a battle of wits. In some ways, it had helped to keep him going in the bleak period after he came out of Stoke Mandeville.

Here was a man who had seen the worst life could bring, had come through by his own courage and was struggling to come to terms with his fate. He was not asking for support, but this is what I longed to give him. His mixture of strength and vulnerability had an irresistible attraction.

The phone was always ringing and he seemed the centre of some little court: visitors coming and going, invitations for him to attend this and that. He talked about everything that was going on and somehow invited you to share in the excitement of it all. In this lay the secret of his charm. Philip shared things. Problems, jokes, good days, bad days; days when he had dark moods and depressions – he didn't often hide what he felt. I went to see him almost daily and felt privileged to be in his company.

At the same time he was living without dignity. The squalid surroundings – commode in the lounge, combined kitchen and bathroom unsuited to the needs of a disabled person – troubled me. Philip was one of the most fastidious people I've ever met. Before he was paralysed, he had taken good care of himself. Everyone testified to that. Now he couldn't get into a bath and couldn't wash up because the sink was too high or the wheelchair too low. With the hordes of people trooping in and out, the place often looked like a tip. Nobody washed up or emptied ashtrays and Philip never asked for help. He was missing his dog, a golden labrador called Winton. Philip was in hospital for a long time so his sister, in Wales, was looking after Winton.

The first thing I did when I went over after work was to start tidying up. I think the home help appreciated it, but Philip wanted to talk and to hear what I'd been doing during the day. He often had good advice to offer.

Summer turned to autumn and Philip's trip to New York was coming up. Chuck Bennett had made all the arrangements and I was helping Philip to sort out the things he would need on the trip. I was disappointed that he would be away on my birthday, 7 October, but we went out, just the two of us together, to celebrate that and his forthcoming trip a few days before he left.

I'd stayed overnight at Eastcote Road before when it was too late to drive back, and later that evening I stayed by his side in a loving embrace.

We made love in the way that was special to us. I fell into a dreamless sleep tucked into the three-foot bed, between Philip and the wall, hoping I wouldn't move and disturb him.

One of the effects of a bullet passing through the spinal cord at chest level is to cut the brain's control of the sexual function, though not necessarily to bring it to an end.

At Stoke Mandeville, Philip had been given a list of things he would never do again. One of them was making love.

Many a man in his position would have accepted his lot. But Philip was a fighter. He wouldn't accept that he would never walk again, and he thought if he could never make love again, he might as well have died on the pavement.

So yes, we did make love. We also planned a baby. This too was a scientific possibility, although it was not to be fulfilled.

Philip was a considerate lover. Sometimes, I think, in the traditional relationship between men and woman, men can be selfish in their lovemaking. Provided they can reach their own climax, they may not always be too concerned about how their partners feel.

Because Philip no longer had the need to satisfy himself in that way, I became the star partner.

Our lovemaking was always good. It was the one thing in our relationship where neither of us were ever disappointed. To us, it was very, very special.

But knowing that many people thought that Philip's disability had put an end to that part of his life, I think it's important to say that there are different ways to have a loving and considerate physical relationship. By heightening the sensitivity of the erogenous zones left and by exploring our sensual reactions, we found an ecstasy that was special to us. Obviously, we knew what the restrictions were from the beginning. But our lovemaking developed with a wonderfully close and tender excitement. We both felt that we had discovered something magical and intensely private in our relationship which was our secret and ours alone.

In June 1981, Philip was faced with retirement by the end of that year. The visit to the States, where he was to be welcomed by the New York City police on a red-carpet tour, was to be his last vacation. I was going to miss him for every minute of the ten-day trip and with a twinkle in his eye, Philip suggested that I might like to move into the house and look after things while he was away. In the four and a half months since we'd met, I had been to-ing and fro-ing from north London and although by now I knew it wasn't in Philip's nature to indicate that he depended on anyone for a permanent relationship, we both knew that this move was going to be more than just a caretaking job.

Philip went to the States accompanied by his friends and colleagues Ron Castle and Pete McKinley. Chuck arranged everything – flight, accommodation and an itinerary that included a tour of police headquarters in Manhattan, a special luncheon and dinner on Long Island and a trip to Washington for a tour of FBI headquarters. At the airport Philip was welcomed with a police motorcycle escort, which took him on a special patrol down Highway One and even held up the rush-hour traffic to take him to a celebratory dinner.

On one occasion he was taken by police helicopter to a shooting range where strict codes of conduct are in force. He was given ear defenders and goggles and allowed to try several different types of armaments used by the New York Police. One of these was a powerful sub-machine gun, which, as Philip let rip, swung his wheelchair round in an arc so that he narrowly avoided spraying the onlookers. Next time the brakes were locked and the wheels chocked. Philip's exploits on the shooting range made a noteworthy topic later at P. J. Reilly's, a favourite police bar known as Ye Old Sod, presided over by Angie, a warm-hearted Irishwoman who became a lasting friend to Philip.

Philip phoned on several occasions, once after taking the New York Police on in a drinking contest. Describing his flight in a 'hollykipper' or 'hillycopper' at about 2.30 a.m. our time, he sounded like Dudley Moore in *Arthur*. Hearing about it all on his return, I wondered how he was able to take what, even by American police standards, seemed like a hectic round of hospitality.

Honoured by American police officers whose list of casualties far outnumbers ours, Philip's treatment by the New York Police was unprecedented. He came home with an amazing collection of memorabilia including an original nightstick – a bigger and, as regarded by those who use it, better, version of the British truncheon – a police cap and numerous patches.

I was thrilled with the gift he brought back for me, a pair of gold earrings.

As soon as I arrived on the scene at Eastcote Road, Philip's home help and all the other professional carers melted away. If I thought before meeting him that I lived a busy life, I was soon to see that comparatively speaking I had been taking it easy.

The daily commuting to north London took precious time and I applied for a transfer. No instant magic carpet was laid at my feet, however, and I was required to submit a report and produce what is known as a 'welfare' reason for the move. This was duly taken into consideration but it was some time before I was given what is entitled a 'compassionate' move to another division.

Leaving the police station I'd worked at for the last five and a half years, I felt as though I had abandoned the friends and colleagues in my old district because my commitments at the other end meant it was impossible to organize that customary police ritual – a leaving party.

With Philip as the centre of my existence, I was caught in a peripheral whirlwind. His needs, my work, his friends and our social activities together added up to a new life in which it was a challenge to get through each and every day.

In addition I was re-taking my Sergeant's exam, which, I now realized, required concentrated study of criminal law procedures. Philip had encouraged me in this ambition and I was determined to succeed for my own sake, but a little bit for his as well. I wanted him to be proud of me.

Philip habitually took large quantities of prescribed drugs. Pethidine for the pain, Normisson for sleeping and Valium for the muscle spasms that frequently afflict paraplegics not in control of their lower limbs. One of my jobs was to collect his prescriptions, which were on a repeat basis, and the trips to the chemist seemed to occur with increasing frequency.

In addition to this, he consumed large amounts of alcohol, mostly whisky, which may have helped the physical pain he suffered, but which often seemed to fuel the psychological distress that rose like a sediment of bitterness as he went into the action replay of the night he was shot.

Sometimes he would be in a poorly controlled state of rage – easily triggered by any feeling of inadequacy or the thought of a future imprisoned by the wheelchair, 'the bloody cage'. When turned against himself – his loathing of his body, 'dead meat' below the chest – his anger precipitated ideas of suicide.

What do you say to someone you love who threatens to kill himself because he can't bear to go on living?

It's not much of a compliment, is it? All I could think to say was that if he did anything to end his own life, a lot of people would be very upset and very hurt and they'd miss him. Myself included.

It must have seemed an inadequate answer. Philip's reply was to turn the tables saying, 'You'll be all right. You'll soon find someone else,' making it seem as though I was totally preoccupied with my own situation. Continuing with this theme he would add, 'I promise you one thing, you'd be a lot better off without me.'

Protestations didn't cut much ice with Philip. Often, the less said the better. His mood could suddenly swing in another direction and sometimes I found I could distract him by turning to another subject. All the same, I took the threats seriously. His pills came contained in leaves like a small book and sometimes if I was worried I would detach all but one of the leaves and hide them. If I was on night duty I would leave behind just enough to get him off to sleep. Not that I was ever sure how much was enough or how much would be too much.

Rows flared over nothing. I can't remember what had been happening the first time he hit me. We were in the hall ready to go out to dinner. I asked him something and without warning, he slapped me right across the face. Nor was it a light slap.

As I fell back, my face tingling from the blow, he at once turned and said, 'Oh, I'm sorry. I'm sorry, I didn't mean to do that.' Then he said, 'Hit me. Hit me back.'

I said, 'No, I'm not going to hit you. Why should I?'

What was going on here? Philip was obviously angry and frustrated about something. Something I hadn't realized. From one moment to another, his eyes had darkened from blue to almost black. It was like seeing a mental eclipse.

He was screaming at me, 'Hit me, hit me. I'm telling you to hit me back.'

Hit him back? Hit someone you love? Someone in a wheelchair? What a wonderful idea!

So I said, 'Don't be so pathetic. I don't want to hit you. I don't want to hit anyone.' I had no feelings of frustration to work off. I was suffering from shock rather than anger. Perplexed and confused, I still thought there must have been something I'd done without knowing.

The back of his wheelchair was against the front door. 'Hit me back!' he said.

So I gave him a light slap on the cheek.

I felt no satisfaction. There was nothing gained. Instead I felt sick and degraded. But even if it was nothing like the blow he had given me, it was obvious that Philip felt a little bit better for it.

When I suggested cancelling the dinner, he wouldn't hear of it.

Over the meal he was bright company, attentive and talkative. Only once when I started to refer to what had happened earlier did his eyes darken and flicker as before – putting the subject out of bounds.

Chapter 4

I poured Philip a cup of coffee. 'Am I wrong or have you lost a lot of weight?'

His clothes looked as though borrowed from a stout friend. In fact, he was down by about fourteen pounds since leaving hospital. I didn't know him before but was aware that most people lose weight in those circumstances.

'Some,' he said. 'It's mostly muscle.' He didn't want to talk about his condition. He had been told it would deteriorate if he didn't exercise. But he had no means of exercising and he wasn't having any regular physiotherapy. The muscles in his legs had already started to waste. His legs looked like sticks and his face was gaunt.

Despite the fact that a couple of local restaurateurs had filled Philip's freezer with many wholesome and delicious meals, at Eastcote Road he had been living on a diet of Pot Noodles and cheese on toast before I moved in. The usual bachelor habit of not eating healthily had been intensified in Philip's case by the fact that the nerves of his stomach didn't function properly. He could taste food like anyone else but when he was paralysed the usual messages which go from stomach to brain were shut off; he didn't know when he was hungry. Conventional mealtimes had gone by the board. He'd forget about food, then decide to have a chilli con carne in the middle of the night.

It wouldn't be unusual for me to be found in the kitchen at about 3 a.m. cooking chilli con carne from scratch. Later, when we got a microwave it was a blessing. But to begin with my project was to organize Philip's diet and as far as possible bring in regular meal-times. I've always been in favour of healthy eating, long before it became a popular cult; so salads, vegetables and fibre foods were on the menu. To start with, Philip wasn't too keen on these innovations and on occasions I was met with a low-flying salad flung across the room accompanied by curses about rabbit food.

The first present I ever gave Philip was an electric kettle, to save having to use the cranky old gas stove. When I was at work, I would leave meals he could serve himself, remembering to put everything in easy reach.

The pattern of our lives together was drawn up in those first six months. I had a lot to learn. I had to find out about Philip's body: what he could do and what he couldn't. And I had to try to be unobtrusive about helping him. He hated a fuss or anything that drew attention to his disability. Emotionally it was an intense relationship, involving demands I often felt I was failing to meet. Our very different childhoods affected our relationship. I had been a happy child, happy in my police job and the happiest moment of my life was probably when I first met Philip. After that there were times of happiness too, but many of misery and unhappiness and most of it had to do with him.

In learning about Philip, I also learned more about myself. I had never lived with just one person before. I had been used to living in a community, and in communal life a lid is kept on the emotions. Living close to Philip subjected me to the most intense scrutiny I had so far experienced. I so often felt myself to be in the wrong; the possessor of emotions I never suspected existed. In contrast it seemed the whole of my previous life had been spent basking in the approval of emotional security.

As time went on, there was more and more to be done. The daily routine often left me too exhausted to think. I would get Philip's clothes ready the night before, put them over the back of the chair and in the morning check everything and leave out hot water and towels before going off to work.

When I got back, there were usually other people there. Apart from his own police mates, there was another stream of visitors who called mostly by day and sometimes stayed on into the evening.

Because I worked shifts, I'd be home at different times, usually to find a different rota of female guests. Often there would be some young lady I'd never seen before and the following day, a different attractive woman by Philip's side. They came in all shapes and sizes and from all over London.

Where did they all come from? That was a good question. Some were old friends and acquaintances who had looked Philip up when they heard what had happened to him. Others were people who knew someone who knew Philip and they were introduced that way. Or they would just phone up having seen Philip's picture in the paper. He was in the phone book and would think nothing of asking them along. It was evident they enjoyed his company.

With time to kill, Philip didn't find it so difficult to pass the days in feminine company. It was me who would sometimes find it difficult. Not feeling I was looking particularly feminine, I would come back from work, dressed in the blue with black stockings, flat shoes and a skirt creased at the back to find some well-groomed female sitting on the bed. If Philip hadn't got up or dressed, there *were* other places to sit but the bed seemed the most popular perch.

With bags under my eyes, having got up at four in the morning, I often didn't feel like blending into the scene. Nor did I feel like deliberately keeping out of the way, doing all the cleaning up and finding we were out of milk or something.

Presumably they saw their role as cheering Philip up and few of the visitors offered any practical help. None of them seemed overenthusiastic to see me, nor did Philip go out of his way to make the introductions. At a pinch, he managed to give the impression I was just somebody who happened to live there. One of Philip's mates described it as the Eastcote Road harem.

Sometimes I'd come home to find one of these visions draped round Philip's neck and I'd get angry. You could say there was safety in numbers, but there were one or two who seemed to be leading the field. One, I remember, wore a short skirt and plunging neckline, tightly belted in the middle. Another had a husband to whom it appeared she was reluctantly pledged to return . . . 'Gotta go, Phil, see you soon – Bye-bye, sweetheart.'

Out in front was Stef, Philip's Greek girlfriend. Whereas Philip and I were just at the beginning of our relationship and it was quite fragile, Stef had known Philip before the shooting. Philip didn't say much to enlighten me about the others, but he sometimes referred to her. Her marriage was going through a difficult time and she was later to be divorced.

Often I would interrupt what seemed to be intense discussions. Theirs was a long-established relationship. Because of the length of time he had known her and because she was so attractive and they had shared so many intimate times together, I found Stef's continued presence hard to accept. I felt she was a threat.

Whatever had happened in the past, Philip confirmed that Stef now ranked as his friend. He didn't say 'just a friend'. The result was I used to feel extremely uncomfortable when she was around. I got fed up with some of the others as well and that caused arguments. Even though I didn't say anything, Philip knew when I had the hump. Jealousy is an unattractive condition.

My transfer from Tottenham to Harrow Police Station meant that I was stepping out of the security of my old life into one where I had the sensation of burning my boats. All at once I was running a house, getting to know Philip's circle of friends – which included sorting out the groupies from the genuine ones – as well as adjusting to a new job, new colleagues and, of course, a new relationship.

The social life I found myself caught up in was something else. Philip was in regular demand at a round of parties, dinners, lunches and various functions where he was often the guest of honour. It was the decade of barbecues and we went to a lot of these as well as parties given by friends. In addition, we often went to the theatre or out to dinner. Because in Philip's case food was mainly a matter of taste rather than eating for hunger's sake, we often went to a couple of local Italian restaurants (the ones who had so temptingly stocked his freezer), where the well-flavoured dishes and warm family atmosphere were always welcoming.

If I wasn't working, I usually went with him on the more formal occasions, dressing up in a style that was quite new to me. I marvelled that Philip had no hang-ups about making after-dinner speeches or joining even the grandest company. As a group, the police enjoy their entertainments and one of the best evenings was a party at New Scotland Yard where Princess Margaret was present and one of the guests was Eric Morecambe. During the evening, he was presented with an enormous cigar and, unwrapping it, solemnly proceeded to tuck all the bits and pieces into the patch pockets of my dress. He was lovely – one of the funniest people I've ever met.

I hardly had time to think about the extraordinary whirl my life had developed into. The work life, the social life, the life with Philip – I seemed to be functioning on three different levels at once, just hoping that I could bring them all together and make it work.

At the same time I was studying for promotion and taking courses. Having previously failed to become a Sergeant I was now driven by a deeper sense of determination. For some reason, everything now seemed more positive. To pass the exam you have to study all aspects of criminal law. As a Sergeant on duty, you have to follow certain time-worn procedures and be very sure what you're doing. Your job is to advise and supervise the constables and ensure that all points of evidence are present and correct to prove a case. You have to know what people's rights are and inform them and be the one to make certain that when it comes to the point, it's a lawful arrest. You have to react quickly, at the same time giving the impression you have all the time in the world to investigate a case.

Philip was equally keen that I should succeed; helpful in supplying examples from his own experience of the various questions set and also where he'd made mistakes in presenting a case in court. We'd do it so that I was producing the evidence and he was the wily defence solicitor overturning my case or vice versa.

He would pack me upstairs to study and although it was sometimes hard to concentrate with all the noise and laughter coming from downstairs, I beavered away determined to succeed this time.

Having decided against specializing, I still found that what I liked best about policing was the everyday contact with a variety of people. I felt I was there to help people and to care. You can't do the job unless you're interested in human nature. You come across all sorts, not just the criminally inclined. I liked talking to the old bagladies I'd find on the beat. Some of them felt that life had given them a raw deal but they were experts in survival and many had fascinating life histories. In winter they would be found in the warmest doorways, beside boiler rooms; anywhere there was a duct or heating outlet you could spot them under their cardboard boxes.

Sometimes there is a real element of rescue to the work. A call can come out of the blue and one case I particularly remember was when a woman left three children in a multistorey block of flats and water had been reported coming from under the door. Neighbours had knocked to no avail. All that could be heard was the sound of the television as water continued to gush under the door. Suspecting that there were children inside, we didn't want to break the door down and frighten them and it took us some time before we could persuade the eldest child, a boy of about six, to open it. It later turned out that none of the three children was over six. Their mother had gone out leaving the washing machine on, which had flooded and was pumping out by the minute.

The first thing we did was to switch off the television as there was an obvious danger of electrocution. The fire brigade arrived, switched off the washing machine, and tried to sort out the fault. We scooped up the children, the youngest of whom was in a cot, dressed them in warm clothes, left a note for the missing mother and took them to the police station. Doing our best to keep the children happy, we called the social services.

This was one of the occasions where human feelings go hand in hand with points of law. With three frightened children on our hands and nowhere to put them except one of the detention rooms on mattresses and blankets on the floor, their welfare was our top priority. When the mother eventually arrived she was far from grateful and threatened to sue us for removing her children. In this case there was a lot of sorting out to be done before the situation could be satisfactorily resolved.

Although the police force receives a lot of knocks in the media, there is still a large section of the public who rely on them for help in a variety of situations. Everyone knows that the police are open twenty-four hours a day and we are often the first service people call on for help. Apart from protecting the public from crime, this can vary from a call where an old person has just fallen out of bed and needs help, to going out with chain saws when fallen trees are blocking roads or have trapped people in their houses, as happened after the gales of October 1987.

The main requirement in a police officer is the ability to communicate with all types of different people. I thought I'd been scoring quite well in that department before I met Philip.

After the first attack, I had become infinitely wary of anything that might upset him. He could be in a wonderful mood, relaxed and enjoying a conversation; then just the smallest thing could trigger off an outburst, his eyes growing dark with anger. Knowing what to say or what not to say was something I couldn't work out at first. Usually I just waited until the mood blew over.

It is difficult to describe all that Philip had become to me in those first few months. He was my mentor, involved in my day-to-day work which we would discuss together. He was my lover and whatever the actuality of our physical relationship, it was precious to both of us and this romantic attachment had become the primary obsession of my life. He was also the person I cared for in the literal sense, our intimacy closer than in the case of many other couples.

It would be wrong to give the impression that except for his inability to walk, Philip was just like any other able-bodied person. Yet sitting in the wheelchair, laughing and talking, this was the impression he often gave. Although he did not often complain directly, at times the pain was so bad it was amazing he could control himself at all. After he left Stoke Mandeville there was no further physiotherapy and no one to advise on the psychological wounds, which remained as firmly imprinted as the physical ones. Philip was still in a state of shock. Despite his high profile and the concern of many highly placed people, his morale was to sink lower and lower, especially when the spotlight of publicity was off and all the visitors had gone home. Despite Philip's high public profile and all the very best medical attention, on the psychological plane advice was as thin as air. Support groups were hardly on the scene and there was no one to enlighten me on the best way of dealing with the increasing problem of Philip's mental instability.

Had I known Philip before the shooting, I might have been more alert to the changes in his personality. As it was, I concentrated on the physical side of his condition, accepting that he was under stress because of continual pain but not knowing how to cope with the turmoil of his emotional reaction.

When Philip was taken to Hillingdon Hospital, the work of a skilled woman surgeon saved his life. Had it been an ordinary bullet that had entered his shoulder, it would have been a clean wound, the bullet easier to remove and wouldn't have caused such extensive damage. But the filed-down, blunted dumdum bullet used by Stuart Blackstock had more far-reaching effects. Entering his left shoulder and puncturing his lung, it knocked a quarter of an inch out of his spinal cord, ricocheted through his chest, finally lodging itself somewhere behind his right shoulder blade. To remove the dumdum fragments from the nest of broken nerves in which they were enmeshed, involved another major operation: a thoracotomy in which the whole of his right side had to be cut open.

Even when lying semi-conscious on the pavement outside the off-licence, Philip had been aware of the first effects of paralysis. As he felt his life's blood flowing out of him, with pain beginning to wash in like the tide, he made what he felt to be one last effort to die with dignity. Speaking of that moment, which he truly believed to be his last, he described the sensations of a man whose body, from chest to feet, will never be within his control again. A man to whom human dignity was important.

'The realization I first had was: I'm dying. But it wasn't so bad, though a bit on the painful side, I must admit. I was also surprised by the brightness of the stars, the softness of the pavement and this ludicrous feeling that my knees were tucked up under my chest. And so while dying, or at least I thought I was dying, I felt I had to stretch my arms down to my knees to straighten them. Because to die in such a ridiculous position, like a cockroach on its back, offended me. While I was alive, I still had enough personal ego to make sure my legs were straight and my arms down by my side so I could die in a decent position. So when I found my legs were straight, I carried on with the honourable process of dying.'

Philip's sensation of having his knees drawn up to his chest is common to those whose spinal cord has been damaged – the first symptom of paraplegia.

To say it could have been worse: that a severer degree of spinal injury could have resulted in a loss of use to both his arms and legs, to have become a quadriplegic like some of the injured people he was to meet, was of no consolation.

With his uncomfortable brand of honesty, Philip could accept no words of comfort when it came to his disability. He hated it and I think this often made him hate himself.

'A carcase of dead meat below here,' is how he described himself, pointing at his chest, 'no bullshitting.'

Philip was to put up one of the most famous struggles ever recorded to overcome disability. But it had to be done his way.

'I call myself a cripple because that's what I am. I'm not disabled, I'm not temporarily out of function, I'm not unwell. I'm a cripple – crippled by a gunman's bullet.'

This was Philip in full, disturbing flood at the top of his rage. And woe betide the unfortunate who tried to sidestep the issue by referring to 'the accident'.

As Philip would point out in the bluntest terms, the shooting of a man in cold blood is no accident. He always called it the shooting, never anything else.

Philip would shock people by referring to himself as 'cripple of the year'. He didn't want to be associated with any disabled group. All he wanted was a cure, to be back as part of the system and everyday society, to be considered normal – whatever that really means.

Cheated, as he often said, of a clean and honourable death, Philip had come round from the first operation knowing he was paralysed. The full implications were yet to sink in. He had set up a mind block to the future and for the time being at least the euphoria of coming through alive sustained him.

When news of Philip's shooting was relayed on Christmas Eve, friends like Gus, his old partner on the beat, phoned traffic control at Alperton to find out where he was. Due to intense media interest at the time, the police press office handled all calls. Little additional information was given out and visitors were confined to family and a few high-ranking police officers.

Mick Rawson, who did get through the security net, spent his off-duty time at the hospital. Perhaps with his background in the service from an early age it was inevitable that Philip was to find that deep in the deepest of troubles, his police colleagues mattered more to him than the family he seldom saw.

It wasn't until he was moved to Stoke Mandeville that he was able to see the friends who kept his morale going. One fellow PC was surprised to see how little time he had for his mother. 'He cut her off as though she didn't exist,' he said. Gus and his wife, Linda, came down from Norfolk and, according to Philip, acted as a psychological lifeline. He, like others, found that Philip's need was not for an oversympathetic reaction. He was not the first injured PC to discover that police humour acts as a better safety valve than any amount of hand wringing. Another colleague, who knew better than to adopt the tragic approach unwittingly given by some bedside visitors, was Roger Webster, a larger than life, colleague and fellow motorcycle enthusiast.

When Roger arrived exuding north country humour, Philip was full of tubes and lying in a side ward. Together they both heard a report on the radio describing Philip's condition as critical. A great hulk of a man and a close friend, Roger was deeply moved while striving not to show his own distress.

To some people their dialogue might not have seemed the world's funniest patter, but to them it was important to play out the traditional code of police humour.

Speaking of the sombre news both had heard over the airwaves, Roger asked him solemnly, 'Are you going to die then, Phil?'

'No, not yet,' said Philip.

'Well, you won't walk again, will you?'

'It doesn't look like it.'

'In that case, can I have your motorcycle boots?'

To Philip, this was hilarious. In fact, he later gave his friend the highly polished boots, which had been his pride and joy. Roger treasured them and kept them in the same good condition as Philip had done.

Somehow the grim joke did more to cleanse the cloud of horror hanging over Philip's future than any conventional show of sympathy.

In the series of flashbacks, which he later relived with me, Philip seemed to be making it clear that the last thing he wanted was anyone to feel sorry for him. From him I learned that sympathy and understanding are not always quite the same thing. It's a very indistinct line. But I was beginning to realize that above all things, Philip dreaded becoming an object of pity. At the same time he did not want to accept his limitations. The only thing he wanted was a miracle cure.

Such awkward equations were not inclined to help his rehabilitation – another word Philip detested. And nowhere were his irreconcilable attitudes more in evidence than at Stoke Mandeville Hospital. At Britain's leading spinal injuries unit, Philip was arguably just about the worst patient they had ever had.

Their philosophy – that once the patient knows the worst, he can begin to come to terms with the possibilities of the future – was not one which fired Philip's imagination, because right from the start, he refused to accept that he would never walk again. Except for physiotherapy and some exercises which he never bothered to do at home, he resisted any idea of improving the quality of his life by developing a new range of interests, let alone the prescribed attitudes.

The prescription was straight from the shoulder. Philip was told: 'You will never walk again; you will never be able to make love again; you will have to learn to live with your disability. Here is what can be done to help . . .'

Ever since the hospital was founded in 1940 the doctors at Stoke Mandeville have known about the many physical and psychological problems that follow spinal injuries. The wheelchair Olympics originated from there. Jimmy Saville raised £10,000,000 for a new centre and thousands of patients have cause to be thankful for the programme of treatment and rehabilitation that enabled them to go back into the world.

Unless the doctors could find a way to mend his spinal cord and get him back the way he was, Philip was not interested.

The problems of paralysis are many and varied. From the point of view of Dr Hans Frankel, Director of the Stoke Mandeville Spinal Injuries Unit, the inability to walk is not in itself fatal.

He explained, 'It's a great inconvenience, but mobility can be substituted by a wheelchair or other device.'

More important were a number of related complications, as Dr Frankel pointed out in the television programme *The Visit* which featured Philip's fight to walk again. He said: 'The inability to feel anything below the point of injury, renders the patient liable to pressure sores which, if they go untreated, will kill. The lesion in the spinal column prevents the bladder from working properly and infections can be dangerous. It also prevents control of the bowels, another severe disadvantage which has to be taken care of and it affects the sexual function which is also a great loss. So the inability to walk is only one of the things patients have lost.'

The list of negatives was eternal. Far from just sitting back in his wheelchair and accepting his lot, it seemed that for a spinal injury patient, it was going to be a life of effort to keep even moderately fit.

In putting up with the humiliations and indignities of his condition, Philip saw no reprieve.

Was it then, or was it at the Old Bailey when the gunmen were cleared of attempted murder that the bitterness took root in Philip's soul, leaving an unreasoning anger and a desire to hurt? These were dreadful enemies he carried within himself. At times as destructive as bullets.

During his time at Stoke Mandeville, Philip discovered no great thunderbolt from heaven to change his attitudes. Doing whatever was necessary to accelerate his discharge, he took part in the recovery programme and even went in for archery to strengthen the upper part of his body. Michael Bentine sent him a bow. But in every way possible, he kicked against hospital restrictions. When it came to being told that he could have one pint of beer a day, he said he would rather save the week's ration and have it all together on Saturday night. He drank. He smoked. All the time he asked why. Why had he stood in the way of a bullet?

Whenever he cast his mind back to these events, thoughts of suicide were never far from Philip's mind.

Trying to show the love that could banish these thoughts, I knew I couldn't even imagine the way he felt. I had the experience of dealing with people in a state of shock, but not with its long-term effects. I knew that what he needed was the promise that someone would make him walk again. That nothing else really mattered to him.

Philip was once described as dramatic. Over dramatic, I suppose they meant. With him, drama and crisis were never far away. Even before the shooting, he had lived a dramatic life. Gus said he was fearless; once he decided to effect his purpose, he wouldn't back off. Gus told me that he was amazed that the pair of them had survived their time together in central London without serious injury.

People thought that with Philip, I was taking up some sort of crusade. But it was nothing like that. I loved him from the moment I saw him. I accepted him for what he was while never being entirely sure who he was. Perhaps he had always had a complex nature. Perhaps I never really knew him.

When I first met Philip, he was at a transient stage. Glad to be out of hospital and back in the land of the living, he was nevertheless, not like someone who is merely convalescing before resuming normal life. There was a large question mark over his future career. In fact, he didn't have a future career, not at any rate with the police force, which was the only career he had ever known.

Surrounded by people who flattered and made much of him, his ego was recovering from the battering it received at Stoke Mandeville. I suppose looking back, I should have been more tolerant of the harem. I didn't have time for lengthy analysis and it was all I could do to keep pace with the ever-lengthening list of things that had to be done.

Philip was by no means helpless, but having had no further treatment at all after leaving hospital, his progress wasn't exactly brilliant.

I suppose you could say that the caring side of my nature was unconsciously modelled on Mum. Because Philip hated asking for help, I developed an awareness of what needed doing and went about it without fuss or bother. I got to know Philip's body with the same kind of detached intimacy as a car driver listening to the rhythms of the engine.

In Philip's case, there were a number of signs if anything was going wrong. Headaches and high blood pressure were signs of infections and pressure sores were a persistent problem.

When I first met him he had a pressure sore on one of his legs, which had started in hospital and hadn't completely healed.

As Philip couldn't feel anything below the chest, he didn't know if a shoe or something was rubbing a sore place. A pressure sore looks like an open suppurating wound or, at worst, a hole. You have to remove the source of pressure, make sure the sore is clean, dress it and if possible, leave it uncovered and give it a chance to dry. If that's not possible and it has to be covered up with shoes, socks or other clothing, you apply a dressing, but you have to be careful when dressing a pressure sore, because if the tape is too tight it restricts circulation and causes other problems; or if the tape is too loose and it breaks down, the dressing rubs and makes it worse.

Kidney and bladder infections are a great danger and with no control over his bladder, Philip sometimes needed some help in this direction and would tap out the residue collecting in the bladder. This tapping helped the bladder to contract, exuding the residue. The urine drained into the bag strapped to his leg, attached to the penis with a medical glue. Bowels had to be managed by manual evacuation, but it was sometimes necessary to use suppositories.

With the loss of control over the bodily functions most of us take for granted, Philip had already experienced the depths of humiliation. Any fussing made it worse. I tried to develop a cool, calm way of dealing with things. Everything was done without asking.

I learned how to organize the routine as fast and efficiently as possible. Hot water, soap and plastic gloves for dealing with his toilet: usually a five-minute operation, but one which could take half an hour if things went wrong. Philip getting dressed with all his clothes pressed and ready – a twenty-minute job. I got ready in the shortest time possible, fitting in any clearing up that was required.

How Philip really felt about the loss of human dignity so casually rated by the rest of us, came out when a TV reporter asked the sort of unthinking question on which Philip was always ready to pounce.

The question, 'Has the shooting made any difference to your life?' brought an answer which I imagine the unfortunate girl will remember for the rest of her career.

'Yes,' replied Philip, 'I really think it has. I can't piss, can't shit, can't fuck and I can't walk.'

A mixture of stifled chuckles and embarrassed silence spread through those present. Needless to say, the film wasn't used and the interview translated into rather different terms by other press reporters present on the scene.

When he chose, Philip knew how to shock. But for a man who had taken a pride in his appearance, the useless body he now saw below his shoulders was an unsightly, unwieldy and uncontrollable burden. The loss of the natural functioning of his body was a deep and dismaying degradation. As bad, if not worse, than the inability to walk.

The automatic but satisfying bowel emptying process after a night of beer and curry, the relief of expelling the last drop of urine from a strained bladder, are not sensations generally talked about, nor even the ones most people imagine they would miss. Not compared to the all-engulfing pleasure of spitting the life force into the body of a woman. For Philip all this had been lost at one blow.

Whatever the emotional state of our relationship, it never affected the way in which I cared for Philip's shattered body. His physical welfare was always in a category apart.

Chapter 5

You have done your best to ruin the life of a young and courageous man for the sake of a few pounds.

Mr Justice Skinner to Stuart Blackstock at the Central Criminal Court, Old Bailey
6 June 1981

Although his words were directed at the gunman, the judge little knew how often they were to ring in Philip's ears. In a series of almost nightly flashbacks, Philip was to re-live that moment when Blackstock raised his gun and fired.

The pointlessness of the crime and the paltriness of the rewards were factors which only served to deepen the bitter well of his anger and frustration.

Out of my depth with so much that was new to me, I didn't always understand what I was hearing. I wanted Philip to leave the subject alone. If there was nothing I could do to blunt the painful past, I could concentrate on building him a more tolerable future. That's what I thought at the time.

I'm looking at my diaries for those first few months with Philip. Random dates and reminders, mostly a list of things I had to do.

Stock bedside drawer – repeat prescription – pills. Food, drink, leg bags, glue. Dry cleaners. Dress for Grosvenor House ball. Ironing – 17 shirts.

Funny how something resembling little more than a laundry list can trigger off so many memories. Some dates look ominous. Underlined three times.

As the able-bodied one, obviously I did all the shopping. Philip's bedside drawer had to be regularly re-stocked with the prescriptions he needed, pills replaced before he ran out. Top priority. No one knew except him how many pills he took in any one day. I was beginning to worry about the morphine cocktail he took at night. Later I got very worried. As it was, when I was on early turn, I'd ring home just to see he was all right and to give him an alarm call. Laying out his clothes the night before was an important ritual because if I'd forgotten something he would sometimes make it the excuse just to stay in bed. Philip letting himself vegetate was very bad news because of pressure sores and poor circulation. Also it was a signal for depression – stormy weather on the way.

I'd get it in the neck if I forgot anything. One extraordinary note says 'Petrol 4.30 a.m.' I suppose I'd overlooked it the night before. Juggling one thing against another, sometimes I'd make it, sometimes not. Often in the morning, I'd wonder if I'd been to bed at all.

I'm amazed at how much I crammed into a day. I probably couldn't do it now. But then I was driven by an energy I didn't know I had. I could get a day's work done in less time than I do now and still stay up three-quarters of the night. I felt I was more efficient under pressure, and prided myself on being able to do several things at once.

The seventeen shirts mentioned, which I ironed most weeks, actually strikes a happier note. We did so much socializing that Philip, who always liked to look smart and clean, often got through two a day. And there were dress shirts as well. Then there were my duty shirts. Philip bought me a portable TV for the kitchen and I used to watch the soaps while I did the ironing.

My first introduction to the world of glamour Philip moved around in, came when we went to Grosvenor House Hotel for a ball given by the Grand Order of Water Rats, a theatrical charity.

At the ball, transformed like Cinderella, I wore a new Frank Usher ballgown – black with a hooped skirt, a present from Philip. I'd never been to anything like this before and for the first time I began to realize how well known he was. People clustered round him and stars came up and introduced themselves. We were up on the balcony and the celebrities trooped up there to shake him by the hand.

As various glamour girls draped themselves round him, Philip naturally showed every sign of enjoying himself. All dolled up in my best, I couldn't, of course, dance with the Prince Charming, and while the assembled diners scrambled over each other to talk to him, I gradually moved further out on the fringes, wondering how the other wives or girlfriends of celebrities coped. I suppose they all knew each other and talked among themselves or danced with someone they knew. I danced with a friend at our table, otherwise I didn't know anyone and no one knew me. There was a cabaret and speeches and I concentrated on taking it all in.

Meeting Douglas Bader was the high spot of Philip's evening. Another bloody-minded individual like Philip, who had refused to resign himself to life in a wheelchair, he had also given them a hard time at Stoke Mandeville. During the evening he had found out where Philip was sitting and walked up the twenty stairs to the balcony on his artificial legs. It was a very hot evening and you could see the effort it had cost him. Philip was so pleased to meet him. They were kindred spirits, similar types who went for the shock effect and didn't suffer fools gladly. There was an instant communication between them that Philip never had with anyone else.

'Don't let the buggers get you down,' he called out as he departed. Undoubtedly, Philip knew what he was talking about.

Philip used to comment that he was glad I was built like a Roman Centurion because it meant I was able to lift, push or carry him in or out of most places. Two paces behind and manipulating the wheelchair in full evening dress round awkward corners or up and down stairs with as much grace as possible. Sometimes when it was a struggle, I'd take my high heels off, give them to Philip together with my handbag, hitch up my skirts and arrive looking like the Bionic Woman. Some lifts were too small for a wheelchair, or access to the function rooms was by stairs, so we'd have to make our entrance from a utility lift, crushing cabbage leaves and carrots on our way. Philip hated attention drawn to his disability so on our backstairs adventures it was very necessary to keep a sense of humour going. We prided ourselves that not everyone gets to check the kitchens before eating in these establishments.

A lot of London theatres were difficult and often it meant coming in through the back door. Sometimes in theatres which wouldn't allow access to wheelchairs, it proved too much of a struggle for Philip to transfer to a narrow theatre seat and we had to give up. We became both streetwise and seatwise, developing our own star ratings for backstairs premises.

Mostly, no matter what the obstacles were, we'd get round them somehow. On our own, we'd sometimes whizz along at a fair old crack with Philip calling out, 'Faster!' We did have a few spills and more than once a sharp swerve resulted in him being tipped out on the ground.

We cursed and laughed about the wheelchair, but at least we got around with it. We were like children let out of school for a few hours of relative freedom. And in love.

Philip even got as far as Downing Street. Edward Fox invited him to a performance of *Anyone For Denis* at the Whitehall Theatre, which was followed by a reception at Number 10.

I was on duty and couldn't go, so Philip took his old stalwart from the Traffic Division, Mick Rawson. After the theatre, the supper party was held in the Prime Minister's private apartment. This turned out to be very informal with about fifty people including Joan Collins who certainly had Mick and Philip's eyes out on stalks.

The party finished, Mrs Thatcher asked Philip and Mick to stay on. There were only about six people in the room when she kicked off her shoes, breathed a sigh of relief and sank down next to Philip. Apart from drinking the PM's drink by mistake, Philip got on with her very well. He said she was just like someone's Mum with no nonsense about her at all. She was very direct and wanted to hear Philip's version of the shooting and subsequent verdict, and his plans for the future. She got right down to it. Philip also said that Mark Thatcher was good company and showed him around Number 10.

In fact, at the time, Philip's future prospects with the police force were far from rosy.

Every policeman knew that serious injury meant the end of his career. He would be required to resign, pensioned off with no further role to play in an active police force. Although Philip knew this, nothing had yet been finally decided. For the time being, he was off sick but on full pay.

Many injured policemen have accepted their lot and retired on an ill-health pension. But being what he was, Philip was not about to salute goodbye to his police career without a struggle. There were things he could do and to hell with the wheelchair was his attitude.

But knowing full well the logic of the situation, Philip went into battle with a commendable detachment, playing his cards coolly and calmly as a number of senior police officers came and went at Eastcote Road.

Basically the Home Office states that we can have an establishment of so many police officers, and the ideal plan is to have the maximum number out on the streets in contact with the public. Obviously there are admin posts which require a certain knowledge and which have to be staffed by selected officers. It also often works out that the ones who are in office jobs are older or have a major medical problem. Maybe they've broken a leg and are receiving physio-therapy, or are postoperational but are expected to get better. But so that they are not just at home doing nothing, an office job is given to them until sufficiently recovered to be able to go back on the beat. But the number who are temporarily out of action is relatively small and the basic structure of the Metropolitan Police is built round a pool of officers who are posted for three to six months in these various jobs, giving them – apart from anything else – an insight into some of the support services on which they rely in everyday policing.

If there is major civil unrest, such as Wapping or a poll tax riot there is a pool which can be drawn from to get them out of the office jobs and to where they're needed. This reserve comes from all over the Metropolitan police area and it's all worked out if possible in advance with a lot of planning and contingencies. Someone permanently occupying an office job that would normally be rotated is a cog in the wheel of flexibility.

Philip was set to put forward a case that had hitherto been regarded as unarguable: despite severe disability, he had something to contribute that made it worthwhile keeping him.

Since the age of sixteen, Philip had dedicated himself to the police force. And at a time when he was literally fighting for his future, he disciplined himself into adopting a low-key approach on the question of how he could function effectively.

It was a high-level decision. Many senior officers came and went at Eastcote Road, discussing the situation with Philip in our cramped sitting-room. Philip's stance was to assure them that he realized that posts needed to be occupied by able-bodied men and that as senior officers, he appreciated that they would have to carry out the letter of the rules. But in showing a subtle detachment, Philip also contrived to send them away with the feeling that his continued presence in the police force would prove an asset rather than a liability.

He was playing a waiting game. The two cards up his sleeve were that he was a good communicator with the excellent all-round experience suited to an administrative post, and had also proved to be a highly effective spokesman to the media. The police force could feel proud of his public performance.

Mentally Philip was as active as a switched-on computer. It might take him hours to get ready physically, but he was always at his best meeting new people. Apart from his reactions to the odd tactless question, I was always very proud of the way Philip conducted himself in public. Talking to the press or on TV, he always seemed to have a suitable answer and the ability to find the right words – not always what they wanted to hear but he was quick at picking up on interviews.

At home he liked watching news and documentary programmes on TV and took a deep and continuing interest in anyone who came to talk over their problems. He could have been an agony aunt. Admittedly, he had time for all this. But sometimes I was surprised by the things he did notice and took an interest in.

One of the things was the details of my appearance. When I first met Philip, I'd only get dressed up if I was going out. Shopping for clothes wasn't something I particularly enjoyed. If I went shopping with a girl friend, I was never sure if I could rely on her opinion or not. She wouldn't say this colour doesn't suit you or that style makes you look tarty, or the whole thing's a mess, for fear of being tactless, leaving me in a state of indecision. Philip changed all that. Although hardly in a position to go window shopping, he always seemed to know where I should go and the sort of thing I should be looking for.

Talking to Andrew McEwen of the *Daily Mail*, Philip expressed himself in terms which were self-consciously chauvinistic on a subject to which he actually devoted quite a lot of thought.

'I consider her my representative and I don't want my woman looking like an SAS reject. If she goes out looking like a bleeding commando, I am not too keen on that either.'

This was a dig at my jeans and jumpers which I automatically reverted to when around the house and periodically caused Philip to explode. However, when he started on my hair, I had to admit the ultimate result was an improvement. Apart from having it cut regularly, I had never gone in for having it styled. I just used to wash it and leave it to dry. Nor did I normally wear any make-up.

Philip thought I ought to be a bit more adventurous about my hairstyle and suggested going to John Frieda. Stef's hairstylist as it happened. So off I went to Mayfair to have my hair restyled and I thoroughly enjoyed it. It was a new experience.

The strict police rules about hair mean that if it's long you have to remember you'll sometimes be struggling to put it back as neatly and tidily as possible at five in the morning, but I chose to keep the same length and John Frieda cut it into a long, shaggy bob.

With all the functions we were going to it was necessary to look as unlike 'a bleeding commando' as possible and the clothes and the hairstyle and the private dentist Philip insisted on were a considerable help to my self-confidence. The problem was that when you're with a hero, you're very much a shadow. Two paces behind, just the bag carrier.

A big date in the diary was 23 November 1981. 'Scrambled egg everywhere,' whispered Philip, referring to the amount of gold braid about as we entered the hallowed halls of New Scotland Yard where Philip received the Metropolitan Police Commissioner's High

Commendation for Bravery. Awarded by the Commissioner, Sir David McNee, the commendation was given out in the holy of holies deep in the celebrated building that houses miles and miles of files.

I'd been with Philip on several official occasions when we were pictured together after he received a certificate for bravery and a cheque for £200 at Bow Street Police Station. The caption described me as 'the smartly dressed mystery girl with PC Olds'.

But the mystery girl in Philip's life wasn't me. It was Stef.

While I was the official girlfriend living with Philip and accompanying him round London, Stef's long-established reign was on a different footing. Because of her marriage, their secret meetings continued to generate a flavour of clandestine excitement.

Stef usually came when I wasn't there.

We were at home together one day, when to my amazement, she walked into the front room. Philip and I were just having a kiss and cuddle. Stef had come by way of her old route, parking her car at the back, walking through the rear garden gate and into the house through the kitchen. It was summer and the door was open.

I don't know why but my hands were shaking as I went to make some coffee. No one spoke as I gave it to them so I went outside into the garden. Suddenly I heard raised voices, then Stef made a dignified exit, fire in her eyes.

A real Mediterranean beauty with long dark hair, slanting eyes and snappily dressed, she looked like a Continental film star. Later Philip described her as a fiery Greek. Now he seemed fairly shaken.

What had happened?

'I told her,' he said, 'Vanessa is special.'

I thought I'd seen the last of Stef.

Meanwhile, as far as work was concerned, I hadn't got off to the most spectacular of starts. On one of my first days at Harrow I was given a beat book and told to take out a panda car. The beat book shows a map of the route you are meant to be patrolling and I suppose I couldn't have followed it properly because coming out of the police station, I came to the main road, took a couple of right turns, then a left-hand one and at some stage found myself in some unfamiliar backstreets. I had driven off the map. I hadn't a clue where I was or in what direction I was pointing. So I had to call up on the radio and say, 'I'm in such and such a road – could you tell me where I am?' I felt a right banana. Impressive, eh?

I was in new surroundings at work, unfamiliar territory at home and with a new relationship that had to be adjusted to. It was a very unsettled time.

Added to this, my family had migrated. After thirty years in the police force Dad had retired and he and Mum had bought a smallholding near Ross-on-Wye in Herefordshire. The terms of service in the police force are based on a span of thirty years rather than retirement at a fixed age, so at a youthful 50, Dad was starting a new and productive life looking after the farm animals, mostly sheep. Neither of my parents had taken to a life of quiet retirement. Mum was working exceptionally hard as a manager of a cosmetics firm, later returning to nursing at an old people's home nearby. My brother, Chris, shortly to get married, had become a teacher in Surrey and my younger sister, Tracey, was at a training stables in Old Redding. Nick Clark, my former boyfriend, was about to leave the police force and join the Fleet Air Arm and, with the exception of Elaine Smith, now stationed in east London, I had lost touch with most of my friends from Tottenham.

Driving off the map seemed symbolic of the way I felt – lost. Or lost, at any rate, to comprehend Philip's unpredictable moods.

How much of it was due to pain? He suffered. You or I or anybody else would no doubt show quite different aspects of our characters if we suffered as he did. Because pain etches a story across a face, I came to recognize the signs. Pain draws the features and colours the face grey. How much pain he was in I didn't know because he didn't say. Pain meant that Philip would be running on a short fuse. It also prompted memories of the night he was shot. I knew that once he got into the swing of the story, he could, and probably would, go on all night. The action replay had many different versions.

In re-living the dramatic events that in the space of a few minutes had ended his existence as an able-bodied person, Philip saw a maze of alternative paths he might have taken.

At times he felt he should have been on the alert to a dangerous situation when he jumped out of the car outside the off-licence in Willowtree Lane. There was a car waiting with the engine running. He knew he should have assessed the situation and not been taken by surprise as he was.

At a deeper level of frustration was the moment when he remembered finding himself face to face with the gunman armed only with a twelve-inch piece of wood. Had it been a gun instead of a truncheon, he felt he wouldn't be in his present circumstances.

This was arguable. Something which could be discussed for hours. As we both knew, the question of whether or not Philip would have been shot if he'd been carrying a gun, was hypothetical. Obviously it was something to be considered. It had to be. If he'd been armed, if we had an armed police force at all, the gunmen might well not have taken up the challenge.

But there again, we were into very much of a 'what if' situation. What if he had been armed? If you're carrying firearms, at some stage you have to make a decision whether or not you're going to use them. It could equally have been that, taken by surprise as he was, Philip would have ended up in exactly the same situation. It was unlikely that he could have anticipated what was going to happen because he hadn't been called to an armed situation. So even if he'd had a gun with him when walking into a shop, he would have been at a disadvantage and the outcome might have been the same.

The proportion of disabled or dead police officers in countries where the police are armed is about the same as in Britain where they don't carry guns. It's only when you start comparing our police force to those in the majority of countries where they are armed and go into minor skirmishes with water cannon and baton rounds that you can see that we haven't an aggressive policing system. Because we don't have firearms, we have to adopt a different approach. We have to learn how to talk to people and it's a far more human response. Philip, as a police officer noted for being particularly good at communicating with people, knew all this. What good had it done him?

The most consistent version Philip stood by was that whatever the circumstances might have been, he could never have just stood there and allowed the gunmen to run away. He called it his one-man Charge of the Light Brigade.

Reasoned and philosophical as these discussions usually started out to be, they inevitably led down the same emotional blind alley.

Other scenarios continued to haunt him – circles of fantasy in which he had single-handedly arrested the gunmen or taken another course of action. The stark conclusion that it was fate which had placed him in that situation, unarmed in front of a murderous criminal, could never satisfy his outraged sense of justice.

When I first met Philip, 6 June 1981 was a date still fresh in his mind. This marked the conclusion of the two-day trial at the Central Criminal Court at the Old Bailey where the verdict on Blackstock and Cooke had been delivered.

Not long out of hospital, Philip had put on his uniform, got to the court early and given his evidence with a noteworthy degree of detachment, determined to see justice about to be done.

The charge had been attempted murder, and the jury's decision to change it overnight into a verdict of wounding with intent to resist arrest brought gasps of surprise in the court. The judge, Mr Justice Skinner, gave the maximum sentences possible under the circumstances.

Found guilty by an eleven to one majority, Blackstock had been sentenced to life imprisonment and was also given fifteen years for the attempted robbery with a total of five years for possession of two firearms. These two terms were to run consecutively.

'I am satisfied you are a dangerous and evil man,' the judge told him.

The judge described Cooke as 'a stupid, weak and contemptible man', who had gone along on the raid knowing that Blackstock had a loaded gun which he was prepared to use to frighten anyone who got in his way. Cooke was gaoled for twelve years for the attempted robbery and was sentenced to five years for unlawful wounding and five years for possession of firearms. The two five-year terms were to run concurrently, but consecutive with the twelve-year sentence.

Considering that both gunmen arrived on the scene already armed, the implication that there had been no premeditation was received with silent disbelief by Philip and close colleagues waiting in court.

Stuart Blackstock had grinned and swaggered from the court after the judge passed sentence. As Leslie Cooke was led to the cells, he swore at the judge and hit out at the dock.

While the judge's sentences had been the maximum, the jury's reduced verdict had left Philip stunned, his faith in British justice shattered.

At the time he had described how the gunman deliberately took aim before firing the shot that was to paralyse him but it seemed to him, as it did to many others, that the verdict discounted his evidence.

Blackstock had been armed with a .22 Luger loaded with three rounds. When he shot Philip, Cooke also brandished a gun. Swearing as they failed to open the tills, they had terrorized the off-licence staff by firing a shot into the ceiling.

Deputy Assistant Commissioner Ian Richardson of New Scotland Yard was in overall command of the investigation into the shooting. There were detailed descriptions of the gunmen and police were holding a black Ford Capri which the pair had travelled in. A gun was found in grass near the off-licence and there were fingerprints.

The search for the escaped gunmen went on over Christmas. Between operations at Hillingdon Hospital, Philip awaited news. Under the direction of Detective Superintendent David Hind, the search was set up with scores of police with dogs, cars and a helicopter looking for Blackstock, who was of no fixed address, in open space at Fryent Way and Barn Hill. He walked with a distinctive limp having had a steel plate inserted after a motorcycle accident. As an ironic coincidence, Philip had only been back on active duty for three months after injuring his leg in an accident while on motorcycle patrol and still had a slight limp.

It was Cooke, known to Hell's Angels as 'The Animal', who guided the police team to his door. After the shooting on 23 December, Cooke and his girlfriend were spending part of Christmas Eve with some friends and looking at the midday news on TV which referred to the shooting. Cooke bragged to the assembled company that it was his friend 'Sunshine' Blackstock who had shot the police officer. Correcting the newscaster's account of events, he added, 'The copper deserved it.'

The horrified hosts at once reported Cooke and he was arrested on 27 December. After a massive police hunt, Blackstock was found in hiding and arrested on 15 January 1981.

Philip received the news in hospital knowing that he must concentrate his mind on recalling the events that in a short flash of time had made all the difference between a full and normal life and the one which now lay ahead. His evidence was required to comply with the highest standards of professional impartiality and for the time being, he blocked his mind out to the huge storm of anger that months later poured into his soul like acid rain from a darkened sky.

In court, medical evidence on Blackstock was produced to show that he suffered from a serious personality disorder and during the trial, Blackstock and Cooke, both of whom already had criminal records, insisted that they had not intended to shoot a police officer.

'Only if he got in the way,' was Philip's bitter comment on this later when going over the details of the trial. Philip never came to terms with the Old Bailey verdict any more than he did with his injury. He was bitter beyond belief.

Of all the people you could name with the ability to accept life in a wheelchair, no one could have made a worse adjustment than Philip. Philip in a wheelchair was tantamount to putting a young jungle animal into a cruel and confining cage. As the nightly saga raged on until the early hours, I knew that nothing I could do or say would make up for that fate.

Why did he have to be crippled at the hands of two petty crooks who didn't even know how to get money out of a till? 'Rubbish,' Philip called them. Why hadn't the bullet passed clean through his head leaving him to die with honour? Why had it happened to him?

I found I didn't have an answer to these questions. There was nothing I could usefully say. We can all make the necessary noises about how sad or how awful it was – 'try not to think, it doesn't help'. Nothing I could say was positive. Once Philip's mind centred on the shooting, the subsequent verdict and a future life, his world went dark, as dark as the night outside. Lost in this darkness he would sometimes break down and weep.

He would talk incessantly through the night. I thought that even if the same scene was replayed ten times in one evening, even when, fuelled by painkillers and whisky, it all ceased to make sense, it must help to hear him out.

This was before the days when you heard about counsellors.

Nowadays you can go along to your doctor and say 'I've got this problem, I need to talk to someone', and he'll find you a counsellor and you go away and talk your problems out. Rape, shock, allergies, divorce – no matter what, there is a counsellor who will listen and give expert advice. And this is what Philip needed – professional counselling.

I had no knowledge of what is now recognized as post-trauma therapy, so never really knew whether I was doing the right or the wrong thing.

Should I say, 'Look, I've heard this story ten thousand times and it's not getting us anywhere. Let's talk about something else'; or should I let him ramble on night after night and get it off his chest? Except he never did. Never got it off his chest at all. There was nothing I could say in consolation. And in my job I'd earned points for getting through to people.

Frequently, I was numb with exhaustion. But I knew better than to say: just let's go to sleep, because if I did, it could provoke a furious reaction. I did sometimes say, 'Hold on a minute. In three hours' time I've got to be at work,' and so on, but I had to be very careful when I said it. Sometimes he'd say, 'Okay, I'm sorry, you need your sleep;' which might spark off some story or other about the times he would have to be up for an early turn. On other occasions he'd turn round and say, 'Right, you don't want to know' – the signal for another row.

I never made the mistake of saying 'I understand', because nothing infuriated him more. However much I cared about him, how could anyone else understand the combined factors which were tearing Philip apart? Like Dad, I learned not to give unasked-for advice.

All I could do was to let him know he had a girlfriend who loved him and try to show it in different ways.

When I was first at Eastcote Road, I looked at everything through rose-coloured spectacles. Philip knew I loved him and I found it easy to show my love.

I'd leave little notes when I went off to work so he would see them later. Sometimes I'd write a poem and leave that. Sometimes I'd buy him one of those silly little love tokens you see in shops, things like teddy bears and Glooks with little messages such as 'The thing I do best is loving you'. Little pottery figures with lovey-dovey words on them. I've got one in my bedroom now.

I remember coming home one day and I'd left him one of these little figures with some loving notion on it, just something light-hearted and cheerful to make him smile. I thought it was quite sweet.

When I got back, Stef or one of the girlfriends was there – I just don't remember which one – and I suppose I was a bit offhand and made her feel uncomfortable, so she left.

As soon as whoever it was had gone out of the door, Philip turned to me and said, 'You've got no right to treat my friends like that. Anyone who comes to my house is welcome. You come back with a face like a wet pudding and you say you love me? Well, just don't give me any more of these cheap junky statues . . . I don't want them.'

I stood there feeling a right silly nit, my love for him cheapened like a fifteen-year-old schoolgirl with a stupid crush. I thought it was a pretty cruel and nasty thing to say, because some of these little things, well, I'd thought they were mildly amusing.

I looked at it. A teddy bear with a hat on saying, 'Loving you is what I do best.'

Then he hurled it straight across the floor.

Lying in shattered pieces, the expression on the bear's face seemed to have turned into a mocking grin.

Chapter 6

My thoughts cold and hungry
Tapped on my window,
Begged to be allowed to enter. I let them in
But made no allowance
For the warmth
They needed so much.

You were my thoughts
And should have warmed you
And cherished you.
I did not believe you or me.

And my thoughts had
The feeling drained from them
And I let them starve
And weaken them so
That they could not move up.

I imagined you were stealing my mind
And my past.
But I could not know
You were not a thief.

So I put myself in a cold vault,

Trapped but safe.
I have only just started
My account with you
And warm up our minds.

Philip Olds
1983

It was the St Valentine's Day party that finally made me realize, if I'd had any doubts, that I was in Philip's domain and that he could do there what he liked. It brought it home that ours could not be called a relationship of equals.

The party was held on the Saturday, 13 February. And although I am not superstitious, I might just as well have been because it all ended in tears.

Philip had been responsible for asking all the guests and it became apparent that the only person I was really going to know there was my friend Elaine Smith. She was about the only person from Tottenham section house with whom I'd kept in touch. A bubbly personality, Elaine was always much in demand at parties and I was particularly pleased she was able to make it. It was planned as a fancy-dress party and the theme was famous couples. Philip and I were Othello and Desdemona, a choice that might have seemed ill-starred had I given the matter more thought. I made Philip a special costume and hired a black curly wig for him together with a velvet Shakespearian costume for myself. We used theatrical make-up to darken Philip's face and arms. We had great fun getting ready, in fact it proved the best part of the evening.

Elaine turned up as Scarlett O'Hara and Philip and I planned to do some matchmaking with a friend who could have doubled for Rhett Butler. But Cupid must have been on his annual hols because like the party, the idea ended up as a bit of a disaster. I'd prepared the food, the *pièce de résistance* being a heart-shaped strawberry flan edged with cream.

The party was in full swing when who should turn up but Stef.

Not only did she appear unannounced as far as I was concerned, but she proceeded to play a prominent part in the evening's festivities. Although at this stage I didn't know many of the guests well, not all were strangers. Some I'd met on visits to Eastcote Road or I had gone to their homes with Philip. Many were flabbergasted to see Stef there as most of them, though they knew of her, had by now accepted me as Philip's girlfriend.

As the evening wore on, the atmosphere became more strained. Finally there was a showdown. Elaine decided to stick up for me and told Stef frankly that even if she had been invited by her *ex* boyfriend, it was a bit of a cheek for her to show up at a party organized by his new girlfriend.

In the contretemps, sides were taken. Philip took up Stef's banner because he'd invited her. I leapt to Elaine's defence because she'd stood up for me. It didn't help that the Rhett Butler character tried to interfere. Before things got too out of hand, Stef made a graceful departure.

The storm didn't break immediately, but in the meantime the clouds were gathering strength. As soon as all the 'famous lovers' had left, Philip and I had a blazing row. Still wearing his wig, Philip banished poor Elaine from the kingdom. Because that's exactly what it was: a little kingdom where Philip held court and made his own rules.

There followed some black days – some very black days indeed. By Thursday the row was still smouldering and Philip told me to leave. He said that if I couldn't handle his other relationship, he couldn't cope with my jealousy. It was out in the open. Just simply like saying, 'If you don't like it – piss off.'

Philip gave the impression of being reasonable. I was given time to leave and find somewhere else. Bearing in mind that I was in a new district and was on relief work I couldn't help feeling pretty much adrift. Worse still, I felt I had stepped out of the friendly security of my old world into a new and more critical one. A place where I hardly knew anybody and where, apparently, I could be slung out on my ear if I didn't fit in with a new circle of 'friends'. I put friends in inverted commas because the assortment gathered round Philip had, for the most part, I discovered, only recently arrived on the scene. Few were what I would have described as real friends, a fact which Philip later admitted when most of them drifted away.

The main reason for the hurt, upset and jealousy I was feeling was, of course, Stef and the fact that unknown to me, Philip had been at great pains to keep in touch with her. He was certainly right in saying I found it hard to cope with the situation. I was on an emotional rollercoaster.

A few days after the row and before my 'notice to quit' expired, we had a talk. About my jealousy. It was then I discovered I had a lump in my boob. We'd had a reconciliation and Philip discovered it actually. I thought it was cancer. No one could have been kinder and more loving about it than Philip. He told me that even if the worst came to the worst and I had to have the breast removed, he would love me just the same. He came with me to a specialist and after all the panic, it turned out to be due to stress.

The doctor's advice to remove the source of stress wasn't much help, but Philip continued to be supportive and sympathetic and in time the lump disappeared.

I was now on a relief at Wembley Police Station, part of a team of thirty PCs and one Inspector. I had three stripes to sew on my uniform, a pay rise and a new set of responsibilities.

I was quite apprehensive about the change of role because if I was no longer one of the boys and girls, I knew that the respect which is supposed to go with the job has to be earned. Being a Sergeant entails making more decisions. You have to give support to the PCs you're working with, and take on additional responsibilities in running the station.

As a Sergeant I no longer had to walk the beat but alternate days were spent supervising officers on the street or working as station officer, a role which includes dealing with prisoners.

Philip was proud on my account and helpful as usual on professional matters, giving an insight into what he expected of a Sergeant: cool decisive action, loyalty, encouragement and support – not forgetting a sense of humour.

I was on night duty when my promotion came through so we didn't celebrate. Five days later Philip was admitted into the neuro-surgery ward of Atkinson Morley's Hospital in Wimbledon.

It was thought that something could be done to alleviate the root pains from which Philip had been suffering ever since his injury. These are sometimes called phantom pains because for someone with no feeling in the lower part of the body, the pain, though real, is fugitive. This is hard to explain unless you are actually looking at a diagram of how all the nerves in a normally functioning body are attached to the spinal cord. The nerves thread your body, sending messages to your brain if you stub a toe or cut a finger and telling you that your toe or finger really hurts.

If you're paralysed and you stub your toe, the message doesn't get to the brain – that's paralysis – but pain can be experienced in a different way. At the point where a bullet went into Philip's spinal cord, he was left with a bunch of torn and damaged nerves, like bare wires. Nobody can put insulating tape on these bare human wires and you can't shut off the electricity.

When these exposed nerves become irritated, the brain reacts to the fact that the nerve, which should go continuously down the leg, has had an interrupted journey. This causes the nerves to jangle and send alarm messages to the brain. So even if he was just sitting there having experienced no external damage, Philip could have agonizing pains in a leg as a result of the torn nerves at the site of the injury. Philip hated the phrase 'phantom pains' because to him they were all too real. At the same time he could also experience muscle spasms making a leg jerk in a way which he was unable to control. He hated it and found it embarrassing. It wasn't like the sudden pain you get from a knock on the shin and which gradually fades away, but a much deeper pain which intensifies as the damaged nerves send out their messages.

Philip was prescribed Valium to help prevent the muscle spasms and painkillers for the 'phantom pains', which could strike anywhere in the body. The Valium worked to a degree but the painkillers rarely seemed to hit the spot.

It seems a very strange and difficult thing to appreciate that if you're paralysed and can't feel anything externally, the brain can still send out messages saying that your legs ache or you have a terrible pain in your big toe for no apparent reason.

As Philip always said, he was dead meat from the chest down – you could pinch him and it wouldn't hurt – but as these erratic and mysterious pains continued to gnaw away, he had been referred to David Uttley, a specialist in neurology at Atkinson Morley's Hospital. Mr Uttley had devised what looked like a mini computer which can help in defusing the root pain. This is done by inserting an implant into the abdominal cavity. Wires run from this to the point of injury while an external stimulus introduces electrical impulses to the body, confusing the nerve endings sufficiently to prevent them from sending false messages to the brain. It was a very complex operation in which the wires had to be fed into the spinal cord while Philip remained semi-conscious, because the surgeon has to have the patient's reaction in order to make sure that the wires were in the right place. So it was a pretty horrible experience, but worth it to Philip if it was going to help the pain.

Philip was to go into Brodie Ward at Atkinson Morley's for preliminary tests lasting just over three weeks with the full-scale operation to follow six months later if the tests were successful.

Considering what he was undergoing, Philip seemed to be coping amazingly well. Positive action always seemed to bring out the strongest of his resources. He would have done anything to reduce the pain even if it meant experiencing more pain in the meantime.

As ever, he was usually surrounded by visitors. One cheerful contingent were policemen from the local station who kept him in touch with the world outside. I went over to Wimbledon every day, either before or after work. I rarely seemed to get more than a few minutes' talk with Philip. Often he appeared offhand and distant, more intent on amusing his other visitors. Usually, his greeting was to ask me to go off and bring him in a Chinese takeaway. I complied but found it hard, when I was so intensely concerned about his welfare, to be swept aside and relegated to the fringes.

Given the circumstances, I hardly imagined that Philip could possibly be forming another romantic attachment – this time to a student doctor. It showed how little I yet understood him. Nothing, it seemed, could destroy his machismo. Not that I wanted to. I just wished he could control it.

Once he was home, the Eastcote harem reassembled. After the ordeal in hospital, Philip seemed quite his old self again.

It must have been 28 April it all blew up in my face, because in my diary for that date I had underlined one word: *Row*.

I had come home from work to find another married woman sitting on his bed, shirt unbuttoned to her navel. It wasn't the first time I'd seen her draped round Philip in what is called 'a provocative pose'. After she left we had a blazing row. I was becoming obsessive, wondering what I was doing coming home after work with the shopping, feeding Philip, clearing up the shit, clearing up after the visitors; being one of the harem.

Once again, Philip stood his ground: 'This is my home. I'll have who I like here. If you can't handle it, you'd better go for good.'

The same aggression, the same unfeeling words.

He was right, we couldn't live like this any longer. It was time I left.

The trouble was where to go. All my friends were over the other side of London. I had nowhere to go except the dreariness of the section house. It was designed for single police officers.

I was rescued by Chris and Steve, a married couple, both traffic officers, who later became good friends. They had been at the St Valentine's Day party and, they later told me, had noted the scene with some foreboding. Their opinion was that if I was expecting Philip to give up his other girlfriends, I was on a collision course to disaster.

In the meantime, I heard that Philip had replaced me. The student doctor he had met at the hospital moved in a few days after I moved out. To prove that the relationship wasn't just a case of someone to look after him, I heard that he had bought her a special dress and taken her to a Ladies' Night dinner we had been due to attend together. I'd already seen her on one of my visits to the hospital. I had remarked on her resemblance to Stef, only to be assured by Philip that he hadn't particularly noticed it.

He phoned once or twice just to see how I was getting on. I had made up my mind I was not going to listen to any more justifications and kept it short and sharp – stilted conversations in which I made no enquiries. He had made it clear he could do as he liked, so what was there to say? I practised sounding bored.

Anything I had done for him now seemed quite beside the point. With his all-conquering charm, Philip didn't need me to love or look after him. When I wasn't looking for flats or working, I slept. I slept the sleep which only those who have yearned for eight unbroken hours can know.

It was May when Philip phoned to ask if we could meet to talk over our relationship. The student doctor had gone and he suggested that we should go right away from everything and everybody, just the two of us and talk.

This sounded a different Philip. Agreeing that we had unfinished business, the idea of talking things over with Philip away from the madding crowd of continual callers was something which I admit, suddenly seemed an excellent plan. He suggested going away for the weekend. If I could get the time off, he already had a plan which he thought I would like.

In for a penny, in for a pound. You only get three consecutive days off at a weekend once a month and I hadn't yet had mine. My distant manner thawed. Whatever else happened, we could be friends again.

It was a brilliant day as we drove off. England at its greenest and best. Philip had planned a trip to Stratford-upon-Avon, booked a hotel and seats at the Royal Shakespeare Theatre. First stop was the Swan at Tetsworth run by Eric Johnson, an ex-policeman.

On the way down, Philip pulled off the road, stopped the car and said without any preliminaries, 'Will you marry me?'

After all we'd been through, it was the last thing I expected. So far not one word had been said about our broken relationship. Totally taken aback, I just looked down and gulped.

'Well, will you or won't you?' he said.

I didn't want to appear completely bowled over, but that wasn't all that raced through my mind. What exactly had happened to bring this about?

'I'll tell you when I've had time to think about it,' I replied.

Philip turned on the engine again. 'I want an answer over the weekend,' he said.

In all, we'd been apart for twelve days. Since then, what had Philip been up to? The student doctor had come and gone. What about the others? All that was behind us. I found I didn't want to reveal the depths of my jealousy. I didn't want to talk about that.

Flowers had been delivered to the room: two dozen long-stemmed roses. The scene was set.

'I do want you to marry me,' said Philip as we gazed solemnly at each other, his eyes the pools of light blue that had caught my heart the first time I met him. It didn't take a lot of pressure for me to say yes.

We still hadn't talked about anything, but there would be time. We had never discussed marriage before either. I felt it put everything on a different basis: the other women, the black moods of violence, were all in the past.

Despite all I had seen in my job of the dark side of human nature, despite the dark side that Philip himself had revealed, I had the outlook of a romantic. I fell for the man, not the heroic reputation or the disabled condition. The wheelchair made no difference to the way I saw him. To me Philip was a romantic figure, as quite evidently he was to many other people. From the first, I had been ready to fight for him.

There were still some hours to go before the theatre and Philip wanted me to be wearing his ring. We found an old-fashioned jewellers in the town and I chose a single diamond set in a pretty and graceful design. I never wear much jewellery, but I've worn that ring to this day. I never take it off. I gave him a briar pipe and chose a mixture of tobacco. I'd always felt that a pipe was a symbol of settling down. I've kept it as a symbol of the happy ever after we never had.

After seeing *Much Ado About Nothing*, which unfortunately I remember little about, I phoned Mum and Dad to tell them I was engaged. Mum was thrilled and asked us to join her in our toast. I don't know about Dad; maybe he had reservations. If so, he wouldn't have voiced them. Philip, who was never in close contact with any of his family, phoned Stef. Just to tell her he wouldn't be seeing her any more.

When Philip and I made love, it was to the pattern of intensity and erotic tenderness we had invented for ourselves. Obviously, we weren't going to be able to swing from the chandeliers or investigate the missionary position. But for two people who had limitations on their physical lovemaking, we had discovered how to compensate and between the pair of us our lovemaking lacked nothing. I suppose the one thing it really taught me was that making love to someone doesn't have to be the main sexual act. It can be an intimate touch; a kiss and a cuddle can mean more and be more exciting than routine lovemaking, which to some people is meaningless once it's over. Rape after all is a sexual act and no one would describe it as an act of love.

Although Philip always said that the emphasis should be on me, it was important to me that whatever we did, he should feel happy and fulfilled. Bearing in mind that Philip couldn't feel anything below the nipples of his chest, I suppose the disadvantages we had to come to terms with gave our love a special quality of sensitivity.

If your most heightened erogenous zone are your nipples, which in Philip's case they were, then that is the centre of eroticism. And if in the case of a paralysed person, his injury had been at a higher level, then his erogenous zone would be higher than everyone else might consider it normally should be. If all you've got left are your earlobes, then these can become the centre of your emotions. I suppose if the highlight of our lovemaking had been rubbing noses, provided that I never found Philip rubbing noses with anyone else, it would have been our ultimate and most special act – the one which meant everything to us because we had invented it.

I'd had several boyfriends before meeting Philip so it wasn't as if I knew nothing. But despite his disability, despite the restrictions on our lovemaking, my response to Philip outweighed anything I had previously felt. One of the things Philip had said to me was: 'You never made me feel I was disabled.'

Another factor was that we shared a special type of intimacy. Whereas most couples, if they need to go to the toilet, go tootling along the corridor into the bathroom, close the door and do what they have to do in private, we shared the most intimate of bodily functions. Clearing up after Philip and dealing with the subsequent mess, I had become closer to him than would ever have been the case with an able-bodied partner. And whereas the situation was not something which could be thought of as desirable in most relationships, it had brought us to a point where I knew Philip's body almost better than my own.

Because we were so close physically and knew the bounds, at least we didn't have any of the modern hang-ups about sexual performance. We were relaxed with each other. We had fun.

One of the remaining functions left to Philip was an erection. It wasn't brought on by erotic feelings but a reaction which could be produced by manipulation, and necessary in order to attach his plumbing properly. Otherwise he couldn't have attached the condom to his penis and been able to apply the glue which held the seal.

But so far as erotic feelings were concerned, Philip didn't get an erection like most able-bodied men. I think that together with the physiological workings of his body, his erotic feelings had undergone a change. Sometimes when he got an involuntary erection, we would take advantage of it. He'd say, 'Quick, quick, come here – get your knickers off.' It didn't always last for very long. We'd laugh about it. It was fun, one of our private jokes.

Philip paid me what I suppose is the nicest compliment he could have by saying that our lovemaking never left him frustrated or disappointed. When he realized that he wasn't letting me down and that there were no regrets on my part, he became more relaxed, more adventurous. If you have a relationship in which you can enjoy a good laugh together and play about a bit like other people do, I don't think you are missing too much.

Now and then we realized that our physical relationship was a matter of speculation. At home the doorbell was forever going and sometimes I'd have to dive out of bed, try and make myself look decent and arrive at the door all flushed in the face. It was obvious I hadn't just been doing the ironing and Philip and I used to have a laugh about that. Occasionally, I think there were some raised eyebrows because when someone is disabled, other people just don't expect that sort of thing.

Once or twice journalists tried to put a few questions to Philip about our lovemaking. He gave them short change. His usual reply was to say, 'Use your imagination,' which is exactly what we used to do, but they didn't realize how barbed the answer was.

Philip had a needle-sharp sense of humour, at times fairly wicked. Soon after I got my promotion and I'd been cross-questioning him sergeant fashion about some of his visitors, instead of blowing up he decided to get his revenge another way. We always slept with no clothes on and one night while I was out to the world, he drew three stripes on my right bum cheek with an indelible pen. It took me weeks to get this stuff off and I was naturally somewhat annoyed. The vestiges were still there on our weekend at Stratford. Philip was often the subject of newspaper headlines and had become adept at supplying his own: 'Cheeky bum Sergeant weds PC', was one of the more outrageous. As well as a private joke it was a reminder that at home I wasn't the senior officer.

Our idyllic weekend at Stratford-upon-Avon, perhaps the happiest we ever had together, was marred only by one small incident. As it happened, there were no ill effects but it was all in line with the back-to-front notion people have in this country about facilities for the disabled. The luxury hotel we were staying at was down in the guide book as providing facilities for the disabled. These often consist of a handrail by the loo – usually too far away to be of much use – and not much else. In this case, the lack of imagination could have had more far-reaching consequences. On Sunday morning, I went to get the papers and just as I had gone off, Philip remembered something else he wanted and went to open the door to shout after me. He pulled at the door, but nothing happened. It was on a spring that made it impossible for anyone sitting in a wheelchair, however strong, to open it. Philip's upper body was as strong as anyone's but even so, the door refused to open. Had there been a fire, he or any other disabled person would have been trapped in the room.

Today, the subject of raising standards in public places for the disabled still brings the same muted response.

It was a slightly discouraging note on which to leave after such a lovely weekend, but one which in our new state of happiness soon went to the back of our minds.

Going off with my ring and flowers I felt as though in a fairytale. When we got back, Philip asked Dad for my hand in marriage and was accepted in classic form. Brought up in a loving household, I was born a romantic and saw my future with Philip as one in which love would conquer all; the stage at which love and affection were expressions of the delight in living which Mum and Dad had always conveyed to me and some of which I hoped I would be able to pass on to Philip. Like nursing a fire which needs encouragement to burn.

One of the things we talked about at that time was the possibility of having children. There are disabled people who manage to have children and our hopes were very high. Women who are disabled but have able-bodied partners usually have the best chance. But in the reverse situation, conception can take place providing the man's sperm has not deteriorated. So what usually happens when a man, especially a young man as Philip was, is found to be paralysed, is that as soon as the life-saving procedures have been taken, doctors free some of the sperm.

This had happened in Philip's case. At the time Philip was fighting for his life but he remembered that someone had come in and taken a sample and told him it was a routine thing to do. Philip had thought little about it at the time but we decided to investigate. The result was a disappointment. The sample was infected and our first hopes were dashed. Later it turned out that there was still a chance. Someone who is paralysed can still possess viable sperm although the probability is that it will have deteriorated, the all-important factor being circulation. In crude terms, whereas an able-bodied chap is going to be a bit careful about his balls when he sits down and moves around, Philip couldn't feel any discomfort so the sperm had been affected by his circulation and the samples couldn't work.

Philip adored children and most definitely had the ability to be a good father, otherwise we wouldn't have considered the idea of parenthood. We thought about adoption but realized Philip's disability would count against us. Because I was capable of having a child, at one stage Philip even suggested that asking someone we knew who didn't look very different to him might be a solution to getting me pregnant. Not by getting into the sack with him, but by means of artificial insemination, as Philip was at pains to make clear. In fact, although this seemed to be the only possibility open to us other than using an anonymous donor, which Philip didn't feel too sure about either, I thought that it would not be a strong enough bond. Rightly or wrongly, I felt that if times got tough, he might have thrown it in my face that the child wasn't his. It was too big a risk even to try and take.

But we both attended fertility clinics and at one time, the prospect of having a child of our own was not beyond the realms of realization. It was something we talked about from every aspect.

97

Philip was one of those people who has a distinctive rapport with kids. I think that to have had a child of his own would have made a very big difference to him. Also, it would have proved his manhood and although he didn't need to demonstrate it to me, Philip still needed to prove himself to the world. He wanted to walk again and show all the doctors to be wrong.

This was one miracle which was about to happen.

Chapter 7

Philip was an articulate guy and intelligent. Too intelligent for some people. He had good honest principles and didn't suffer fools gladly. But you could talk to him about anything.

Vanessa improved and affected his life for the good. It was appalling of him to smack her in the face and treat her with violence. He would get annoyed about something and put on a show of rudeness and arrogance.

Two views of Philip Olds by his friend and colleague, Police Sergeant Michael Rawson.

Immediately after Philip was shot, donations started to pour in from the public. At Hayes Police Station alone, about £100 was handed in within a couple of hours of the incident being reported in the news and by the end of the month the sum was well over £1,000. People also left money at local police stations and at Hillingdon Hospital.

No official appeal had been launched but unsolicited donations came from people from all walks of life all over the country. Friends and colleagues started collections for Philip and as the news of his paralysis spread, scores of tributes and goodwill messages continued to arrive.

Philip would open the post to find a five-pound note from an old-age pensioner, or £20 from a school collection; even a pound from someone who was unemployed saying what had happened to Philip was a hell of a way to lose your job.

Society was saying thank you in an unprecedented way to our police. There might be demonstrations in Trafalgar Square and anti-police stories circulating in the media, but people still sent money, gifts and letters to Philip to thank him for what he did and what he represented. The amazing thing about the British public is that they do respond in this way when their imagination is caught by a cause or a person they see as deserving of help and support.

And how did Philip feel about this response? Humble and very, very grateful. Being disabled is about the biggest unwanted expense anyone can have.

The first thing you notice when you walk into the home of a disabled person who is being adequately cared for is that the atmosphere is like a sauna. Because of restricted circulation, anyone who is paralysed is peculiarly vulnerable to the cold. Even with the temperature kept at 75 degrees, Philip would often feel cold – cold to the touch that is, because except for the upper part of his body, he didn't know if he was hot or cold. The unawareness was damagingly deceptive, for bad circulation could mean hypothermia; even death. For disabled people relying on their savings or the social services, heating bills alone can read like a death sentence.

If you are a paraplegic, almost everything from the kitchen sink to the front doorstep suddenly becomes of no further use to you. The structural changes needed to meet your new way of life can mean a new home or a large-scale capital investment.

Donations made by the public provided a contingency fund, which was added to by an ever widening circle of charity events. Fund-raising activities for Philip took off in a big way.

A few days after Philip was shot, Hayes Police Station and the Alperton Traffic Garage combined to organize a fund-raising evening on Philip's behalf. The dinner was a sell-out weeks in advance with over 450 people buying tickets. The charity cabaret dinner held at a Heathrow hotel less than a month after the shooting raised a cheque for over £11,000, wildly exceeding the total expected, with stars, including Michael Aspel, Michael Parkinson and Roy Castle, giving their services.

Scotland Yard administered a Philip Olds Fund while further donations, big and small continued to flow in. A raffle at the Barnshill School PTA raised £155. A local football club announced they were to hold a series of benefit events.

Some people preferred to send gifts. Pupils of Waddesdon Secondary School raised money to buy Philip a cassette player. The Lord Mayor of London gave him a ceremonial ice bucket. I wish I had a list of all the individuals and organizations who wanted to thank him for carrying out his duty so courageously, but when he died all that was taken out of my hands. A lot more charity dinners and events were organized by fellow policemen from different divisions, which, whenever he was not in hospital, he would attend and usually I would accompany him.

Philip was both touched and pleased with all this generosity and the kind thoughts and gifts from complete strangers. It gave him a sense of hope and a wider belief in the future. Invited to take part in all sorts of charities, he saw another side of life. Children moved him to tears and the cancer ward Teddy Bear Appeal at Great Ormond Street Hospital was one that he did everything he could to help.

The realizations of finding yourself disabled and, on top of that, discovering how expensive it is to live like that, come as twin blows. The most precious thing you lose when you're disabled is your freedom. The freedom to come and go as you please. Replacing that freedom, even in the most limited way, is an endless cycle of expense.

In order to get in or out of the house you need to build ramps, you sometimes need to alter awkward doorways and although wheelchairs are available on the National Health Service, they are very heavy and not very practical. Philip was able to buy himself a lighter type of wheelchair, which was easy to pull close to the bed or car. Some people need hoists and specialist equipment, all of which cost money, but one of the biggest expenses is a car. In this country, public transport is virtually inaccessible to paraplegics. Without cars, their limits extend to the four walls of their homes and short trips to the shops where help is needed from an able-bodied person to negotiate awkward pavement levels. To Philip his car was a symbol of freedom. Fitted with hand controls, another expensive operation, his car was his passport to the outside world. Philip had qualified as an advanced driver before the shooting and only behind the wheel of a car did he feel on equal terms with the world.

Donations from the public made Philip's life a lot happier than it might otherwise have been and I think it's probable he wouldn't have lived so long as he did without some of the things which minimized the everyday frustrations of life as a severely disabled person.

The main thing it gave him was hope. Philip never gave up hope of finding a miracle cure and most of the money was kept in a contingency fund which he called his 'backbone money'.

Because I had nothing to do with it, I don't know how much it amounted to, but Philip always said that if someone somewhere in the world – it might be Tasmania or Outer Mongolia for all he cared – devised a method of sewing his spinal cord back together, he would use every penny of it to get there and get it done. The 'backbone money' was invested but in such a way that he could always get his hands on it at a moment's notice if ever and wherever the miracle cure turned up.

One of the things he also said was that we ought to have a contingency fund for my backbone, because as he said, 'In a few years' time you might be feeling all of this.' Although I used to have the strength of an Amazon, there were times when I strained my back, heaving Philip round in the wheelchair over the bumpy terrain of a social life that generally contained as many stairs as a Palladium spectacular.

When Philip was awarded the Queen's Gallantry medal in 1982, he became one of the many who have received their sovereign's recognition from a wheelchair. The Palace, with its spacious corridors, might almost have been designed for the wheelchair brigade. Philip said that such was the smoothness of the organization and the unobtrusive competence of the uniformed footmen, that he was hardly conscious of being borne aloft to the upper regions of the throne room.

As he waited his turn for presentation to the Queen, his pride at being given this prestigious award suddenly gave way to extreme nervousness as all his thoughts centred on the fear that his plumbing might go wrong at the crucial moment.

Asked his impressions of the splendid surroundings, Philip told me later, 'All I could think of was what would happen if I pissed on the carpet.'

Philip wheeled himself smartly forward as his name rang out, and found himself gazing into what he described as the Queen's 'kind, lovely eyes' as she pinned on his medal. After a few words of conversation in which he remarked that he hoped Prince Andrew would soon be returning safely from the Falklands, Philip had forgotten his moment of nervous embarrassment.

He had taken as his guests, Laurie Howarth, the policeman who was with him at the time of the shooting, and Andrew McEwen, whose sensitive coverage of Philip's story in the *Daily Mail* had led to a lasting friendship. Philip enjoyed Andy's company and had rated him among the more intelligent and honest reporters he had met, as well as having the art of making his stuff very readable without descending into sensationalism. We had attended Andy's wedding to Rita, a warm-hearted Italian girl and our links with him were to go far beyond the usual bounds of a journalist and the subject matter of his story.

It was at the Palace that Philip met David English, Editor of the *Daily Mail*, who was there to receive his knighthood. Philip enjoyed the encounter but didn't expect anything more to come of it. Though neither knew it at the time, Sir David English was to be instrumental in Philip's fight to walk again.

To tell the truth, I would have loved to have gone to the Palace. Well, who wouldn't? I couldn't help feeling disappointed that as his fiancée, Philip hadn't asked me to accompany him.

In fact, as Philip's fiancée, I wasn't exactly billed as the supporting role. Stef might have acknowledged our engagement – at least she had kept away – but to the rest of Philip's fan club it had made little difference.

Among Philip's real friends such as Mick Rawson, who remained one of his closest buddies, there were those who were sometimes uncomfortable with the way he behaved on occasions. To people who liked us both, Philip's attitude towards me was often embarrassingly chauvinistic. To the hangers-on, it gave further encouragement.

I was finding I could have done with some support. From Philip's family, the only regular visitors were his stepmother, Josephine Olds, whom his father had married shortly before his death and who was not much older than Philip, and Philip's cousin Sarah, a nurse in whom he took a brotherly interest. Discouraged by Philip, his mother hadn't visited him since he left hospital. Philip behaved as if he didn't have a mother. I could always tell by his body language if she was on the phone. Philip's face would tighten, he would raise his left arm and wave it around in the air, talking in a cold, dismissive voice.

I wished that there had been a better relationship between Philip and his mother. I felt it would have helped him if he could have talked to her. But the lines of communication between them had been damaged a long time ago and there remained a conflict of personalities. According to Philip there had never been a time when they could sit down and talk.

Chris, Philip's brother visited a couple of times, but said he found Philip's condition too upsetting to come again. Of all his immediate family, Philip was closest to his sister Jenny, but living in Wales with a young family meant that her visits were limited.

This left the cast of the Eastcote soap opera as a continuing presence. After the engagement, their activities took a new and more active turn. This took the form of drawing Philip's attention to any of my bad points, pretending to sympathize with me over his aggressive attitude then, as a sidewinder, telling him I was complaining. With Philip's volatile state of mind, these proved dangerous tactics that seriously undermined our relationship.

When Philip's reinstatement in the police force was officially confirmed, it seemed to give his life a new momentum.

Staying in bed on days when he didn't feel like making the effort to get up, his morale had been on the decline and the inactivity wasn't doing his physical condition any good. Also I have to confess that the day I didn't come home to find the place littered with unwashed cups and overflowing ashtrays with a disturbing atmosphere in the background, was going to be a red letter one for me. With Philip back at work, I hoped that the Eastcote harem would be disbanded.

Using a mixture of diplomacy and sound reasoning, Philip had been given the job he wanted: an officer in charge of communications at the Police Traffic Centre at Alperton – the man behind the radio control. It was a job in which his knowledge and experience would be invaluable. Philip's arguments had been based on management sense rather than an emotional appeal. He was to work office hours and could get himself to the police garage. At the other end a colleague would be ready with a wheelchair to help him out of the car. This was the only extra help he would require. His reinstatement was a popular decision. Popular with the media as well. The day Philip donned his uniform again, reporters and cameramen were waiting to record his first day back at work. Ever since the shooting, he had been regularly in the news.

Philip was concerned to prove that in taking a disabled officer back into the fold, his bosses wouldn't be let down. But more than the average person could ever imagine, just getting to work and seeing to the complicated plumbing arrangements that were to see him through the day, was a testing process. There were days when he had infections or felt unwell, days when things could and did go wrong.

Worse than this were the times when it seemed as though demons returned to afflict him. Whatever private hell Philip still existed in, the underlying problem of his sudden violence had not gone away.

The first time Philip hit me it had come as a short, sharp shock. I almost thought it was a mistake, a nightmare which would never be repeated. He had apologized, been remorseful. But it had happened again.

I never knew why it happened, but I had to face the problem any intelligent person must ask: why did I let it happen? Philip was in a wheelchair – why couldn't I just get out of his way? I didn't because he'd say, 'It's all right for you – you can walk away. I can't. I can't follow you. You're just proving to me that I'm disabled – a cripple in a bloody pram.'

It made my blood run cold. I didn't want to hit him back like he insisted I did before. It was a detestable scene and I didn't want to take it any further. So I used to stand there and think, well let him hit me.

For the most part, I had no idea how these situations arose. An unbearable sense of frustration bubbling over? Something that had been said during the day? Me?

Living in close proximity with someone, you come to realize you have your share of annoying habits. I don't any more, but I used to wake up in the morning full of the joys of spring. I didn't realize I was doing it, but my routine apparently, was to jump out of bed when the alarm went, scratch my right bum cheek and go off whistling into the bathroom. Always the same maddening routine. Sometimes it made Philip laugh – he used to tell people about it – but sometimes it didn't. I could see it was especially maddening to someone who couldn't jump out of bed, wasn't experiencing the joys of awakening to a wonderful world and couldn't feel his right bum cheek even if he had been in the habit of scratching it.

I used to hear this voice coming from a tousled head stuffed under the pillow: 'Oh, shut up . . . Do you have to?' But I used to carry on singing or whistling because that's what I'd always done. Later, to save bad feeling, I had to pack up being quite so bright and breezy in the morning. So I'd hum and whistle out of earshot, or at least what I thought was out of earshot.

I knew that Philip did have dreams and that in his dreams he was always walking. So in his dreams he was happy: walking, moving about naturally, without effort. An able-bodied, thirty-year-old man, able to walk free as he had always done. And in the morning he'd wake to find he couldn't move his legs. That he was paralysed. Remembering in a great flood of consciousness, what had happened. Coming back to reality.

For most of us it's the reverse. A brief nightmare, then the relief of waking to a familiar world. I've thought about this a lot lately. I've put down here:

'To him, nothing was as it was before and everything was an effort. The once simple act of getting up and dressed took more willpower than I ever possessed. But acknowledgement took years to sink in. Initially, I didn't realize how much it meant for Philip to wake in the morning and come back to reality. His days were his nightmares and his dreams were his release.'

I've written after this, 'Unfortunately.' Because unfortunately, it took me a long time to understand this. I had to think about how literally to manage the days. I couldn't really afford to have any off days, but I did have off days. Days when things were forgotten and routines rushed – with unhappy consequences.

I knew I was fighting a battle, but with what I was unsure. Really, nothing made any difference to Philip's inner turmoil. It was as though he was striving to keep the adrenalin going, the adrenalin you need in a fight. Then you need the fight to use up the adrenalin.

Both in our backgrounds and in our respective situations, Philip and I were of two very different breeds. I can only remember Mum and Dad having one argument and that hardly amounted to anything. It must have been a rare occasion for me to remember it. We were in the car, going on holiday. Mum was map reading and she got the directions wrong. Dad got furious and only recovered when we were on the right road again. When we arrived, I think somewhere in Devon, where we had our family holidays, we all had a good laugh, which cleared the atmosphere. This was the difference: there was no way of laughing off Philip's anger. Or his violence.

I felt it was his problem, and that he should find a way to deal with it. I don't think he talked to other people about it because he wasn't proud of it. But some people did know. They might say, 'Leave it out,' when he started to get abusive, but at that point, they usually left because they were treading on dangerous ground. He once hit me in front of other people and they were completely shocked, but they weren't going to say too much because what goes on between a couple is regarded as private business. In any case they had no reason to suppose he could really hurt me – a man in a wheelchair.

I'm not talking about being hit on one or two occasions, I'm talking about being hit on many, many occasions. There were too many to remember one from the other, except for three which have stuck in my mind.

I remember thinking after the first time: I don't like this sort of thing, but the next time, you know, I took it.

The next really major incident was the time I'd made up my mind I wasn't going to take it. It only made things worse.

We'd been out somewhere for the evening. We'd had a nice time and came back late. Like most of the arguments, I can't remember what it was about. The subsequent shock blots everything else out of your mind. We hadn't been back long when Philip started to get aggressive so I went upstairs knowing he couldn't follow me. One very decisive way to put a stop to the argument. I just went and got into an unmade bed intending to go to sleep and deal with the situation in the morning.

Downstairs I could hear Philip shouting, 'Get back down here!' and calling me names. I ignored him, and eventually I went off to sleep.

The next thing I knew, there were blows raining down on my head. Philip was pummelling me as hard as he could go. Once I realized what was happening, I tried to get out of arms' reach but to start with I was numb with shock and he'd already had a good few hits while I was asleep.

In a surcharge of aggressive energy he had climbed the stairs on his elbows.

An overpowering anger at the way I'd walked off and gone to a place where he couldn't get hold of me had fuelled this incredible feat. He had thrown himself out of the wheelchair, used all the strength of his upper body to get up the stairs, then heaved himself up on the bed. That's why it had taken so long and why in the meantime I'd fallen asleep.

All I'd done by walking away from him was to increase his anger and frustration, because the circumstances were so different from those of an able-bodied person and because he was the one who was at a disadvantage. This, unfortunately, was the way I was looking at the situation, rather than asserting my right to self-preservation.

Of course, looking back I can see the question of whether someone is able-bodied or disabled doesn't matter. Why did I accept it?

But I did accept it for a few years. Later I would leave the house – running away Philip called it. The other thing was that I always tried the best I could to make life easy for Philip. I never wanted to feel I was letting him down. I would ask myself why he behaved like that.

'The day he climbed the stairs and beat me up. Why?' I put in my diary. Obviously, if not consciously, I was making excuses for Philip's behaviour. I could never really know how he felt. There were reasons, God knows, for the anger and frustration always evident below the surface. I felt I should have recognized them and been able to deal with them.

With hindsight I realize that by taking the brunt of these outbursts, I had taken the first steps towards becoming a whipping boy, a destructive role that I should never have accepted.

I'm not an aggressive person, but I still wonder if maybe a reciprocal attack or at least some kind of defence would have made Philip think twice before assaulting me. Was that really what he wanted? I had hit him once and then only at his insistence, but I'd hated myself for doing it and never wanted to go down that path again.

At the police station I was dealing with women who had been battered, advising them on their legal rights. Few ever took them up. A serious assault can be where a woman comes in with her face hanging open after an attack by her husband or boyfriend. Lesser attacks are everyday occurrences but nevertheless still serious.

Obviously there had been some embarrassment when I turned up at work with a bruised face the day after Philip had attacked me in bed. I got strange looks but only one person challenged me about it. I explained it by saying that my horse had done it by throwing back his head. Laughing it off killed any further enquiries.

As time went on, so did the batterings and their ferocity increased. Philip was showing the sort of behaviour patterns which get other people locked up. But I was committed to him, prepared to cover up for him and still deeply in love. The situation couldn't be turned round now.

Drama and crisis were never far away, but given that so many other things were happening at the same time, it was not surprising that my own concerns took second place.

In August 1982, Philip returned to Atkinson Morley's Hospital for the final stage of the painstaking procedures to fit a device in his abdominal cavity to inhibit pain. He was there for three weeks and although it worked for a time, unfortunately it proved no long-term solution.

This time round, he formed no romantic involvements in hospital. There were other things on his mind. For some time it had been obvious that the domestic circumstances at Eastcote Road were far from ideal for someone in a wheelchair, let alone for two of us sharing. It was desperately inconvenient living only on the ground floor and it may well have been that the unsuitable conditions were putting an additional strain on our relationship. Philip was now working office hours and in his free time had been house hunting with friends.

Built in the 1950s, 79½ Barrowpoint Avenue was as distinctive as its address. A one-storey house of character, little had been done in the intervening years to bring it out of the austerity era. The odd-sounding ½ had been adopted when the bungalow was built between two larger houses with spacious gardens. Rather than re-number the whole road, the new house became 79½.

Two features instantly recommended themselves: apart from being all on one floor, there was a three-foot-wide ramp up to the front door as it had previously been lived in by another disabled person. The other advantage was its peaceful location in a very nice part of the world. To me, another plus factor was the garden with a wooded area at the bottom in which Philip pretended to imagine a contingent of Japanese combat troops. Admittedly there was an air of mystery to that part of the garden. Apart from that there was little in the way of amenities. The kitchen was primitive with a butler's sink and an equally old-fashioned clothes airer that went up and down on pulleys, there was no central heating and the whole place had to be completely re-wired.

Philip decided that it was worth knocking down virtually the entire place to make it habitable. What lay ahead was a complete reconstruction with cavity filled walls and central heating. Two special concessions were a kitchen with ceramic hobs and a built-in microwave where the units were slightly lower than the standard level. The new bathroom was given a tiled floor which tilted towards a plughole over which was a special shower Philip could use while in his wheelchair. Apart from this and the ramps, there were no special gadgets or any other reminder that this was the house of a disabled person. Philip emphatically did not want a house which looked as though specially designed for the disabled because he hated everything that reminded him of his condition.

There was a parquet floor in the lounge and Philip found a craftsman to make some plaster beams for the walls and ceiling, and he designed a lovely fireplace made from York stone and slate.

Designing the details of the house gave him a great deal of satisfaction.

One of the larger projects to be taken on board was a heated swimming pool. This was donated by the CID who had raised money with a series of charity nights, boxing matches and all sorts of sponsored events in the early 1980s.

A great deal of the work on the house was carried out by police officers who turned out to be among the world's best handymen. From plumbing and electrical work to decorating, they seemed to be able to tackle almost anything. For some reason, policemen always seem to be doing something to their own homes and you would be surprised at how many DIY experts there are in the force, many of whom have been in other trades before joining the Job, as we always call it. They came over on their days off and after they had finished their shifts. Thanks to them the house was finished in record time. We had quite a lot of fun choosing bits and pieces. I was particularly pleased with a 1930s bedroom suite with an art deco inlay, which was bought at an auction. The house, when finished, came up to a high standard of design. Even Rhona, Philip's ex-wife, came round for a look.

We were lucky to have had so much help from friends, lucky indeed after the restrictions of Eastcote Road to be living in such attractive and civilized surroundings. And particularly lucky as it later turned out, to have such good next-door neighbours as the Griffiths family – a retired parks superintendent and his wife. Their son, David, was to become one of our best friends.

We might have been very happy at Barrowpoint Avenue. But Philip couldn't be happy anywhere. The house hadn't changed him.

He continued to have the same explosive emotional reactions to anything that upset him, usually out of all proportion to the occasion. So although life was a lot easier and pleasanter in the new house, for me to have been cheerfully bustling around seeing to things while Philip was in the same state as before, enraged him. At the same time, he reminded me that this was 'our home'. When I suggested we went home to Mum and Dad on one occasion he took me up on it by saying, '*This* is your home.'

One thing Philip had not lost was his ability to hope for a miracle.

Neither of us had given up hoping that something would come along. Philip was always ready to listen to the news of any scientific advance or medical discovery, always hoping to hear of some far-flung genius who had found a new way of knitting together spinal cords.

Nearly a year had elapsed since Philip had received his decoration at Buckingham Palace. We could have papered a room with all the medals and framed certificates for bravery Philip had received in the last couple of years. They were of little comfort compared to the news Andrew McEwen brought with him one late autumn day as the leaves began to settle on the CID pool which Philip so seldom used.

Philip had made a lasting impression on Sir David English when he had wheeled himself forward in the Buckingham Palace throne room. In New York recently, Sir David had watched a sixty-minute television documentary on the subject of a Professor Jerrold Petrofsky and the work he was doing at Wright State University in Dayton, Ohio. It was hoped that paraplegics could be helped to walk with the aid of the new Petrofsky system.

Sir David English lost no time in phoning Andy in London and asking him to find out what Philip's reaction would be to this project. All Andy was able to tell Philip at that stage was that it was some kind of scientific project to help people with spinal injuries to walk with the aid of electronic equipment. Would Philip be interested?

The problem was to restrain Philip's enthusiasm. The first thing to establish was whether the idea was a viable proposition rather than something in the realms of science fiction which might vapourize under the cold light of investigation. If it was on, the next thing to be decided was the practicalities of Philip going out to the States for an unspecified length of time. How he could get on the project, for a start? And how he was going to live? And who was going to look after him while he was there?

Although I didn't know it at the time, this last question was to become important to the final decision because the fact that I would be there to support him made it more likely that Philip would see it through to the end. Petrofsky was not looking for drop-outs. In fact, he was not looking for anyone from as far away as Britain at all. All his guinea pigs were to be home-grown, young – preferably under twenty-five – and most were to come from the University so that while taking part in the project, they could keep their minds occupied with their studies.

The one quality Petrofsky required from his guinea pigs was that they should be fighters. They could be as awkward and bloody-minded as they liked, but they needed guts and they needed staying power. The role sounded tailor-made for Philip.

As it happened, Petrofsky would be attending a seminar in London in a few weeks' time. Andy was to contact Petrofsky and ask him whether or not he would be prepared to accept Philip as one of the guinea pigs on an otherwise all-American project.

Petrofsky was only to be in London for a few days and when the time came, Andy was dismayed to find that the Spinal Injuries Association who had sponsored the visit were firmly in charge of Petrofsky's schedule.

It turned out that there was a long queue of eminent people wanting to meet the American scientist and Andy's chances of getting an appointment were becoming thinner by the hour.

Chapter 8

I'm said to be a great man to have around in a very dangerous situation but no good when everything is all right. The trouble is that everything is all right 97 per cent of the time.

Philip Olds

For a whole day Andy McEwen had been trying to speak to Professor Petrofsky without any luck. So when he came on the phone to say Petrofsky was going back to the States the next day, things didn't sound very hopeful.

Jerrold Petrofsky was staying as the guest of the Spinal Injuries Association in London and it looked as though they were going to protect their eminent speaker from any outside intrusions up to the minute he boarded his plane home. According to Andy, the Spinal Injuries Association had fixed up a tight schedule for Petrofsky's diary, leaving him little time for any diversions from the plan. Messages had been left by Andy but continued to go unanswered. The trouble was that in order to get Philip on the project, it was essential for him to meet Petrofsky face to face.

All Petrofsky's guinea pigs for the research programme had to be hand-picked by him. They had to have some special quality which wasn't on any formal record, a quality of character that apparently only he could recognize. If Philip was to have the slightest chance of being accepted, he would have to meet Petrofsky in person within the next twenty-four hours.

Philip had obviously become very excited at the prospect of having the chance to walk again, and it seemed brutal that all his hopes were simply evaporating.

As repeated phone calls between us confirmed, Andy wasn't getting anywhere very fast. At least, not fast enough to catch up with the soon-to-vanish Petrofsky. Time was running out, so what were we going to do?

'This was my chance,' said Philip, sinking into despondency. 'I've fallen at the first fence and that's all there is to it.'

I told him that Andy hadn't given up yet and had promised to phone back yet again.

Philip's reaction was to shut himself off from disappointment by going off in the car. He couldn't bring himself to sit and wait for a message that might never come. As frequently happened when upset, his way of relieving tension was to drive the car at speed. In this mood he wasn't going to be too careful.

'Please don't go out,' I begged. 'Not in this frame of mind. It's not too late yet.'

'Don't get this way!' I yelled after him as he got into the car and disappeared into the night in a cloud of exhaust fumes.

Philip had often described me as the eternal optimist. That was one side of me; there were others. Once I got a bee in my bonnet nothing would stop me. I was like a sales person with confidence in her product. I felt that in Philip I had a good quality product. It only remained for the customer to see it.

Reckoning that by now Andy's name was on the blacklist of callers to be discouraged, I decided to try Petrofsky myself.

Earlier Andy had given me Petrofsky's hotel number and speaking in a fake American accent, I gave my name as Mrs Petrofsky.

'Sorry,' said a cool English voice. 'Professor Petrofsky is not available.' Maybe the accent wouldn't have fooled anyone. I phoned Andy and told him what I'd done and how it hadn't worked. I also told him about Philip driving off into the night.

Andy had done his utmost. 'I don't know what we do now,' he admitted. His disappointment was almost equal to Philip's.

I wasn't going to be beaten if I had to stay up all night. 'We can't give up,' I said. 'I'll go on trying.'

The next time I phoned the line was engaged. Then I tried again, this time using no particular accent but endeavouring to sound briskly confident.

'Yeah,' said a sleepy voice. 'This is Petrofsky.'

I was so surprised, I nearly tugged out a lock of hair I'd been idly winding through my fingers. Getting as much over in as quick a time as possible, I explained what the story was.

'I don't suppose you've ever heard of him,' I said, 'but there's this policeman, PC Philip Olds, who was shot. His spinal cord was severed and he'd do anything, absolutely anything, to be able to walk again. Would you just see him?'

As I was still talking, Petrofsky cut in and said, 'Yeah, sure I'll see Philip Olds. Tell him to be at my address at 9.15 in the morning.'

Without replacing the receiver, I dialled Andy's number and told him the news. Half-way through the conversation, I heard Philip's car coming down the drive. Asking Andy to hang on, I dashed out to help Philip into his wheelchair and explained I was in the middle of a phone call.

'Andy again, I suppose,' he said morosely. Looking out of the corner of my eye I could see that, refusing to hope, he was not a happy chappie.

'You'll never guess what,' I said, 'you've an appointment early tomorrow morning.'

It took a moment or two for Philip to react so I told him the whole saga, warning him that Petrofsky had promised nothing.

There was no guarantee that Petrofsky would take Philip on. But getting to see him was the first step.

'You didn't think I was going to let it go at that, did you?' I said.

Philip's face just broke into a big, big grin. 'What am I going to wear?' he said, pulling me onto his lap. Laughing, we went for a spin round the room in the chair. We didn't dare to get too emotional, but a cuddle seemed in order.

The next morning we were at Petrofsky's hotel right on time, having allowed more than the usual forty minutes to get Philip ready. We had estimated correctly that in the morning traffic it would take an hour to get from Pinner to NW1.

Petrofsky, who had been in the middle of packing, came bounding down the stairs all in a bit of a tizz about having enough time to get to the airport. Both Philip and I immediately registered that he wasn't at all the type of person we had expected to meet. Somehow, our mental picture of the typical professor had been someone small and skinny with light-socket specs, a shock of white hair and a dry manner. Professor Jerrold Petrofsky turned out to be the complete opposite. A tall roly-poly man in his mid-thirties with an exuberant manner, he looked like a young Orson Welles.

After my phone call of the night before, Andy at last got through to Petrofsky and had been able to explain a lot more about Philip's background than I had managed to gulp out in our brief conversation.

It had definitely been quite a coup to get to see him at all and with Petrofsky's imminent departure, Philip felt he had to talk fast. Compressing the reasons why he wanted to have a go at the project and what it meant to him, Philip made it as short and to the point as possible.

Petrofsky listened, nodding as if Philip had come up with the right answer. Clearly not the sort of man to hang about where decisions were in the balance, it took Petrofsky only a few minutes to agree to Philip coming out to the States to be evaluated. The emphasis, as he explained, was very much on evaluation and we gathered there were many hurdles to be overcome. The situation was that yes, he would accept Philip as a guinea pig on the project providing the evaluation was good. But he wanted the tests done by Wright State University doctors in Petrofsky's unique laboratory according to their own medical criteria, the same as with the other volunteers.

He explained that this was a research project *not* a complete project, so Philip would be going to America to take part in a test to see if he was suitable to take part in another test that would prove if he was ever to walk again.

'D'ya think ya can make it?' asked Petrofsky, shaking us both by the hand and departing in a whirl of farewells to important medical colleagues who had gathered to say goodbye to this extraordinary pioneer in the field of spinal injuries.

Petrofsky had mentioned hurdles, but he had left us feeling that the most important one had been cleared in one soaring jump.

It looked as though at least one important thing had been decided before breakfast – particularly as we hadn't yet had any. The next was the question of how Philip could make it to the States, existing in Dayton as an outpatient. Petrofsky didn't say for how long.

If the outcome of the first test of Philip's suitability as a research subject was favourable, he would have to return to Dayton to take part in the project, a programme which as yet had no specified time limit.

Right from the start, Philip's euphoria at the prospect of walking on his own two feet again had to be matched by a cautionary realism. We learned that Professor Petrofsky's work in the field of electronic equipment designed to give victims of spinal cord injury some mobility was still at the experimental stage. His tests with Nan Davies, a young student paralysed in a car crash, were about to prove successful but each individual case was different.

Petrofsky's offer of a fighting chance – and it had been no more than that – left Philip in little doubt about taking up the challenge. What remained were a chain of decisions which had to be made with some speed on this side of the Atlantic.

In all, we were to spend the best part of 1983 in Dayton, Ohio, but at that stage, because the project was an open-ended commitment, it was anyone's guess how much it was going to cost.

There was no knowing whether Philip's original 'backbone fund' would stretch to flights backwards and forwards to America and long-term visits of an unknown duration. Also, as neither of us were free agents, permission had to be sought from the police force to allow us to go.

When Sir David English made an immediate decision to sponsor the trip on behalf of the *Daily Mail*, it was as though a magic wand had been waved. Andy McEwen asked for my assurance that I was willing to accompany Philip on the trip and although this was hardly in question, we both had to submit reports to the police authorities. In describing the purpose of our journey, we also had to request to be allowed to take part in the resulting publicity. Unless authorized, police officers are not allowed to make statements to the press, let alone play a central part in one of their stories. But as Philip had long since won the media's heart as a police hero, and his fight to walk again could only be regarded as a worthwhile endeavour, permission was speedily granted. All we had to do was arrange for our visas and get ourselves organized.

With the eyes of the nation upon him, Philip was about to start on a new career as a figurehead for the disabled. Even if the project fell flat on its face and the brave new walking system wasn't a success, Philip's determination to overcome his disability gave new heart to thousands of paralysed people like himself and we left Gatwick on a tide of hope and good wishes.

Flying presents a challenge to anyone who is disabled, but in this spirit of goodwill and publicity we were treated like royalty by British Caledonian who had provided the tickets and smoothed out all the problems we'd been anticipating.

Given time to settle in before the other passengers embarked, Philip was spared the undignified struggle of getting into his seat with everyone else milling around. As his wheelchair was too wide to go down the aisle, the airline provided a narrow chair to bring him up to his seat and Andy McEwen, who had learned how to lift Philip without hurting him, eased him in without any problem. We were flying first class and there was room to raise Philip's legs on the long flight, a necessary precaution because the last thing we wanted on arrival at Dayton was to find he had developed pressure sores, which could prevent him from taking part in the tests. No way though, could he get near the toilet, so it was up to me to be fairly inventive about seeing to Philip's plumbing department which, judging by the way he was pouring drinks down, was going to be a constant problem throughout the flight. I decided to trust the sick bags provided and developed a system whereby I emptied the leg bags into the sick bags and disposed of them in the loo. The number of times I had to walk down the aisle clutching one of these bags, I should imagine that quite a few passengers thought I was suffering from a bad case of airsickness. Despite all the luxury and the supportive presence of Andy McEwen and *Daily Mail* photographer Graham Wood, Philip hated flying and the trip was what we came to call a 'pouring job': Philip pouring down drinks at one end, me emptying them at the other and then pouring him off the plane when we got to New York and from there to Dayton.

We arrived in Dayton early in the New Year of 1983. Settling into the warmth of the Marriott Hotel, we looked around to find a compact and elegant city, where business flourished and the achievements of the Wright brothers – who made the first powered flight – were commemorated in street names and buildings.

Our first visit to Wright State University was a bit of a culture shock. I think I'd expected something ultra modern out of the twenty-first century rather than the distinctly archaic look of Petrofsky's control room draped in a tangle of overhead wires. It looked as though an eccentric professor had just discovered the wonders of electricity. A Meccano set of pieces of equipment I dimly recognized from chemistry and physics labs at school were strewn about the room.

Philip and I were utterly silent as we contemplated a battered wooden chair on a stand. Connected to a forest of wires, it resembled nothing so much as an example of an early electric chair borrowed from a museum. Brimming with reassurance and enthusiasm was the jovial professor himself. Larger than life, his white coat hanging open, he seemed to fit the part of the eager boffin ready to plug Philip in to his latest experiment. But before this could happen, various trials and tests had to take place. Petrofsky proved a model of caution.

José Almeyda, one of the lab technicians, connected Philip up to equipment that would monitor his heart beat and blood pressure. Philip was put into the 'electric chair'. Leather straps were attached to his ankles and connected to the straps was a wire which went through the back of the chair into a pulley system. At the end of this were weights which could be varied according to how much tension Petrofsky wanted to put on the exercise and how the muscles were responding. Three electrodes were placed on Philip's wasted thigh muscles with wires leading off to a computer connected to an electronic box. Petrofsky controlled this by means of a knob which he gently turned up and down as though tuning a radio.

The leg exerciser was designed to build up the tone of the muscles, which in the case of someone like Philip who had been paralysed for some time, had wasted to the point where his legs were little more than skin and bone. To a large degree, the chances of him walking again depended on whether these leg muscles could be sufficiently restored and made flexible enough to bear the weight of his body.

We always had to remember that what Philip was taking part in was a research project, not a recognized medical treatment. We heard that for years, Petrofsky, a physiologist and a computer scientist, had practised his technique on damaged cats, making them walk again with feline grace. Experimenting on the human frame had a number of dangers. Although closely monitored by the laboratory team, the guinea pigs, with their wasted muscles and brittle bones, ran the risk of fractures. Petrofsky also warned there was a chance of electrical burns. Electrodes were strapped on Philip's legs. They looked like large medical plasters but each had a black plastic patch at the centre which conducted the electric shocks. These were smeared with a white cream to improve the electrical contact and put on the leg with small coloured wires attached.

In fact Philip suffered several electrical burns, but on this first occasion he was totally absorbed in what to him seemed proof of a minor miracle. When Petrofsky turned on the power it instantly produced a twitching movement in the top muscle of his leg. It was wonderful to witness this because the leg which had looked so wasted and powerless was suddenly brought to life. Philip felt quite strange about it because for the first time in three years, he saw it lifting out and stretching smoothly. It was to take months of work to build up strength before he could walk, but this was the first step in discovering whether or not his damaged frame would respond to Petrofsky's electronic system. The principle clearly worked. Within minutes of trying the new miracle equipment, Philip had seen movement restored to his lifeless limbs.

It was as Philip put it, 'bloody mind-blowing', because not only had he forgotten how his leg looked when it worked normally, but had there been damage to the peripheral nerves, there would have been no hope for him of the scientific miracle Petrofsky's brilliantly eccentric-looking box of tricks might bring.

Another important part of the testing process was to do with the bones. One of the most serious threats to anyone who is paralysed is the fact that enforced inactivity frequently leads to osteoporosis: brittleness of the bones. This means that just by the very action of walking, a person who has been confined to a wheelchair for a number of years can run the risk of breaking or fracturing a bone. Given a bone scan, Philip was luckily pronounced okay on this score.

Petrofsky explained that by regularly stimulating the circulation so that calcium is deposited into the bones, osteoporosis can be checked. Later on, Philip was to have a heel vibrator which, by lightly hitting the heels, had the same effect as walking. It is the shock waves produced by putting your foot to the ground in the everyday process of walking which stimulates the deposit of calcium in the bones. Just drumming your heels on the floor can do wonders for the circulation, while a long stay in bed can cause muscles to waste and bones to become brittle.

Next Philip was put on the computerized exercise bike, another device that was eventually to restore his wasted leg muscles to near normal. Thanks to a variety of exercises under electronic stimulation, everything was geared to improving the general health of the volunteer patients and particularly the cardiovascular system, which in turn helped to sustain bone density.

How much Philip and the other guinea pigs had been in need of this team of experts came home to me at Wright State University. After Philip had left hospital in England, nobody ever gave any hope, encouragement or professional guidance. He was on his own with me scurrying around trying to learn the job of looking after him. All he had been given was a standing frame and told to heave himself up into an upright position for so many hours a day. This, presumably, was meant to help his circulation. But the dislocated sense of balance from which all paraplegics suffer makes it almost impossible for them to get on their feet unaided and just standing up in a walking frame had been too static to do any real good. Philip found it pointless. Few other suggestions had been forthcoming to lead him to believe he might be able to walk again. He'd been told that he would never use his legs again and that because of illnesses, infections and deterioration to parts of his body now cut off from the brain, he would be lucky if he lived to be forty-five. All along, what the doctors had really been saying was: you're disabled, come to terms with it and that's your lot.

Petrofsky told Philip to forget all this. At the laboratory, he had assembled a dynamic team. Philip and the other guinea pigs drew on this mixture of enthusiasm and scientific feedback like children who had been starved of play. They were carefully monitored but it wasn't a passive regime. A lot was required of them in this crusade to walk again. Inevitably, there were to be some clashes. But if you are someone in a wheelchair, setting out to prove traditional medical wisdom wrong, you need some degree of contrariness, not to mention bloody-mindedness. Petrofsky and his team provided hope and encouragement. At last someone was talking in terms Philip could appreciate and understand.

Although he wasn't up and running after three weeks in America, Philip had met the necessary criteria of the assessment period. And although Petrofsky had already chosen his volunteers – six from the thousands who had applied – he was willing to consider Philip as an addition to the project. Before we left Dayton, the decision had been made that Philip could return to Wright State University as a full-time member of the programme. The programme that really was going to put him back on his feet.

That our journey home was not the triumphal progress which might have been expected was due to a number of factors. Stress, delay, the energy cost of travelling – it all built up to a climax in which Philip behaved at his worst. Throughout the trip, his attitude to me had been short-tempered and arrogant. I realized that he had been under pressure to succeed and get accepted on the programme but I resented playing the role of a necessary evil: just there to help him dress and undress, take him to the laboratory and supply whatever was needed.

Our 'great romance' had been written up in the newspapers but anyone reading about it would have been surprised that I was the girl of his dreams had they seen the way he snapped his fingers in the air, demanding I should fetch and carry.

The homeward journey was to be routed through Paris. Philip's success story in Dayton was sensitive material so far as the *Daily Mail* was concerned, and they did not want other press reporters scooping them at Heathrow where his arrival might be noticed. We were to change planes in New York, fly to Paris, then take the ferry from Boulogne.

Despite the break in New York, the lengthy journey caused problems. Sitting in the same position for hours on end, Philip developed a pressure sore on one leg. There had been a mix-up over the car that was to have taken us to Boulogne and by the time we got on the ferry Philip was totally out of control: as drunk as a skunk and loudly abusive. By this time nerves were frayed all round and Andy McEwen, who had shown the patience of a saint throughout the trip, was coming as close to desperation as I was ever to see him.

I had great confidence in Andrew, both as a friend and as one who had deep insight into Philip's psychology. The next trip to Dayton wasn't going to be like plugging Philip into an electric light socket and away he would go. It was going to be a long, hard slog – how long I'd no way of knowing. When I told Andrew how difficult things had been on a personal level in Dayton and that I had some doubts about how well I was going to be able to cope with a much longer period, he took it pretty seriously.

Talking on the ferry while Philip continued to throw back the drinks, we were like two people offstage watching helplessly as the star performer goes over the top. One suggestion was to hire a nurse for the return trip to Dayton. But how could you hire anyone to deal with Philip? It would only take one of his tantrums and maybe a quick lashing out from the wheelchair and any nurse would have been back on the next plane.

One of the questions David English had asked Andy to look into that of sending Philip and me back together. Our relationship was an important factor because without me there to look after him, it was doubtful whether Philip would complete the project. The *Daily Mail* were ready to shoulder the necessary expense; all they wanted was to be sure that Philip would see it through to the end.

I hoped that with Petrofsky, Andy and myself all committed to Philip, he would now spare a thought for his support team.

Chapter 9

Re: *APPLICATION FOR SPECIAL LEAVE*

Assistant Commissioner 'D' Department. 26th January 1983

I refer to my previous report dated 20th November 1982 and report that in company with my fiancée W.P.S. 98 'Q' Vanessa Perkins, between the 3rd January 1983 and 24th January 1983, I visited Wright State University, Ohio, U.S.A.

The prognosis after the initial tests is excellent. It would appear that given good fortune I will walk again. Professor Petrofski [sic] carried out a number of tests on me, and I attach a Daily Mail photograph taken during the course of his research.

The total expense this far (whatever that may be) has been borne by the Daily Mail. It is my understanding that that newspaper will publish a feature article concerning the story (and my prospects) together with photographs, on Monday 31st January preceded the previous evening by advertising on Independent television. Prof. Petrofski who is apparently limited to a total of six patients has asked me to return to the U.S.A. as one of them. He believes that by modern computerised electronics he can make me walk again and be partially independent of my wheelchair.

Prof. Petrofski did not want me to leave the U.S.A. A major

consideration that made me do so was the fact that on 14th February I am due to commence Recruit Instructor Training, at Hendon. Today on the telephone, sir, you have very kindly indicated that I should disregard the timing of that course and I could be accomodated [sic] on another course at a later date.

I therefore seek your approval to return to the U.S.A. for further treatment in or about mid March 1983.

I further ask that my fiancée be permitted to accompany me though projected duration of the visit is somewhere between two and six months.

Submitted.
.... P.C. 163 'TD'
Philip Olds WT. No. 162218

No sooner had we got back than Philip applied for Special Leave to return to Dayton. With the police force agreeing to give us six months' leave, (Philip was to be on full pay while I was to receive half pay), and the *Daily Mail* meeting travel and hotel expenses, everything had been taken care of.

There was no question in my mind that Philip was to come home walking, living proof of a scientific miracle. It was Andy who warned that the single biggest risk of the entire project would be to raise Philip's hopes and then have them dashed. But if that was to happen, everything would have been done in the most honest way possible.

Philip understood the terrible risk of disappointment but at the same time, he couldn't allow himself to be anything but optimistic. Swept along on this tide of hope, the question of my dropping out never really surfaced.

At one level our relationship was still at the same point as when we met. Basically I was saying: 'Whatever I have to give, I give unreservedly to you. If you treat me as someone of help and succour, it pleases me.' Underneath, what I wanted to say was: 'I'll come, but don't abuse me.'

I was sending out mixed signals. But I was so confused about my feelings, it wasn't obvious to me at the time. I loved Philip. I wanted him to succeed in America. And I wanted to stay with him for all time. Yet I feared the Mr Hyde in his character and there were times when I just wanted to run away from him.

To Philip, it was either I came along or I didn't – no buts. He couldn't have gone to the States on his own, but if I'd chucked a spanner in the works – the last thing I wanted to do anyway – he'd just have said, 'I can get along all right without you.' There was no bargaining ground. Gratitude was the last thing I wanted from Philip. A sense of team spirit, 'We're in this together', would have allayed the insecurities. As it was, I felt trapped.

The only reason we had returned to England was to report to our respective bosses. Philip had been due to take an instructor's course at Hendon. He had proved at the traffic garage that he had the art of communication. And when he wanted to, he could get the best out of people. What he couldn't do was to get the best out of himself.

Throughout, no one had been more supportive than the Met. Not many bosses would let two employees off on indefinite leave, assuring them of a job to return to when they were ready. They had agreed to Philip's taking an instructor's course because they thought he would be good at teaching. Now they agreed to postpone it. In my case, they had raised no objections to time off on an open-ended basis. The only stipulation being that instead of retiring after the regulation thirty years' service, I would work off the extra time. Eventually, I'll be tacking another year on to my working life.

Philip had continued to capture headlines, but he was now more than a good story. His struggle had become a newspaper crusade and he was about to be the subject of a television documentary, later described as one of the most compelling and hard-hitting films remembered on TV.

On the night in April before we were due to fly out to America, the documentary team with Desmond Wilcox, Jan Riddle and Alex McCall, together with various camera and sound men, came to the house in Pinner to interview Philip. Called *The Visit*, the programme was to show various people who had travelled to different parts of the world to pursue their own particular hopes and dreams. In Philip's case, the fight to conquer his paralysis and the 4,000-mile journey he was about to take in order to achieve this ambition obviously had a strong emotional appeal. What Desmond Wilcox and his team perhaps hadn't realized as the lights and cameras were positioned in our sitting-room was that Philip, far from sentimentalizing the issue, was about to unleash the painful and explosive truth.

When Desmond Wilcox questioned him about coming to terms with the wheelchair – a subject that at any time was a bugbear – Philip didn't mince the facts about what it meant to be paralysed.

'I don't get anything from this damn wheelchair,' he told Desmond and several million viewers. 'I was a motorcycling, fornicating, beat-walking, criminal-catching cop. I've been robbed. Robbed of death because being in a wheelchair is worse than death, worse than a bullet going through my head or through my heart.'

Worked up at the prospect of the impending trip and his underlying fear of failure, Philip seemed bent on showing the most tortured side of his personality.

In 1980 it had been the Year of the Disabled and if Philip wanted to create an awareness of the disillusion anyone experiences when suddenly becoming disabled, he chose a controversial way of putting it:

'The Year of the Disabled rapidly became the Year that Was and during that year I happened to be Cripple of the Year. I didn't enjoy that very much but a lot of people identified with me and I want to prove to them and everybody that we have the right in Britain to some hope.'

For Philip, disability was a fight. He did not want to say 'poor me' and resign himself to a wheelchair. Nor did he want pity. Nothing could have been further from his idea, but I winced as Philip responded to Desmond's questions about living with the rage and frustration which was becoming all too evident as the interview progressed.

Refusing to co-operate with the sympathetic interview envisaged, Philip, who resented Desmond's bone-dry style of interviewing and his carefully phrased questions, seemed bent on embarrassing his questioner as much as possible.

'Like I said,' he continued belligerently, 'I want to fornicate, perambulate, defecate and urinate because I quite enjoy doing all of those things. You don't have to understand me to believe what

I'm saying – I'm just a thick, pig-ignorant bobby – that's who I am . . .'

Various friends had foregathered at the house to watch this performance and it was clear to me that Philip was playing up to an audience.

It says much for Desmond's unshakeability that in an interview that was taking on the appearance of a deadly sort of double act, he was able to highlight Philip's courage in taking up a crusade.

Dramatic as his words sounded when he said, 'I died when I was 28,' Philip knew that he owed a duty to the people who believed in him. He made a pledge: 'I'll do my damnedest, not particularly for PC Olds, but for the people in this country who'd like to see me make a success out in America. I'd bloody well like to achieve it, because I owe quite a lot to the people who are making me into a crusader – the people who have made me into something special and never realized I wasn't. So for them I want to succeed and give some hope.'

The interview made a deeply disturbing impression on everyone who saw it. It was the first time that disablement had been shown as anything other than a condition where the victim resigned himself to his fate as gracefully as possible.

Afterwards, Philip received thousands of letters from the public including many from disabled people. His bravery had never been in doubt and the brutal honesty with which he expressed his anguish caused many to think he had shown disablement in its true light.

The Visit team were to follow us out to America to complete the documentary, which later won a gold medal at the International Film and TV Festival.

'Wilcox brings out the light and shade in the personality of a man you can alternately love and detest but never ignore, in one of his most uncomfortable moods,' said one review.

The impact of Philip's frustration provided a fairly dramatic curtain-raiser to our trip. Nothing had been rehearsed and the atmosphere in our sitting-room was tense. Not that Philip's perform-ance had taken place unfuelled. Out of sight of the cameras had been a bottle of Scotch, which he availed himself of between shots. I also noticed something else: throughout the filming, Philip was continually looking at his watch.

As soon as the interview was over, Philip bade farewell to the crew and visitors and disappeared into the night. It turned out he had made a previous arrangement to meet Stef for a farewell drink and was late for the appointment.

I knew he had been seeing something of Stef since our return from Dayton in January and I felt pretty upset about the whole thing, but before anyone could argue with him, he had heaved himself into the car and was away.

Philip had a passion for fast cars. We were always buying and selling them. This latest model, a 2.8 fuel injection Capri had been bought for me and fitted with hand controls so that Philip could drive it. I fortified myself with the knowledge that Philip was an advanced driver and would be unlikely to want a crash on the very night before he was due to set out on so important a journey.

All the same, it was annoying to be left with a houseful of people, suitcases to close and everything to put into shipshape order before we left. I did a very brief interview with Desmond which later, not surprisingly, showed me in rather a soulful mood and when the crew asked me to go with them up the road for something to eat, I thought Oh, why not?

It was about 11.30 when the crew dropped me back at home. And who should be there sitting outside the house in his wheelchair but Philip, with a police officer, who was a stranger to us.

My car was nowhere to be seen. On the way back there had been an accident. No other vehicle had been involved, Philip had simply run out of road on a bend. The car, I learned, was now a write-off though, according to the police officer, Philip wasn't injured.

Altogether, I didn't feel too sympathetic. It was a farcical situation. There was Philip, brought home by the police, sitting on his own doorstep and locked out because he hadn't taken a key. The first thing he said was, 'Where the hell have you been?' and the first thing I said was, 'What's happened to the car?' It wasn't a particularly warm night and Philip, who had been there for about half an hour, was shivering from cold and the effects of shock. This didn't stop him from acting as though outraged by the fact that I'd been out rather than being at home dutifully waiting to welcome him back.

We were barely on speaking terms as we set out for America

131

next morning. Philip had been hurt, but hid his injuries for fear of being barred from taking part in the research programme. However, it soon became obvious various things were wrong. He had broken a bone in his wrist and had either bruised or cracked a rib so it hurt him to breathe. With Philip blotting out the pain with Scotch, to the embarrassment of those travelling with him, it was hardly a good start.

Andy stayed for a short while, settling us into the Marriott Hotel as long-term guests, and accompanying Philip to Wright State University for his first check-up with Petrofsky. Luckily, nothing was found that would prevent Petrofsky's tests. The injuries eventually healed themselves, Philip pretended his ribs didn't hurt, and with all efforts concentrated on building up the muscles he started a Monday-to-Friday regime at the laboratory using the leg exerciser. If the omens were right, Philip was going to have a trial on the walking apparatus within a few months. Hopes were once again high.

Meanwhile, we both became more familiar with the mysteries of Petrofsky's electronic system and often talked to Nan Davies, pioneer of the project and the equivalent of Philip in the States as far as a high profile with the media went.

She had been a basketball player and a high-achieving university student when, at the age of eighteen, the car in which she was travelling crashed on the way to her graduation ceremony. Everyone else in the car walked free apart from Nan, who was paralysed with spinal injuries. When we arrived, she had already achieved some success in the laboratory and was to be Petrofsky's star pupil, the first of the guinea pigs to leave her wheelchair and walk on legs jerked back into life by the battery of the computer.

You could see in Nan Davies many of the same qualities that also fired Philip. When told by the staff at the hospital that she would never walk again, she had replied, 'Rubbish, I am going to walk again and you're going to see me.' Philip was fascinated to learn that her refusal to accept her lot was originally diagnosed as a sign of psychiatric disturbance. Sending Nan to a psychiatrist only strengthened her determination to get on her feet with the result that she was the first to find her way to Petrofsky's laboratory. She received a tribute from Ronald Reagan and the event was relayed on television. For paraplegic people everywhere, Nan Davies's walk in November 1983 was the equivalent of Neil Armstrong's walk on the moon.

Another car crash victim was Dennis Walters, a young golf champion, whose partially paralysed legs responded so well to Petrofsky's bio-medical engineering that he was eventually able to stand in a brace and take part in golfing displays. He even got Petrofsky playing golf. In the afternoon around three o'clock, Jerry would often open the door of the biggest computer and lift out his golf clubs from a space between the terminals. Dennis would give him a fifteen-minute golf lesson with Jerry teeing off from a piece of rubber-backed grass. However, Petrofsky's system was based on individual attention and the exercise sessions were organized on an appointment basis so it was only when our times crossed over that we met the others taking part in the project.

Progress was always the main topic of conversation. In almost every other case, the injuries received had been the result of an accident, usually a car crash. Generally speaking, how the injuries had come about and how their lives had been altered were subjects none of the volunteers seemed particularly anxious to discuss.

An exception was Gene Lieber, a young student who had accidentally been shot by an American policeman. As a policeman who had been deliberately shot by a thief, Philip obviously felt he had more grounds for bitterness. But later he found that Gene felt pretty much the same. Gene blamed the stupidity of the police; Philip could never forget that Blackstock and Cooke had shot him for some paltry amount in the till. Understandably, the situation between them was a little uncomfortable to begin with, but after Philip took Gene aside for a good old gas one day they shared their thoughts and it helped ease the tension. No doubt the other people on the project lived with their own nightmares, too. No one suggested any discussion groups, though Philip and Gene had both benefited from some plain speaking.

Perhaps the most outstanding example of willpower and positive thinking was Sue Steele, a quadriplegic who, despite the loss of movement in both legs and arms, went on to lead an independent life that would compare favourably to many an able-bodied person.

Though the best Petrofsky could do was to offer a chance of getting out of the wheelchair albeit for a short time, what all the people in the lab were hoping for was to further their degree of independence. While in their heads they knew that going back to the way they once were was impossible, in their hearts the experiment still allowed them hope.

A lot of the time, visits to the lab were largely composed of pain and boredom. Apart from the burns on Philip's legs from the electrodes, once or twice there were electricity leakages, which made him feel sick. There were days when we went in and the equipment wasn't available or working, days when Philip wasn't well enough to make any progress and days when it was hard to see much improvement.

I was there as an aide, to help Philip get ready in the morning, make sure he had everything he needed and go with him to the laboratory. As time went on, I got to know the system and the schedule. I became quite well acquainted with how to put the electrodes on and with Philip helping we could virtually plug him into the system. The same basic things had to be done every day, such as using the leg trainer and increasing the weights as Philip got stronger. Then there was the bicycle which used other groups of muscles. It was all geared towards fitness and lung capacity; routines which would prepare him for walking and make the process easier.

In essence, it was a training programme, and like an athlete, you don't start by running marathons. As Philip's body had been inactive for a long time, all the routine work had to be put in before he could even be considered fit enough to try the main harness and take the first computerized steps.

Financially, the project was run on totally different lines from anything we'd met in Britain. For part of the time it was necessary for Petrofsky to be out and about trying to raise funds to keep it going. Often he seemed caught in a bit of a vicious circle: he had to have the money to continue with the research to keep the laboratory going; at the same time he had to be producing results in the laboratory to keep the interest going. Eventually, I think this caught up with him. There were wrangles over the financial side and obviously he couldn't be in two places at once. The haphazard side of the operation later showed itself in delays and mysterious breakdowns of machinery.

The mainstay that kept the laboratory running on a sweet note was the manager, Debbie Hendershott, who had been with Petrofsky right from the beginning when he had been working on animals. Debbie looked after the lab, booked in the appointments, checked everyone's records and monitored the decisions on whether the subject in question was fit enough to carry on to the next stage.

We had been in Dayton nearly three months when it was decided that Philip's condition had sufficiently improved for him to go on the walking project for the first time. But before the great day when he was actually to get on his feet X-rays had to be taken to ensure there was no bone damage. The X-ray showed up what looked like a hairline fracture just above the right knee, an indistinct line that could have been a crack in the femur due to a previous accident, or old scar tissue – or at worst, the first suspicious sign of softening of the bone. They weren't going to take any chances. John Gillen, the GP in charge of the project, was forced to delay the walk for at least a couple of months. In the end it was longer. Ten weeks were to go by before the X-rays were pronounced clear and Philip was allowed to make his first attempt at the great walk. It might have been the summit of Everest, it seemed so far away.

Feeling let down and overwhelmed, it wasn't an ideal moment for Philip to run out of painkillers. He drank, he smoked. Prescriptions were on repeat. These were the props he had brought with him from England and while he was prepared to summon all his reserves of patience to wait and train until pronounced fit to walk, giving up the painkillers had not been on his agenda. By now he was dependent on them.

Philip had been accustomed to taking daily doses of Pethidine, a strong morphine-like pain reliever. On bad days his intake could be around eight times the recommended dose.

When his prescription ran out, he went to Dr Gillen to ask for a repeat.

Philip was confident there would be no problem so it came as a considerable shock when he heard the doctor say: 'I'm sorry, we only give Pethidine to patients who are terminally ill.'

Philip made an effort to control his anger. 'For God's sake,' he said, 'it's prescribed by my doctor at home – I've got a letter to say I need it.'

The argument continued for about half an hour but Gillen's words were final: 'The law says I cannot give you this drug.'

Things got very heated but it was obvious that however much Philip argued, he was not going to get a prescription for Pethidine out of Dr Gillen. In America, this drug was on the danger list. I had mixed feelings. I knew how much Philip relied on this particular painkiller. But I also knew that Dr Gillen was right. Not for nothing had I stayed awake at night when Philip had taken one of his drink and drug cocktails, wondering if he would still be breathing in the morning.

Philip knew that what he was taking was dangerous, but his attitude was that the risks were down to him. Told he had a curtailed life expectancy with only deteriorating health to look forward to in the intervening years, he had adopted a philosophy of living to the full – often to excess. If he needed painkillers, he'd take them until the pain dulled or he got to the point of not caring – whichever came first. If it was a self-destructive course, Philip felt he had little to lose.

A testing time now lay ahead. All the doctor was willing to prescribe for him was an interim painkiller not much stronger than is usually prescribed for toothache. He suggested that if Philip needed further help, as obviously he was going to, he should have a consultation at the Pain Clinic. This turned out to be a pain management clinic which was part of the Medical Centre at the University where expert doctors were on hand to advise in cases of chronic pain. One slight drawback was that in the land of the free, nothing is really free and it was going to cost him $600 dollars to be assessed. After that, he still wouldn't be prescribed the drugs he was accustomed to.

Philip called everything connected with his disability 'the pram business', so it was as part of the pram business that he decided to give the Pain Clinic a go.

The Pain Clinic turned out to give a psychological as well as a physical assessment. Philip had to go through a series of tests and it took all day. While I was sitting in the waiting-room reading magazines and drinking coffee, Philip was apparently pouring out his life history. It went from where things had gone wrong in his childhood to his reactions to the shooting.

At the end Philip asked me if I would like to be present when the doctors gave their conclusions. It came as quite a shock to hear what they had to say.

Among other things they made it clear they knew all about Philip's assaults on me. 'Would you agree', said one of the doctors 'that after you've struck Vanessa, you generally regret your actions?'

Philip nodded tautly. 'I feel very bad about it,' he said. 'It's something that happens. I can't help it.' Out in the open like this, it all sounded very different. A matter of deep concern.

The doctors were also seriously concerned about Philip's self-destructive tendencies, the nothing-to-lose attitude that he justified as being logical under the circumstances.

Now the American doctors were saying that he needed psychiatric help. The conclusion of their diagnosis was that when he returned to England, he should become a voluntary in-patient at a clinic where he could be treated. In the US, Philip's eruptions into sudden violence had a name: post-trauma syndrome. A syndrome of extreme behaviour brought about by shock. We were told the condition had first been recognized when treating soldiers from the Vietnam war.

While all the emphasis had been on treating Philip's physical wounds after the shooting, the effects of the psychological shock had gone unrecognized.

The doctors were so accurate in their description of the situation that it came as a shock to both of us. We had accepted that most relationships have their ups and downs and in our circumstances we expected a few more than usual. When Philip attacked me I used to think afterwards: yes it was that argument we had that did it; or: he was under stress from pain. Was it something I didn't say? I always tried to rationalize his behaviour as understandable – even justified, blaming the physical effects of pain and extreme frustration.

What the doctors were saying was that as a couple we weren't handling the problem properly. That basically the situation had gone out of control. They were insistent that Philip's need for professional help was an urgent necessity.

I was shell-shocked quite frankly. Shocked at the accuracy of the diagnosis and by the fact that Philip's mental condition was considered in such a serious light. Although in the past we had discussed finding some professional help, we had never taken any positive steps down that road, probably because we didn't want to open a can of worms. And although by now that can was already open, between us we stuffed the worms back and shut the lid. Philip wouldn't accept he needed psychiatric help. He said it was something we could sort out together – 'a problem shared is a problem halved'.

Later, when telling a friend in the Dayton police about the tests, Philip was able to laugh it all off – 'You go to the doctor for a few pills and he wants to shut you in the bin.'

For the next few weeks, fighting the battle of the pills was to take precedence over everything else. Even the laboratory. For days while Philip fought the pain and his dependency on Pethidine, we never got out of the hotel bedroom.

Withdrawal symptoms from Pethidine are the same as for any other hard drug: shakes and shivers, sweating, upset stomach, no appetite and a deep disturbance of mind.

He was given Demarol, the strongest painkiller the doctors could prescribe. He was allowed enough to last a week at a time and told he wouldn't get any more if he used them up in the first few days.

Although the withdrawal of Pethidine seemed to Philip like the last straw in a life dogged by ill fate, he used every single ounce of willpower available to him to fight his dependency. He was determined to show Dr Gillen that he could crack it.

It was a battle we fought together, a road through hell which took many twists and turns. Sometimes there was abuse: 'Why don't you just fuck off and leave me? What are you waiting for? I'm telling you to bloody well go home and leave me.' More often there was deep depression: 'I can't take this any more. Why didn't the bugger shoot me in the head? I could have died with dignity on the pavement. Why have I been left like this?'

Philip was fighting for his sanity and sometimes it was as though he was a small boy crying out against the injustices of a cruel and incomprehensible punishment. Pethidine had taken Philip back into the past and what he saw there would often make him weep. It had made him a traveller through time, giving him the facility to

Made a Sergeant in 1982, I had three stripes on my uniform and a new set of responsibilities.

Above: Philip returned to work in the Traffic Division 18 months after the shooting.

Above right: Officially Philip's girlfriend.

Right: Philip received his High Commendation for Bravery at New Scotland Yard in 1981. Left to right: Sergeant Mick Rawson; Chief Superintendent Henwood; Philip; me; Commissioner Sir David McNee.

When Philip emerged from hospital in 1981, his future in the police force was uncertain.

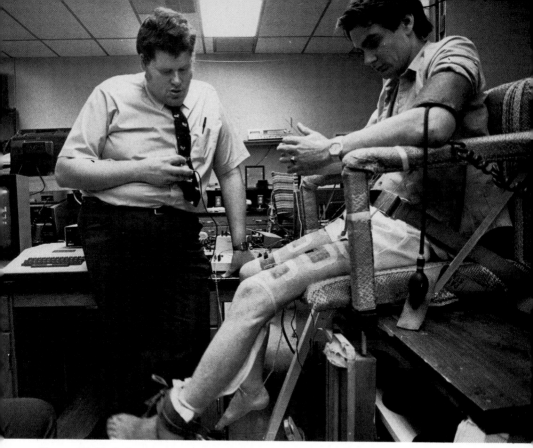

Above: Philip's legs were wasted when Professor Jerrold Petrofsky did the first tests at Wright State University.

Below: Lab technicians Brad and Don apply the electrodes which brought Philip's muscles to life.

Above: Philip on his thirty-first birthday in America.

Left: Philip received the Queen's Gallantry Medal at Buckingham Palace. Left to right: PC John Betts; PC Laurie Howarth; Philip; Sergeant Mick Rawson.

Above right: Philip spent many long hours on the exercise bike.

Above far right: Connected to trailing wires and the computer, Philip took his first steps supported by a safety harness.

Right: Philip on night patrol with the impressively mustachioed Dayton Police.

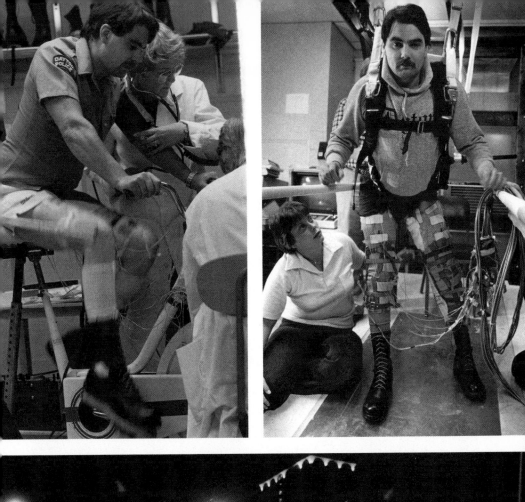

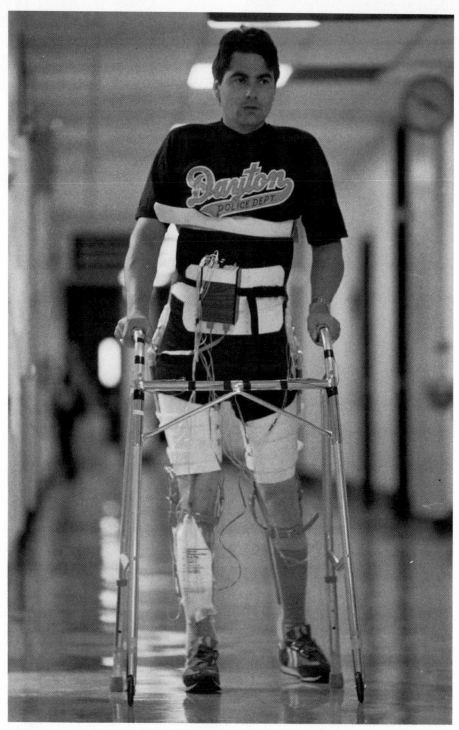

Philip wearing the combined system: the brace and miniaturized computer.

In New Orleans, Philip posed in uniform for the cameras.

Left: On a Mississippi river boat with Andrew McEwen.

Below: Philip with Roy Douglas, designer of the brace, and his receptionist, Eunice.

Right: Riding my horse, Simon, in Epping Forest, my problems would disappear.

Far right: At our bungalow in Pinner, Donny and Woody were our family.

Below right: We were godparents to the son of Hugh and Leslie Connolly. 'Little Philip' symbolized the child we once hoped to have.

Christmas 1983 in America – and we both longed to come home.

pass from a recent conversation to another twenty years before. In the past I had often been unsure if it was Philip speaking or the drug. Now he was facing the effects of raw pain.

When he wept, I'd cuddle him – oh so tight – wanting to heal the pain in his soul even if there was little I could do for the pain in his body. Pain in both body and soul seemed to fill the close confines of the bedroom where we were together twenty-four hours a day. Throughout, Dr Gillen was wonderfully supportive. He had arranged that we could speak to him on the phone at any time of night or day and I think that without him as a human lifeline, Philip would never have come through.

Seeing out the storms of withdrawal took nearly a month. About the only time we left the hotel was to see Dr Gillen. It was a month of nightmares but it seemed to strengthen the bond between Philip and me. Able to give strength, I felt less confused about the relationship between us. I felt that despite everything, we were meant to be together.

I was proud of Philip. He never went back to Pethidine and in beating his dependency, he won the congratulations of the doctors and my admiration.

Philip had won the battle. The war still lay ahead.

Chapter 10

Let me begin by saying that we have a special respect for the British police officer who is visiting our community and who was struck down while trying so bravely to protect his own community. And as a small token of gratitude for the spirit he represents, we would like to present him with the keys to the City of Dayton.

Philip, we hope that the next time you come back to this community, you will be able to shed that wheelchair and walk into these chambers and shake our hands as a prize product of the pioneering work which has been performed at Wright State University.

The Mayor of Dayton, Ohio
July 1983

Now into the middle of Dayton's long hot summer, there was nothing for us to do but wait until the signal came from the laboratory that it was time to re-examine Philip's leg and take him back on the programme.

After spending twenty-four hours a day, seven days a week in the hotel bedroom, it came as a welcome change to take a look at our surroundings. A city with an old part in the middle, Dayton was on the map as a business centre with the headquarters of the National Cash Register Company representing very big business indeed. A

140

nice, bright, environmentally clean Midwest city, Dayton was a place to work and be prosperous in rather than somewhere you would choose for a holiday.

Time was going to hang very heavily indeed without a focus for our activities. Already the hotel bar was threatening to become our front room, so it was a lucky chance when we got talking to a couple of detectives from the Texas Police Department who introduced us to Skip and Donna Beutle, detectives with the Dayton Police.

Philip established a strong bond with Skip and the Beutles became very special friends who later visited us in England and whose friendship made all the difference to our stay in Dayton.

They had a very attractive house in the old part of the city. Their standard of living was much higher than anything a married police pair could expect in Britain and their status in the community was also more highly regarded.

So far away from home, it was obviously interesting for us to swap stories and to find, when all was said and done, that there wasn't such a lot of difference between Britain and America where policing is concerned. Probably, the police have more in common than most other professions. What they're principally dealing with is human nature and whatever language they speak or race they belong to, there are only so many situations people can get themselves into and just so many traits, emotions and behaviour patterns common to human nature.

The friendship between Donna and Skip and Philip and myself was cemented, like so many things in life, by a freak tragedy. It happened when Philip and I were driving to the Beutles' house one bright and sunny day to spend the afternoon and evening with our new friends. We were both in good moods and, for once, all seemed well with the world. We were travelling in our hired car along Route 35 towards Entrada Drive where Skip and Donna awaited us. We stopped talking as Philip concentrated on pulling off the freeway into a three-lane suburban carriageway travelling towards a main junction where we wanted to turn right. Before reaching the junction, a car pulled out of another junction on our right. The driver, who didn't look our way, slowly drove across our path. Philip braked and tried to take evasive action. But there was no way of avoiding a collision and we hit the car on the driver's side. From there on it was all bad news. Philip and I both had minor injuries. I had whiplash and bruised legs and Philip injured his wrist and bashed his legs and chest on the steering wheel – injuries that were discovered in the fullness of time.

While police and ambulance were called, I got out to check the occupants of the other car. The passenger, an elderly lady, who had been knocked into the footwell, assured us she was all right. Looking across at the driver, it appeared fairly obvious to me that he was dead. Because of the position of the two cars, I couldn't get him out and it was only when the emergency services arrived and managed to remove him that it became apparent he'd had a heart attack at the wheel of the car.

Philip was devastated. He knew he'd done all he could to avoid the accident. The passenger confirmed that the driver had gone through a stop sign before the crash, but Philip agonized over the accident for a long time afterwards. For someone who had seen scores of accidents in the course of his job, Philip's reactions showed an extreme and unexpected degree of shock. Skip and Donna who came and fetched us from the scene of the accident, cared for us both and for the first time saw behind the mask which usually hid Philip's emotions. Skip in particular gained a fuller understanding of Philip's vulnerability and the layers of shock and disturbance still so close to the surface. The incident established a long-lasting bond between them and Skip was one of the few people in whom Philip felt he could confide his deepest thoughts.

While we were there the Dayton Police invited us to go out on a couple of patrols: raiding suspected premises, breaking up drug deals, fights, arrests, just everyday stuff to them. Taking Philip along was a gesture of real affection on the part of Lieutenant Labatzky who ran the Dayton Police Academy and had taken a great liking to him. But arriving on the scene of the crime with sirens screaming and lights flashing came as a reminder to Philip as he looked on from a patrol car, that to work this job you need to be able to function both physically and mentally at 100 per cent.

At home Philip had qualified as a police shot, although ironically, he had never carried a gun on duty. We were both allowed to use the shooting range at Dayton Police Academy and given some instruction, I was surprised to find I had an unsuspected talent for accurate shooting, even managing some trick shots such as splitting a card edgeways on. For Philip it was inevitable that target practice should bring to the surface the troubling memories that were never far from his mind. As he sighted his gun from a wheelchair, the paper silhouette facing him from the other end of the range came as a bizarre reminder of a man pointing a gun: Stuart Blackstock.

The question of whether or not he would have been in a wheelchair if he'd had a firearm with him on the night of the shooting was especially poignant in America with an armed police force.

This was to come up again when Philip was asked by Labatzky to speak at the Academy. The class was composed of older, streetwise cops who had seen it all, but who were nevertheless brushing up on survival techniques.

I think I would have found them a bit intimidating – it would be hard to imagine a tougher audience – but Philip decided to accept the challenge, keeping the tone as low-key as possible. Starting by very briefly telling the story of how he was injured, he spoke very informally as though talking to colleagues in the canteen. Listening to this relatively young police officer and seeing for themselves what had befallen him, it was fascinating to watch the reactions of these hard-nosed, tobacco-chewing cops with life etched on their faces.

Compared to the firepower most of them were accustomed to carrying, the thought of a British policeman going into action clutching a twelve-inch piece of wood appeared crazy beyond belief. Either we must be very stupid to go around unarmed, or insanely brave. Whichever way, I think they started out by thinking we must be entirely bonkers. It was only when they realized that Philip was talking from real street experience about the basic needs of self-preservation, that he began to hold their attention.

Philip had devised a keyword for the occasion, which I was to write on the blackboard.

'I don't know if you've heard this word before, but I will ask my lovely assistant to write it on the board.' Feeling rather as though I was part of a conjuring show I chalked the word ASSHOLE in large letters vertically down the board.

The seasoned audience whose faces were by now cracking into a few smiles, loved this but the mnemonic had a serious purpose.

The letters of the mnemonic spelt out the seven important points to be kept in mind in moments of panic or inattention.

A – Assume Nothing
S – Scan the Area
S – Senses – all 5 – used in a plan of campaign
H – Help
O – Open Mind
L – Lazy Attitude
E – Ears and Eyes Open – Mouth Shut

Using himself as an example of someone who had wrongly assumed he could tackle two gunmen without help and without fully assessing the situation, Philip continued with illustrations from his own experience, lecturing not from a book, but speaking in language familiar to everyone in the audience. He was talking about the pitfalls that could be forgotten by even the most experienced of cops – a living reminder of what could happen in a split second.

Philip ended with the poignant reminder that if you're gassing away with your mouth instead of watching out with your eyes and ears, you're likely to miss things.

'And if you miss things,' he concluded, 'that's when you could quite possibly end up in the same situation as I'm in now.'

By maintaining a modest stance about his own bravery and using his own experiences as an example of the mistakes that can happen, Philip had managed to bring his audience round to a consideration of the fact that armed or unarmed, any police can find themselves in an equally vulnerable position.

The impression was of an 'ordinary' PC who wasn't really ordinary at all. This might have been an unreceptive audience, but although not a polished performer, Philip had the magnetism of one who can readily hold an audience.

According to Ron Labatzky, it was a lecture which made a lasting impression on the Dayton Police Academy and he later sent a letter of recommendation to the Commander of the Metropolitan Police Training School at Hendon, praising Philip's capabilities. The genuine support and affection Philip received from the Dayton police revived his faith in himself, and the goodwill and hospitality they showed did much to alleviate the growing tedium of waiting for a recall to the laboratory.

No one except the clinic doctors and myself knew quite how much the struggle to beat his dependence on painkillers had cost Philip. Still swamped at times with moods of black depression and frustration, alcohol had to some extent acted as a replacement. Philip rarely showed the darker side of his suffering to the outside world. I knew only by the pallor of his skin when the pain was winning and that recourse to a mixture of alcohol and pills would be the only gateway to the freedom of his dreams.

Raw emotion quickly raised to fever pitch without any perceptible build-up was still a dominant factor of his personality. Post-trauma syndrome – now at least the symptoms of imbalance had a name. But given the present circumstances and his headstrong attitudes, talking Philip into taking psychiatric help was out of the question. In essence, Philip and I wanted the same thing – each other, and relief from the energy-draining effects that constant pain was having on him.

While alcohol played an increasing part in replacing Pethidine, it would be wrong to give the impression that Philip was constantly drunk and out of order. We both enjoyed TV documentaries, and long after the programme was over we'd be discussing the implications of the subject over cups of coffee. It was true that the bad days would come along, wiping out the good and easy days, but for eighty per cent of the time, Philip was one of the greatest companions you could have had. His understanding of human nature made him a good listener. Keenly observant, he frequently acted as a magnet of charm to a wide variety of people I would otherwise never have met. The other side of the coin to his volatile temperament was that Philip opened my mind to things I'd never thought about before. In Dayton that year we went out a lot together and although time dragged because of the circumstances, Philip had a spirit which could light any occasion with a feeling of festivity. There were times when we were happy together like other couples, when we shared a mutual dream. We were still engaged and we imagined the days when all this would be over. With Philip healed in body and spirit, we hoped to marry the following year.

Meanwhile, we looked for as many ways of filling in the time as possible. Always ready to try anything, Philip suggested having a swim in the hotel pool. Cool and inviting, it was built half in and half outside the hotel. I thought it a shame to discourage him, but was not at all sure how we were going to manage. Because of the slippery steps which led down to the pool, it was a hazardous operation from the start, but this was nothing to getting him into the water. The best system seemed to be to take the footrests off the wheelchair, push it to the very edge of the pool, put the brakes on, place Philip's feet in the water and when he said 'Ready', tip the chair, depositing him with an inelegant splash in the water.

Philip was a powerful swimmer with huge arms and shoulders built up from manoeuvring himself around in the wheelchair. Once afloat he swam like an otter. Every day we'd have races up and down the pool and play at the usual sort of water antics. The reverse procedure, getting out, was a lot more physical. First I'd have to help to lift him out of the water and turn him round to sit on the edge of the pool. I would then bring the chair up and place it beside him while he put one arm on the edge of the seat and one arm round my neck. With one last big heave, I'd lift him up and across into the seat. Such things took a lot of planning and a lot of effort, but we really loved swimming together and on one occasion had a marvellous day out at Indian Lake where Skip's parents lived. With a huge inner tube and a few cans of beer for company, Philip floated freely around, at length having to be coaxed out. Only in the scorching Ohio summer was it really warm enough for him to enjoy the pleasures of a swim. Because of poor circulation, anyone who is a paraplegic is subject to a chill factor. At home the pool donated by the CID was rarely used. When we were there the weather was hardly ever warm enough and when the weather was really warm, ironically we always seemed to be in America.

Although we knew little enough about American football, one of our greatest friendships was with a team of American footballers whom we met at the Marriott Hotel. Known as the 'man mountains', they were students, huge specimens with biceps bigger than the average thigh – not an ounce of fat on them and not one under six-foot tall. Terrific company, they adored Philip and six of them would turn up for parties in our room bringing along a concoction called Wildrose. Going out with them to a restaurant was sometimes a problem. With eight or nine of us together and the footballers taking up more than the usual amount of space, plus Philip's wheelchair, the restaurant had to be virtually re-organized to get us all in. Black and beautiful, the man mountains treated us like royalty, placing Philip at the head of the table and drawing enquiring looks from onlookers who must have wondered who we were to be protected by these enormous men. Philip, who at times ate hardly enough to keep a mouse alive, was fascinated to watch as gargantuan platesful of food disappeared round the table, followed by a bill of equally amazing proportions.

Urban Suburbans was the name of another bar we often visited. It was close to Wright State University, and a lot of the fund-raising parties took place there. It was usually full of students and staff, there was a good spirit about the place and after only a few weeks we began to feel we were fitting in.

It wasn't until the end of the summer that Philip was called in for a reappraisal of his leg injury. After some consultation, it was believed that there had probably been some fault on the original X-ray because the new set of pictures showed no decalcification or attempt by the body to mend what had earlier been thought to be an injury. A smudge or a false perspective or something – after all it had been the X-ray, not Philip, that had been at fault.

So after nearly three months of disappointment and hanging about, Philip had to start on building up his muscles all over again.

It was clear that we were going to have to stay for at least another three months before Philip could get to his feet and take the first magical steps. The *Daily Mail* found more money, the Met extended our leave and I got our visas renewed.

It was back to the laboratory with Philip resigned to the routine monotony that the build-up required. The days when nothing seemed to happen, the machine had broken down so we had to go home again, or we'd arrive to find nobody there.

It was no use losing patience. Philip had talked often enough about packing it in and coming home but soon rallied with some help and encouragement backed up by our new-found friends. We always had to remember that this was a research programme, an experimental project where delays, disappointments and things not working out as expected were a normal part of the progress.

Not that the laboratory with its coils of wire everywhere and atmosphere of turmoil could be mistaken for a spanking new medical centre where everything worked on oiled wheels. It was September. We were to have gone home in October and my heart did not lift as I surveyed the scene.

Apart from Debbie Hendershott, Brad McCoy, one of the technicians, and José Almeyda, the staff were students from the university. They were usually studying in the fields of science and engineering and had been chosen, I think, for their enthusiasm and caring personalities. Back from vacation, they kept up a buzz of conversation, pleased to see us and busy getting to grips with the Byzantine complexities of the computer.

Our ultimate goal stood in a corner of the room. Philip was to stand between parallel bars with a safety harness taking about twenty per cent of his weight. It was like the framework of a rectangle with the weights and harness at one end of the parallel bars and half a dozen paces away, at the other end of 'the walk', the bank of computer technology. This represented the culmination of many years of hard labour by Petrofsky and was designed to take over the functions of a damaged nervous system, releasing electrical impulses to the body, stimulating the leg and hip muscles. It was this machine which would make the tedium of exercising finally seem worthwhile.

With its trailing wires and complicated machinery, the system could work only in a controlled environment with Petrofsky releasing the power. When it was refined and miniaturized, the system might one day, it was hoped, get paraplegics walking under their own steam.

At this moment the prospect seemed a million miles away. It represented our hopes and our frustrations.

We both had to be home by Christmas and back at work in the New Year. With the hold-up, there was much time to be made up in the laboratory. Every morning I helped Philip into the hired car, a silvery blue Buick with a boot large enough to take the folded wheelchair. Every day, I watched and waited while Philip was worked on. Toughened up and brought back into shape, his legs which had looked like matchsticks when we arrived in April, now seemed to belong to a footballer.

Apart from taking Philip to and from the laboratory, there was little for me to do. I began to feel like a zombie, a permanent bystander and wished that I could have enrolled for a course at the university. We were in a learning institution where everyone else was busy stretching their brains. With no real stimulation of the kind I was used to at work, I began to worry what on earth must be happening to my mind. I had to accustom myself to being on standby, waiting in case we were going home, or Philip wasn't well or the exercise bike had gone wrong again. For me, waiting about in the lab was the hardest part.

It was tough on Philip, too. There was a growing feeling of disappointment. We both felt that Philip wouldn't be coming home with the goods. At least not with a practical system with which he could walk triumphantly out of the plane.

Petrofsky wasn't around for a lot of the time and lacking his inspiration, the sense of motivation seemed to be seeping away.

Within the first month or so of our visit, Philip had known in his heart of hearts that although in time a practical walking system might be developed, what we had here was not the answer he was looking for. With time running out, we tried to press for results. The prospect of going home without having once tested the theory of the whole project would have seemed like an appalling failure.

In press interviews he had sounded optimistic: 'Soon my wheel-chair will be redundant . . .' 'Thanks to the incredible genius of Jerry Petrofsky, I'm going to walk again . . .'

But it wasn't going to be like that. At least not on this trip. And not in the way Philip had hoped.

With his mind in a state of conflict about his own personal hopes, Philip knew he was a standard bearer for thousands of paralysed people keeping hope in their hearts. Whatever he felt about the viability of the walking project for himself, it could, in the long run, become a vital alternative for many other people. He had shown courage on his own behalf, now he had to show it in a different way. Philip had wanted not just to walk, but to be a whole person again. This dream now had to be abandoned, although at the same time, he knew that what he was doing was for the greater good.

The prospect of setting up a similar project to Petrofsky's in

Britain had already been discussed and although the present system had a long way to go, there was hope for the future.

The strain of keeping up a public face had its repercussions. Outwardly optimistic as a public symbol, in private Philip's black moods were traumatically evident and the strain on our relationship grew as the day of the great scientific miracle approached.

Arriving in great anticipation on the day Philip was to have tried out his first steps, anti-climax set in when it turned out that Petrofsky had forgotten the appointment and gone off fund-raising in his aeroplane. After some basic exercising, we went back to the hotel to await the next appointment.

The date was 5 December and in Dayton the Christmas trees were already appearing in the streets. Petrofsky had stayed up half the night before, adjusting his computer programme. In heavy, clumpy boots that needed guiding, Philip was strapped into the safety harness and ready to walk.

It was his own muscles that enabled him to stand, not the harness or the parallel bars, but he was still weak in the hips.

'Five – four – three – two – one –' Petrofsky checked the electrodes and turned up the power and Philip did the first few faltering steps. The steps were noticeably uncertain because due to a hitch in the preparatory work schedule, he had done no exercising of the muscles which lift the legs ensuring the toes don't drag on the ground when walking.

Although the toe dragging was obvious to everyone watching, it was impossible not to be deeply moved by the sight of these first clumsy steps. As the computer charged first the right and then the left leg into action, theory had at last been put into practice. Watching from the sidelines I felt like doing a bit of a twirl round the room. As Philip's grin lit up the room, I was really choked.

Unpredictable as ever, Petrofsky had decided to try Philip out on the first walk at 8 a.m. so there hadn't been time to warn Andy McEwen and *The Visit* team who were all back in London. After hastily getting the word back in England, Andy, Graham Wood the photographer and Desmond Wilcox all dived into a plane and were at the laboratory as soon as possible ready for Philip to stage the whole thing over again.

With Philip in the safety harness holding on to the parallel bars, two people guided each leg as Petrofsky manned the controls and Philip took a few awkward steps. Wires trailed from his body to the computer while the cameras recorded the scientific miracle. The reality was a crude travesty of what we'd hoped and dreamed about, but Philip was never to let his disappointment show, describing it on film as 'a giant step forward for mankind'.

In fact, the technicians in the lab were already working on the smaller and handier version of the same equipment. This was the carrot that was going to bring us back to America – an electronic box of tricks no bigger than a wireless set, which would allow Philip and all the paralysed people who came after him to walk with dignity, free of all the grotesque paraphernalia.

For the time being we had little to show for Philip's efforts, and it was with the feeling of a big question mark hanging over the future that we left Dayton. All the same, there were some pleasant memories with which to idle away the homeward journey.

Through Donna and Skip, we had got to know many policemen and women. Before we left there had been a softball tournament with police officers coming from all over the States to take part. Donna and Skip were part of the organizing team and in the end it seemed as though every policeman in the whole of the States wanted to shake hands with Philip. While we were there we really got drawn into the life of the American police and by the time we left, I think we knew as much about their policing methods and way of life as we did about our own. Both camps are great off-duty socializers. We almost had to organize a shift system to cope with all the hospitality we received.

Our memories were of warm summer evenings, barbecues and beer. As we lived in a hotel it was always great to walk into a family atmosphere and another couple of young police officers we enjoyed meeting were Bill and Debbie Elzholz and their toddler son, Zack. A real little boy, Zack was gorgeous. When he took a dive off something he wasn't supposed to be climbing, or had a major pile-up on his trike, there would be a quiver of the bottom lip, a quick brush down and then on to the next challenge the garden had to offer. Zack became the apple of my eye and Philip's, too. He stood for the child we still hoped we might have one day. Another frontier of medical science still to conquer. Zack couldn't say the name

Vanessa, so there in Dayton I became Vessa, a word which Philip adopted as an endearment. It was Vessa when we were closest and when Philip used his little-boy act to charm something out of me.

During the summer the RAF Nimrod 42nd Squadron came to take part in the Dayton Air Show. We spent a wonderful day with the team sitting by the hotel swimming pool, singing British songs together and being British all over the place. In fact it was great to hear English accents and in a summer which seemed to be dragging as far as Philip's progress was concerned, the high spirits of the airmen were a tonic. They took Philip to their hearts and later some of them ran in the New York Marathon putting the money they raised in sponsorship towards the British charity which was to fit hundreds of paralysed people with the walking equipment later developed.

Now destined for a few days' break in San Francisco while Andy got his series together for the *Daily Mail*, I had time to take stock of what had happened to Philip and to us over the last six months.

To all intents and purposes, Philip looked a different person. His general health had improved; the regime in Dayton had brought him back to a standard of physical fitness which was in contrast to the emaciated body that had flown out from England. He had put on weight and had now grown a moustache – a tribute to the prevailing fashions of the Dayton Police, impressively moustachioed almost to the last man.

He had beaten his addiction to painkilling drugs, he had been the only Englishman on the project and after all he had something to take home as an achievement.

He had wanted to say: 'I've come home with this. I tried it out and it works and it will make life easier for the rest of you.'

It wasn't going to be possible for Philip to make a speech like that, so yes, he was disappointed, but there *was* a purpose to it all and he told me he would be coming back.

Now in public, he chose his words more carefully. Not using 'cripple', the word which everyone tries to avoid and which Philip used on television because he wanted to shock; not speaking of his own true feelings which were far from being optimistic.

'There is no doubt I will be able to cast off this wheelchair I'm sitting in,' Philip had told the Mayor and assembled audience to loud applause when he was presented with the keys to the City of Dayton: '*It will happen.*'

I wasn't there to hear those brave words. I heard about it afterwards when Philip returned in buoyant spirits with Skip after the reception. And later, I read all about it in the local papers. Philip had made a wonderful impression.

I wasn't there because I'd gone down with a flu bug. I could no more have appeared smiling in public than I could have done aerobatics with the Red Arrows.

The trip to San Francisco before the long journey home had been a nice idea on Andy's part.

We wandered round the Napa Valley, the wine-growing region of California and sampled some of the wines. We went to the famous Pier 39, literally an old wooden pier with restaurants and touristy shops on it, and to the lovely Redwood forests. We saw the place where Clint Eastwood had made some of the scenes for the Dirty Harry films and the spot where someone dived off the cliff. I quite enjoyed all that because I think Clint Eastwood is great. He was our silver screen hero. We both enjoyed the Dirty Harry films.

'Having a lovely time,' I wrote on my postcard to Mum and Dad, describing all these exotic attractions we were lucky enough to be visiting. But we weren't having a lovely time at all. We weren't enjoying ourselves. I was getting reactions to the last six months and was so demoralized I could hardly speak. Sorrow and profound fatigue were at the heart of my silence.

It had been all right for Philip to tell me a different story to the one he told the world. To be chief encourager and can-carrier, to have gone through the drug withdrawal together, and *together* stuck it out until the end. What we hadn't realized was how much it had taken out of us both.

We knew before Philip stood up in the harness that this wasn't going to be the great get-up-and-walk. Due to the slowness of the research work and all the money that needed to be raised, the realization of the final objective had become more and more like pie in the sky. Now Andy was saying that by next year, Philip would be back in America to try out the new system. The research was going on. Positive steps were being made.

Although the driving force behind the last six months had been to see Philip walk, to see the whole thing through, there had been many times in the close confines of our daily life when his traumatic behaviour had strained our relationship to its furthest point.

Without the job to provide mental stimulation, I felt that by the end of another trip I would be a mindless moron with no identity of my own. I viewed the thought of returning to Dayton and going through it all again with a heavy heart.

Chapter 11

I didn't know Philip until months after he was shot. The *Daily Mail* sent me to interview him at his home, and I kept in touch from then until he died, though there were sometimes gaps. Any reporter forms a relationship with his contacts, and usually it has good and bad points. With Philip, the link was much more complicated, while the good and bad points became intense. I still can't untangle my own feelings about him, but we were quite close, even if we sometimes drove each other mad. I often felt there were two Philips fighting an internal war which might have been resolved if he'd had more time. He could be extremely good company and very witty; he could also be frightening, morose and full of self-pity. Violent and gentle, articulate and uncouth, often clever and wise, but sometimes foolish. A man of intense moods, good and bad, which could change in seconds. He had more physical courage than anyone I have met; yet there were times when his psychological courage let him down. If I had to suffer what he went through I might not have been such a pain, but I wouldn't have been half as much fun either. You had to accept both sides of his character to appreciate him. Some people didn't understand that and walked away. One person – Vanessa – understood it perfectly. She showed more love and loyalty than I could have imagined. I don't think I am being harsh if I say

Philip did not always deserve her love – he admitted as much himself.

There was one aspect of Philip's character which remained consistent – his generosity. How many people in his condition would have taken part in the American experiment, knowing that it would probably help others much more than it helped him? Our attempts to put him on his feet gave him a challenge and some new experiences, but it was disappointing not to have had more success. I still feel that if the scientific work in the United States had not come to a virtual halt we would have achieved a practical electronic walking system. I don't think it would have made any difference to Philip, but it would have helped others. However, the mechanical system is a lot better than I would have imagined before we tried it.

Philip's death was a terrible blow, even if no great surprise. Perhaps I was foolish to think a reporter could do more good than harm. In the end we failed him, and one half of Philip failed the other half.

Andrew McEwen,
now Diplomatic Correspondent of *The Times*.

Their names were Woody and Donny and they were waiting for us when we got home. Two beautiful golden retrievers, they were named after the press photographers Graham Wood, (who ironically didn't like dogs) and John Downing of the *Daily Express*.

Living on his own after the shooting, Philip had been forced to give up Winton, his golden labrador and had sorely missed having a dog around the place. Philip had felt pretty badly about Winton. A portrait of him painted by Terry Spinks, an ex-police constable, hung over the mantelpiece. It had been commissioned by Met officers and presented to Philip by Sir David McNee at a police dog show at Keston. But a portrait was no substitute for the real thing, and Winton had now settled down with Philip's sister, Jenny, who had married a policeman and lived in Wales. It wouldn't have been fair to uproot him.

In the meantime, we had Genghis, a rough-haired Jack Russell with big ears unusual in a terrier. But then Genghis was an unusual terrier. We'd found him in Epping at the stables, where on rare occasions I still managed to get over to see my horse, Simon. Philip came with me and while I went out for a ride, this little brown and white puppy snuggled up to him and that was that; Philip had to have him.

Philip used to take him round on his lap, entertain him with fights under the duvet, getting his nose bitten and generally allowing him to break all the dog-training rules. Living up to the spirit of his name, Genghis quickly developed the big dog personality. Every time the door opened, he was out in the middle of Eastcote Road, barking fiercely at whatever came by and trying to herd up juggernauts. Even I had my work cut out to catch up with Genghis and when I wasn't there, his exploits became too much of a liability for someone in a wheelchair, so Mum and Dad were persuaded to give him a home in the country where, to this day, he gives the postman's van a hard time whenever he gets the opportunity.

We were both pretty soppy about dogs, so when we moved to the bungalow at Pinner with its big garden, it wasn't long before we had the urge to get another dog. We had both fallen for the golden retriever owned by our dentist, so Philip got the name of the breeder in Cornwall and put his name on the waiting list for the next litter.

Deciding that two would be company for each other when we were at work, we had asked for brothers and Woody and Donny arrived while we were held up in the States. A local dog lover called Inga had agreed to act as foster mother until we got back and Woody and Donny were five months old and very nearly house-trained by the time we returned home just before Christmas.

They meant some extra work, but affectionate and well-behaved, the dogs were a joy. When I was on early turn, I'd get up at 4.30, put them out into the garden, whizz into the shower and get dressed, prepare the dogs' meal, lay out all Philip's clothes and take the dogs round the garden before driving off to get to work at half past five. They were company for Philip if he was on his own and always ready with loads of kisses and cuddles whenever we got home. They were more than just the perfect family dogs: for us they were the family.

With me back at work and Philip on an instructor's course at

Hendon early in the New Year, life had snapped back into its accustomed shape: hectic activity, with the sense of motivation that had deserted me in America. I was better under pressure. I needed the hard work, the long hours, the shopping, the cooking, the constant monitoring of Philip's health. I needed it all because I'm temperamentally programmed to pushing myself to the limit and probably because constant activity stopped me from a too close examination of where I was going with Philip.

Where *was* I going with Philip? By June 1984, the wedding date had come and gone. When a reporter enquired, Philip told him that when he got married, he wanted to walk down the aisle on his own two feet. That got quoted in the press. But the truth was Philip was quite upset when I said that there was too much happening to get a wedding organized and that we'd do better to wait until Petrofsky got the next stage of the research project sorted out.

Too busy to get married? It sounds like a lame excuse but even if things had been perfect between us, which they were not, I'd have wanted something more memorable than a quick dash into the register office.

Without analysing my feelings at any great depth, I suppose I was less eager to marry Philip than I had been three years ago. We had arguments in which I stood up for myself; also, I was no longer prepared to stand there like a human sacrifice every time he felt like hitting me. I learned to duck and dive – almost to tap dance. I got out of the way whenever I could. Despite the wheelchair, his reactions were incredibly quick. A sudden lunge when you're not expecting it comes like a bolt from the blue and it wasn't always that I got out of his reach in time.

These symptoms of what had been diagnosed as post-trauma syndrome seemed to happen according to an unseen cue. One moment Prince Charming; the next, enter the Demon King.

Once I wrote him a poem starting, 'Dear Dr Jekyll, or as you read this, Mr Hyde . . .' At the time I was in a patrol car watching some 'insecure premises' – police terms for a place insecure due to a burglary or damage which left it vulnerable to further abuse until it was boarded-up or had new locks fitted. I remember feeling total bewilderment. If Philip had been a police case, I could have taken advice. But I had no one to turn to.

Yet for 97 per cent of the time, things were going well for Philip in 1984 – better than he could have hoped for a few years earlier. Far from being on the scrap heap, he had finished his course and was doing a good job at Hendon. As an instructor, he was both popular and effective.

He formed a true bond with the recruits he taught, enjoyed their enthusiasm and understood their desire to get out on the streets and take a chunk out of what's really termed as life. It was quite obvious that what he called his 'babies' meant a lot to him. He worried when they went out on the streets for the first time and wished he could walk with them and guide them along the way. In his classes he aimed to instil an awareness of street survival techniques that would become like second nature by the end of the course. Like, for instance, not standing squarely in front of a door when you don't know what to expect on the other side. Like always keeping in a position of advantage so that if someone wants to make a sudden move, you're going to have some warning of it.

When it comes to going out on the streets for the first time as a probationer, it's the teaching behind the practice that counts: knowing where you are, what you're looking at and remembering everything you've been taught. It's not a lot of use radioing back for help, for instance, if you're not exactly sure about the name of the street you're in. It sounds an obvious precaution, but it's easy enough to let your mind drift in another direction. Then when an emergency comes up you can't very well run off down the road looking for the street name.

Philip was thrilled when some of his ex-recruits came to visit and told him about occasions when his words had rung in their ears and prevented them from stepping into unnecessary danger.

The irony that the advice Philip gave was all too late in his own case didn't escape him. Nor was he unaware of the effect that a police instructor in a wheelchair might have on raw recruits. But with this job, he developed a sureness of touch and the ability to turn his own fate to the benefit of his students. He got good results from them and instead of focusing on his own limitations, found a great deal of satisfaction in getting to know and like the recruits, and preparing them as thoroughly as he possibly could for the great big world outside.

Another area in which Philip scored was with my family. Mum loved him. Philip often used to say he felt like an adopted son. My sister, Tracey, came to regard him as a second brother. When Philip died, she was absolutely devastated and to this day keeps a picture of him with the family photos.

Philip also got on well with my brother, Chris. They shared a common enthusiasm for motorcycles. One particular Christmas in Herefordshire, they disappeared off together and a short while later, guffaws of laughter could be heard echoing round the valley. We went out to find that Philip had conned Chris into pushing him up the steep hill outside, then letting go to see how fast he could whizz down in the chair. Their estimate was between 30 and 40 m.p.h. with Philip braking like hell on a bend. Mum and I arrived on the scene just after Chris had scooped him out of a ditch.

Dad was welcoming to Philip, but rather more reserved. They had nothing particular in common. Dad is a practical man. He enjoyed sport and apart from motor racing, Philip wasn't interested in sport. Dad also thought Philip drank too much, which was true. Philip was first and foremost a ladies' man, and Dad had memories of Philip's father at Hendon where rumour had it that he had acquired quite a reputation in that direction.

Although he tried not to show it, Dad was wary about our relationship. He was concerned for Philip too and he worried about the way he mixed drugs and drink. Although Philip was no longer on Pethidine, he was taking Fortagesic, a strong painkiller – potent when washed down with Scotch – as well as Valium and sleeping tablets.

When my parents bought their house at Ross-on-Wye, there had been no reason for them to consider the question of access for the disabled. It was probably the most inaccessible place you could have found for someone in a wheelchair – a tiny cottage on the edge of a hill, nothing on one level and steps here, there and everywhere.

We used to go there at Christmas and Mum and Dad did their best to make it less restricting for Philip. They put ramps down for the wheelchair and took a lot of thought to moving furniture around before we arrived. Although they never told him of all the efforts they'd made, Philip was always very appreciative, particularly of the calm way Mum dealt with everything.

Staying there, it was impractical to have the wheelchair upstairs, so Philip and I worked out a sit and lift system to get him up the stairs and a more dangerous and back-straining one to get him down again. One night we'd all been out together and had an hilarious evening and when it was time for bed, Dad offered to help Philip upstairs. Dad is very fit and strong so he picked Philip up in his arms and carried him. Philip had his arms round Dad's neck and on impulse half-way up the stairs, Philip planted a big wet kiss on Dad's cheek. They both started to laugh and collapsed in a heap on the stairs.

There were many times when a laugh and joke were the saving grace. Going down long flights of stairs was always a hazardous venture and hard work for both of us. Philip would use his hands as brakes on the wheels as we went down, but occasionally as I felt the muscles in my back groan, our combined strength would give out. When this happened, what started as a sedate and controlled descent would turn into a rapid, scrambled dive ending in a big bump at the bottom of the stairs. With me following behind, Philip would make a swift handbrake turn – rather like a ski turn – to avoid mowing down people in our path. While trying to look as though there was no problem, we'd often find ourselves stifling almost hysterical giggles.

We were staying at Mum and Dad's one Christmas when something happened that very nearly rocked the whole household. I had arranged to go hunting on New Year's Day and had got up early. Beforehand, I had asked Philip if it was okay if I went because I always tried to avoid upsetting him. I didn't really get a reaction, but before I went, I left his clean clothes laid out as always. Mum said she would bring Philip in a basin of hot water and all the other bits and pieces he needed later, when I'd gone. Mum got on so well with Philip, I didn't think he would mind.

So I went on the hunt and had a really good time. When I came back, Philip was still in bed, so I asked him if he was all right. He said, just close the door and come over here. So I closed the door, went over to the bed and he grabbed me by the arm, pulled me round and bang: punched me straight in the face. I hit the deck.

Of course, in a small cottage you can hear everything. So Mum and Dad asked what had happened.

I called back, 'It's okay, I just dropped something.' I had a bloody nose and a split lip. I thought he'd broken my front teeth, but he hadn't. The blood had congealed on my teeth. In the bathroom I bathed my face in cold running water. After wiping away all the blood I went back into the bedroom and said, 'What did you do that for?'

He said, you didn't leave all my stuff out. So I said no, because Mum said she would do it. He said, I didn't want your mother to do it. So I said, well *I'm sorry.*

There had been no sign of Philip working himself up to a frenzy. Lying in bed, he had looked as cool as a cucumber. Within seconds, he'd decked me.

I thought, if Mum and Dad know this they'll go mad, so I didn't dare to go downstairs for some time. Later, I told them I'd walked into a door. Years after Mum told me she knew it was something more than that.

Dad didn't know then that Philip was hitting me, but he did try to speak to him. I wasn't a party to it, but I think he told Philip that he didn't like the way he sometimes spoke to me. For a time, it did have an effect. Philip respected Dad.

I enjoyed the fact that Philip and Mum got on so well together. Mum didn't fuss over him, but he enjoyed being mothered. With Dad and Philip, I often used to feel like piggy in the middle. I used to have to think: do I go up into the woods and out into the fields with Dad like I used to, or should I stay indoors with Philip because he is so restricted as to where he can go? So it was a constant dilemma. It took a lot of the pleasure out of staying with Mum and Dad.

For most people, coping with the disabled is foreign territory. All the time I was with Philip we went out a lot: to restaurants, theatres, people's homes, and I'd always have to think ahead wherever we were going. If there was a party at a friend's house, sometimes we'd arrive and find we couldn't get the wheelchair down the hallway because it wasn't wide enough. More than once, it had meant going round the back of the house, over a muddy lawn and through the French windows. Then if someone's got to move all the furniture about and there's a tremendous amount of fuss, you don't feel like going through with it because it focuses too much attention in the wrong way. You want to cause the minimum amount of embarrassment to the people who invite you to share their hospitality and you can't expect everyone to rearrange their homes just in case someone in a wheelchair visits them. But perhaps just a little more education on that subject would help. If you can't get a wheelchair into a room or down a corridor, you're stuck and there's an end to it. Short of going round measuring people's houses, I always tried to work things out beforehand to save embarrassment.

Had we been put off by every unexpected snag, we'd never have got anywhere, and as Philip was the type willing to take a chance on most things, we'd occasionally make some unusual entrances.

We had been to Andrew McEwen's wedding before the first trip to America and when he and his Italian wife, Rita, invited us to dinner in Bell Street near Paddington, their flat was up three flights of stairs at the top of an old Victorian house. Andy got round that by putting Philip over his shoulder and carrying him, something Philip wouldn't gladly have allowed anyone else to do, but with the ever-resourceful Andy there were never any problems or embarrassment. At the time, Philip's legs were like pieces of string and his emaciated body weighed little more than a child's.

It was a different story when we came back from Dayton. Philip's legs were about three times the size and his weight had almost doubled. Poor Andrew couldn't believe how heavy Philip had become. Getting him upstairs the second time almost broke Andy's back and although the two of them collapsed laughing about it in the sitting-room, they both knew that unless something was done fairly rapidly, Philip was going to end up where he'd started.

It seemed a great shame that he had come home healthy and strong and that, after months of work building up his strength, all that was going to happen was that he would waste away again.

In Dayton, there had been further delay. Petrofsky had been working on plans to reduce the computer to the size of a pacemaker and implant it in the body. This didn't work out and he was now testing a more practical piece of equipment in the shape of a computer about the size of a camera case which could be attached to the body, hooked onto a belt.

As it became apparent that development problems in Ohio might take months to solve, David English got together with Andy to

163

decide that they couldn't leave the project where it was. So plans were made to set up a smaller research facility in Britain.

Every time there was a story about Philip in the papers more donations came in from the public and when the first part of *The Visit* was shown on television in January 1984, a big fund-raising operation got under way. The Philip Olds Spinal Cord Research Fund was set up with the aim of extending the research and sending him on the return trip to Dayton.

By June, the scope had widened to make a modest start on setting up an experimental project in Britain. With contributions from thousands of readers and donations from over a dozen leading companies, the *Daily Mail* Fund for Victims of Spinal Cord Injuries was formed. The charity began research work in a rented outside ward in the grounds of St Vincent's Hospital, Northwood in Middlesex.

It began in July, with four paraplegic research subjects in addition to Philip. First the subjects had to undergo tests arranged by the Medical Research Council at Northwick Park Hospital in Harrow, and after about six weeks, further tests were made to measure changes in muscle development and to safeguard the general health of those taking part.

The project opened with a major contribution from Nissan UK, and the muscle-stimulating machines powered by computers donated by Apple, plus other equipment given by British firms.

Professor Petrofsky came over in June to launch the scheme and Debbie Hendershott and José Almeyda set up the leg exerciser and bike. The four youthful pioneers – Shane Colley, Frank Doherty, Adam Thomas and Rena Zdaniewicz – all had similar disabilities to Philip. They had been chosen out of many applicants as a control group. Apart from being young and only recently paralysed, they were able to give time to the project and had pledged themselves to attend on a regular basis.

All the money donated was channelled into a central fund with Deputy Assistant Commissioner Hugh Annesley then of Scotland Yard, Stuart Marshal of Coutts Bank and Desmond Wilcox as principal trustees and Sir David English as chairman.

Andrew McEwen also became a trustee and to him fell the task of co-ordinating the work of the charities, organizing the events connected with them, keeping abreast of developments in America and providing the incentive to keep everything going.

Andy, who worked from a special office put aside for the charity at Northcliffe House off Fleet Street, spent many long hours working like a Trojan into the night to bring to fruition the dream that eventually allowed thousands of paralysed people to leave their wheelchairs behind for long enough to savour the joys of independence.

But one stumbling block remained: if Petrofsky's computer failed, the paralysed person could fall. The solution came when a London-born orthopaedic surgeon, now working in New Orleans, heard of Petrofsky's project. Since the early 1970s, Roy Douglas, who had trained as a prosthetist at St Mary's Hospital in Roehampton, had been developing a type of reciprocating brace, medically known as an orthosis. After many prototypes, Mr Douglas had perfected a design that had got large numbers of spina bifida children as well as over fifty spinal cord accident victims, on their feet. He had always intended to add electrical stimulation to his design to help the effort needed to walk. So when he heard about Petrofsky's experimental work, he felt it was time to join forces.

What was now awaited was the combined system using Petrofsky's computer and Roy Douglas's walking brace.

Worried by the delays in Ohio where Petrofsky seemed to spending more time on fund-raising projects than making progress in the laboratory, Andy set about bringing the scheme to fruition. It says a lot for his diplomatic skills that although unqualified in the field of science, it was he who acted as the driving force, bringing the two doctors and their two different walking systems together. He worked enormously hard, sometimes under difficult circumstances and without his relentless efforts, I doubt if Philip would ever have got as far as he did. Together the two inventions offered hope to thousands of paralysed people. It was not a cure. Paraplegics would not be able to say goodbye to their wheelchairs. But it would allow them to stand and to walk and to stay upright for a limited time.

With the financial support of Sir David English, everyone concerned was now pledged that, however long it took and however much it cost, the world's most advanced scientific walking system was to be brought back to Britain with Philip as its first exponent.

In the end it was eighteen months before the recall signal came from Petrofsky. I think in the frustration of waiting, we had lost sight of the fact that this was a research project where everything has to be tried and tested very many times before being attached to a human being. Reducing a computer from the size of a milk float to the dimensions of a cufflink box was obviously more complex than we could realize.

Meanwhile, Philip went regularly to St Vincent's, which was only a few miles down the road from us, working out on the leg exercisers to keep bones and muscles in a state of fitness.

At the time there were rumours about his prima donna-ish behaviour, but I don't think this was entirely fair. If someone gave Philip an explanation for what had to be done, he would accept it if it rang true. If it didn't ring true to him, then he'd never accept it. All the people who were on these projects had a similar type of personality. They had drive and determination, and probably, they were equally difficult to live with as Philip. It needed a certain type of person in charge to understand the way their minds worked and the frustrations they experienced. No one had done this sort of work in England before and to begin with there were some personality clashes – not just with Philip – that had to be ironed out.

Throughout the summer and into the following year, Philip went round doing a huge amount of fund-raising for the project. Every week there were sponsored walks, runs or swims, there were fêtes, dinners, lunches and functions of every description. Philip was welcomed as the guest of honour and celebrity hero and I usually accompanied him whenever I was off duty. We had an amazing social life and looking back I can't believe how much we packed into the time.

Described by Sir David English as 'the spearhead, the focal point, who dramatizes and draws attention to the work', Philip was no longer just the recipient of other people's help and charity. It was estimated that there were some 20,000 people in Britain who could benefit from the work of the *Daily Mail* fund. In publicity terms, Philip had become its chief contributor.

Any personal donations Philip still received from the public were channelled into the fund. As the subject of the BBC's hard-hitting documentary, his honesty on the subject of disablement had gone a long way to altering public perceptions. His natural and unaffected manner made him a popular speaker at functions. He was sought after, he was doing good: his story had gone far beyond just holding out hope to paraplegics. As David English had put it: 'It is a story of hope for anyone who is sick in cases where science and medicine are attempting to make a breakthrough.'

So how could I have not wanted to go with Philip on the return trip to America? When in May 1985 we were told that the long-awaited walking system was at last ready for Philip and the others in Dayton to test, there were celebrations all round.

My presence on the trip was taken for granted. Everyone except Andy assumed I would be only too willing to go, so how could I explain the trepidation I felt about a repeat performance in the States?

The intensity of our relationship was more tolerable at home. When things blew up between us, I could get away from it. I could go out in the garden with the dogs. I could immerse myself in my job twelve hours a day. I would accompany Philip in public where the darker moods were seldom seen. When they were, it was usually because someone else had put his foot in it, not me.

I'd learned to be very, very careful. Philip was still showing the same violent changes of mood which, thrown together in America, would be impossible for me to avoid. No one seeing us in public at all the parties and fund-raising events, would have guessed at the volatile situation underlying our relationship.

Also I didn't want Mum and Dad worrying, so I pretended everything was all right. But there was a price to be paid for putting a lid on my emotions. I often longed to be loved for myself without having to put a guard on all my words and actions.

In contrast to my life with Philip, in my job I was gaining more confidence. As a Sergeant, I was taking on more responsibility – serious decisions for which I was accountable.

In the job you have to be very alert, using all the senses, plus a sixth sense, I suppose you could call it, where in fractions of a second you may have to make life-threatening decisions.

Sometimes you're in a very tense situation involving several people where one of them might attack another one – or you. My own method is to look for a rapport whenever possible. It doesn't matter if it's a criminal or a victim you're dealing with, somewhere along the line you can usually find a rapport with them given the chance.

So if you're trying to assess a situation, you may have the opportunity to try a couple of different approaches, but usually your reactions have to be very quick. You may be in a situation where someone is throwing their arms about and shouting. Now if you're a probationer and not terribly experienced it's easy to come to the conclusion that the person throwing wobblers all over the place is possibly the most serious threat. But the person responsible for all the noise and verbal abuse isn't necessarily the problem. Maybe it's the quieter person standing there withholding his feelings who is the real aggressor. If you're too busy dealing with the one letting off steam, you won't have noticed him until he suddenly hits the button and explodes.

There can be a lot of distractions. Someone wagging their fingers in your face can be irritating beyond belief. But you mustn't let it rile you or you lose control of the situation. You're the steadying influence. So you ignore the finger-wagging and get on with dealing with the real problem.

You always hope that speaking clearly and quietly and putting it all in a logical way will help defuse the situation. It doesn't always work, unfortunately. And if it doesn't work, you have to resort to other means. The other means sometimes involve standing there in the station and saying 'QUIET' at the top of your voice. I frighten myself sometimes when I hear it. It all goes quiet for a minute and everyone looks astonished. Because apart from anything else, they don't expect a woman to come out with something like that – I don't know why.

I don't like having to yell because I don't think shouting like a fishwife is particularly feminine. It doesn't always work, but just one word can sometimes work miracles. A voice is a very, very powerful weapon. It depends on how you use it. It's like a Mum saying to little Johnnie: 'I told you not to do that,' and he doesn't take a blind bit of notice, and she can say it another way and put the fear of God into him.

Needless to say, it didn't work with Philip. For one thing, I didn't believe that treating fire with fire would solve anything and for another, he always got the better of me in an argument.

Meanwhile, Andy was busy laying on all the arrangements for our next trip to America. He'd booked the tickets, doing a publicity deal with British Caledonian on the fares and he'd rented us an apartment in Dayton. He was doing everything to make a success of our trip. There was never any question of Andy taking sides, but he knew how I was feeling and sometimes he must have racked his brains wondering what to do for the best.

To minimize the effects of body shock on Philip, we were to have breaks in Paris and New York. Like royalty, we didn't have to bother about the cost of anything. All expenses were paid.

Desmond Wilcox and *The Visit* team were coming to make part two of the documentary – this time to record the scientific miracle when Philip eventually achieved the first walk and, they hoped, show him in a more philosophical mood.

From our bosses, the Metropolitan Police, we had wholehearted support throughout. We both knew that the Met are usually sticklers for the rules and how hard it is to come by special leave. Even normal leave is often hedged about with difficulty. Plans can sometimes be altered at short notice if there is an emergency and it is not unknown for an officer to be flown home while on holiday if he or she is needed to give evidence in court. Yet once again, the Met were giving us a further six months' extended leave with their blessing.

If ever there was a goodwill trip with everyone behind us, this was it.

So what was I to say about my inward reservations: 'Sorry, I don't know if I can cope'?

Philip knew about my apprehensions. I no longer tried to hide my fear of his aggression but he was practised at shrugging off matters like this, making me sound muddled in my reasoning and over dramatic.

'Up to you,' he would say. 'Take your choice. We can still cancel everything.' His casual way of putting it did nothing to reassure me.

The answer was quite simple really. If I didn't go, he wouldn't go. I'd be taking away his opportunity to walk. It was emotional blackmail but I didn't think I had a choice.

There was another reason why I knew our relationship would be under strain in America, but it was a problem I didn't want to face yet.

Back in Dayton after the hectic activity of the last year and a half, I had time to think. Assessing Philip for myself, I could see he looked very different from the pale, thin, fierce figure who had first arrived on the American scene; nerves jangling. Fitter and plumper, some of the increased weight was due to alcohol, but he looked stronger and more relaxed. The rather alarming moustache he had grown on the last trip had been shaved off. It had proved a turn-off to some of the women he knew. Even if his relationship with Stef was no longer a frontrunner, he still had a few on-going flirtations and had not lost his vanity.

If the fierceness was less evident, Philip had not rid himself of that morose and billowing cloud that could suddenly descend to darken our relationship and the world at large. The light and shade of his personality made many people wary of him. But self-hatred had become his worst enemy. He hated himself as he was. He hated the degrading rituals of his incontinence. He hated the wheelchair and the restrictions it placed on his life. The wheelchair acted as a barrier in so many ways. When people talked to him with unconscious condescension, I could see him trying to control his emotions as best he could, finally explaining with electrifying honesty that the bullet had damaged his body, not his brain.

I loved Philip for his honesty and if he sometimes shocked people I knew it was because no one who has not suffered the appalling trauma of paralysis can ever fully understand what he went through.

On our first visit to the laboratory, we saw that it had been slightly tidied up and now looked a little less like the domain of a mad magician. There were fewer trailing wires and pieces of machinery to fall over. There at last was the new battery-powered computer consisting of a pack that could be clipped onto a belt. Looking rather like a trendy bumbag or a personal stereo, eighteen months of scientific purpose had gone into shrinking the unwieldly apparatus Philip had been attached to before, into this neat-looking box.

In fact, several of the research subjects were now walking round the corridors of Wright State University with their new electronic boxes.

They moved with less jerkiness than before, but without a bracing system to hold them up, the risk of collapse if the computer failed, was a serious one. They used crutches or walking frames; for a paraplegic person to fall and break a bone was a disaster involving many complications and a lengthy setback. There had also been insurance problems.

Although Philip had been physically built up to the point where he could have walked around with the computer guiding his steps, it had now been decided to combine the electronic equipment with a fail-safe body brace which was to come from Roy Douglas in New Orleans. It was known as the Reciprocating Gait Orthosis.

After Jerry Petrofsky and his team had run the rule over Philip, we were sent off to New Orleans. We met Roy Douglas at the Louisiana State University. He is a chirpy Cockney, rather like a professional Michael Caine and, like most of his patients, Philip immediately took to his warm and encouraging personality.

'You don't have to sit there wonderin' if this Charlie boy is ever going to walk again,' he told me cheerfully, 'because I don't believe in turning people away and I don't accept that there's any condition of paralysis or disease which can't at least be helped by this treatment.'

As a prosthetic engineer at Roehampton, Mr Douglas once had another bloody-minded patient determined to walk again: Douglas Bader. Roy Douglas and his team had worked for fifteen years to perfect the brace Philip was now going to try. Each one is individually made from a plaster cast in plastic and steel, and it clutched him from just below the chest to his toes. No tailor's fitting could ever have been so exact.

Worn under or over clothing, the Roy Douglas brace was a brilliant piece of engineering. As Philip pushed down with his arm on a walking frame or elbow crutches, the brace, which was spring-loaded, would lift the pelvis slightly, giving the leg sufficient clearance of the floor to swing through and forward. As he shifted his weight over and pushed down with his arm again, the trailing leg then moved forward and the procedure was repeated. A key aspect of the invention were two cables passing between the hip joints which swung the leg through for the next step.

A huge army of people suffering from a range of neuromuscular disorders, including a notable number of children, had been successfully fitted with the brace. It lacked the electronic system to be added on our return to Dayton, which meant that the full strength of the upper body had to be used to make it work. Because they were more adaptable and weren't worried about falling over, the children learned faster than the adults.

For most people, it took a lot of energy and concentration to learn how to use it properly: a matter of practice rather than instant magic. But two and a half thousand people have now been fitted out with the brace invented by Roy Douglas and his friendly and charismatic personality did a lot to inspire patience and confidence.

Philip took the attitude that if anything came out of this for him, it would be a bonus. He said that just looking at the children gave him a reason for carrying on. We would see these tiny tots looking frail and scrunched up in their wheelchairs, then a few weeks later they would be laughing and chattering and whizzing about with their braces on, utterly transformed. Roy Douglas's first patient had been a child of only six. She was now nineteen and proud of her independence. She wore her brace daily, putting it on with the rest of her clothes in the morning.

Philip felt that if he could take the idea back to England, he would have done his job. Not that it was an easy task to get used to wearing the brace. At first it was difficult to know whether or not the technique he was using was wrong, or whether it was the brace that needed adjusting. It could be that the wires that went over the back were not at the right tension, or that he wasn't properly balanced in the brace. Either way, for Philip to get moving it had to be exactly right. The plumbing problem had to be overcome, too. You could put the tubes over or under the straps, but if they were going to restrict the tubes, then the way the plumbing was arranged had to be altered because you couldn't risk any damage to that.

Getting into the brace was another art that had to be learned. Everyone there devised their own system. As it was moulded to the shape of the body, most people literally rolled into it. To start with it took ages to get everything just right, but the idea was for the patients to learn how to do it all themselves.

The first thing we'd noticed about the brace was that compared with the heavy and cumbersome types that made Philip shudder, this one was light and flexible. The flesh-coloured straps also made it more attractive than the heavy brown leather we'd seen on most other bracing devices. It was built of thin strips of metal running parallel from the pelvic band up to the armpits with a chest and stomach strap to support the upper body. Then there was the specially moulded hip band which contained the reciprocating wires. Each leg had a locking and unlocking hip and knee joint with plastic cupping at the back for the thighs, calves and feet. The thighs were held back by a pliable Velcro cover, the knee secured by a padded strap underneath.

After several trips backwards and forward to New Orleans, it was a poignant moment when Philip was at last standing upright in front of me secured in this amazing device. More so in a way, than when he actually walked for the first time on the laboratory platform hanging on to the parallel bars. Then I'd hardly dared breathe, counting the number of steps he was taking and wondering if he was going to collapse in the safety harness. Now he was standing there opposite me for the very first time and we fell into each other's arms in a long and loving embrace.

Face to face, I realized for the first time that we were much of the same height, Philip just a little bit taller. Standing eye to eye with him was a different situation altogether. When someone is in a wheelchair, you are literally talking down to them. The brace wasn't going to be a complete answer, but it gave Philip his first real opportunity to stand up and walk about on the same level as everybody else.

He was now ready for the next stage, the electronic system which would take a lot of the effort out of moving about. But before we left for Dayton, Philip had to be seen walking. A big publicity operation swung into action and he was taken here, there and everywhere to be filmed and photographed.

In the sweltering summer heat, he posed for pictures wearing his police uniform: 'British bobby walks the streets again'. His uniform had to be flown out from home. He was pictured standing up against a bar in his brace having a pint – that was quite enjoyable. We were filmed 'sightseeing', which was stretching the point a little at this stage. However, it was not beyond the realms of possibility for the future.

In the steady, almost golden air of New Orleans, we walked together for the first time, the cameras following our slow and rather painful progress.

With the temperature touching 90 degrees at times, Philip got physically tired and was often under stress. He was getting used to the new brace and at the same time was having to conform to filming schedules like an actor. *The Visit* crew were running short on time schedules and it meant Philip putting on his brace and being driven around to various locations and asked to walk here or stand there. It all got very tiring and very testing; it would have tested anybody.

On one occasion, *The Visit* crew wanted to film Philip walking down a long corridor in the hospital. He was tired and had an upset stomach, and just as they were all set up and ready to go, his bowels went wrong. That really put a stop to things. I jumped into a taxi and went back to the hotel, got him a change of clothing, came back and got him washed and back into his brace. By this time he was looking really ill.

The film crew had a flight schedule to keep to and this last shot needed to be done that day. So like a good trooper, Philip did what was asked of him. But he was sweating a lot and I knew that the stomach bug was making him feel unwell.

Under the circumstances – just being taken out of his box, told to put on his brace and stand up and perform – I feared Philip might have lost his temper. But he never did. He now got on well with Desmond Wilcox and apart from winding him up once or twice over some of the questions, co-operated fully throughout the filming. If Philip said he'd do something, he would always go through with it, even in circumstances under which a lot of people would have given up.

The shooting had gone on for some time and it was in the middle of all this razzmatazz that I was called to the phone one morning to take a personal call from London.

One of the reasons I hadn't wanted to go with Philip on this trip was because between our first and second visits to America I had met someone else.

Now he was calling to say that he had found somewhere for us to live, and would I be ready to join him when I got back?

Chapter 12

THE WRECK OF THE TITANIC

What's it like to be in a ship
Lost at sea?
Is it like my mind?
All murky and misty
Frightened to death
Of the doom I envisage beyond
Will I be rescued by a beautiful ship?
Or watch her pass by
And with it my ship dashed on the rocks –
Still watching my lifeboat
Disappearing in the distance,
Unaware or uncaring as to my plight.
Where's my signal flares
Or my flags?
How can I get the message through?
I need you,
To love
And therefore survive
Where are my flares?
Why are you drifting away?
Come back I beg you – and save my sinking ship. P.x

Philip Olds
1986

Having our own apartment in Dayton meant that when times were a bit tough, when we were having an argument or just wanted some space to ourselves, there was another room to go into.

I think Andy thought it would solve our problems. And it did – some of them. Having the apartment gave me something to do. We had a couple of dinner-parties and stuff while we were there, something I enjoyed doing. Even if it was just housekeeping, washing, cooking and ironing and all that type of thing, it gave me a purpose, more healthy and normal than just being there at Philip's beck and call whenever he required me.

In one respect I felt a lot more positive about things on that return trip to Dayton. Different from the shadowy figure I'd been before. Now we had a circle of friends and a comfortable feeling of belonging. I felt that because the friendships in America were ones we had made together, they were warm and loyal and I was not in danger of betrayed confidences.

On the other hand, it was also a very difficult time because I knew that I had left someone behind who was waiting for me; expecting I was going to leave Philip as soon as I got back. Naturally, he'd been making plans.

When Philip's part in the project was completed he would be going home with the combined system, able to walk when he wanted to; more capable of looking after himself and organizing his own life.

I had turned to Ian because, as much as I loved Philip – which I did – I needed somebody to show me love. Someone who showed that he appreciated and cared for me. Philip always said that he did, but he didn't want to show his dependence on me, either emotionally or physically. His broken marriage and childhood had left him with a fear of putting 'all his eggs in one basket', as he put it, and often it seemed that he showed his charm and consideration to almost everyone except me.

Having said he wouldn't take professional help for his psychological condition, Philip had promised that he would be able to control the violence that was underlying our relationship. His attitude that it would take time for the trauma of the shooting to work its way out and that he could only manage it with my help, was no longer quite as feasible.

I was tired of being on the receiving end of all the anger, frustration and broken promises. Every time Philip attacked me, I found it harder to get myself together and carry on.

It had just so happened on one particular morning, I had been beaten up at home and was sitting alone with my head in my hands contemplating my lot, when Ian appeared on the scene. I was quite bruised and as I ran my hands through my hair, there were handfuls coming out.

Ian had been a fireman, one of the people we often liaise with in the job, and we'd got to know each other. Ian wasn't part of the usual scene. He hadn't been there at the beginning and he wasn't one of Philip's group of friends. We had got on well and he was probably one of the first really independent friends I made after moving to Pinner. After leaving Tottenham, I'd lost most of my old friends apart from Elaine who was with me at the first police station. But she was now over in east London so it wasn't often I saw her, although Philip had officially reinstated her on the visiting list.

Ian became my independent sounding board. When he came across me tearing my hair out, so to speak, we weren't close friends, so it wasn't as if I was going to be worrying him by confiding in him. Philip and I were the only ones with the ability to sort ourselves out, but I needed someone to confide in and Ian turned up at the right – or the wrong – time according to how you look at it.

Ian acted as a tower of strength. He picked me up when I was down. Later on our relationship grew into something more special. I think anyone seeing us in the same room together would have recognized that we meant something to each other. I think Philip knew as well. He asked me a direct question once and my nose grew two inches from telling the lie.

But I also loved Philip. I wanted to be with him, I wanted what was best for him. He still fascinated me. But I wanted the affection and consideration I was getting from Ian.

With Ian, I could let off steam – not by crying on his shoulder; that wasn't going to help at all. I'd always loved the countryside and together we'd go off to some local woods, playing silly games with the dogs, running through the trees, doing acrobatics and generally behaving like overgrown kids who had been let out of school. We must have cut a strange picture, jumping off logs and duelling with twigs pretending to be swashbucklers from another age.

Come rain, hail, snow or shine most of our stolen moments together took place out in the elements giving us a sense of uninhibited freedom. We were unlikely to bump into anyone who knew us, and anyone who didn't probably regarded us as mad.

The horseplay that was a feature of our relationship was like a safety valve for all the emotions I'd kept bottled up with Philip for so long. Ian also had a relationship which wasn't going right so both of us had problems we threw off for the time being in this manic release of energy.

A late snowfall in March proved to be my undoing. We'd been throwing snowballs for the dogs, laughing hysterically at their surprised expressions as the snow melted in their mouths, when Ian decided to give me a piggyback down a hill. Half-way down he slipped and fell and, catching my leg as I went down, I felt something snap in my calf. I hobbled back to the car and after getting washed and changed at home, went into work. A couple of hours later I was in Accident and Emergency being told by a doctor that I'd probably broken my leg. The X-rays didn't show a break but something else had twanged in my leg causing a big bump so I had to have a soft plaster and crutches.

Philip and I made a right pair appearing at, of all things, a dinner-dance together. With him in a wheelchair and me on crutches, it seemed almost like poetic justice. I told Philip I'd slipped and fallen over in the snow and, rather unfairly, got sympathy from both sides. This episode put a stop to any more romps in the countryside with Ian. From then on we had more serious matters to discuss – our future together.

I can't describe the way I felt at the time, but there was a song called 'Torn Between Two Lovers' which summed it up as well as anything.

I used to feel horribly guilty about seeing Ian and feeling the way I did about him. But on the other hand, I desperately needed his love.

If I could have combined the two, I would have had the perfect relationship. Philip was central to my life and the emotional support I had from Ian had become vital. It was only knowing that however bad things got at home, I had someone there who really loved me, and showed me that he really loved me, that enabled me to stay with Philip for so long.

When we flew out to America, I thought the best thing to do was to run with the project; get all that sorted, so that if Philip was independent with the use of the brace, then from my own selfish point of view, I wouldn't feel quite so guilty about leaving him. The situation put a strain on our relationship and we were under enough strain as it was in New Orleans while he got used to the new brace, and then again in Dayton with the demands of working out at the laboratory and hoping that the new system would be successful.

Petrofsky's new development was a pair of shorts which looked like cycling shorts, elasticated and fitting close to the skin with electrodes sewn into them. The electrodes were attached to wires joined to the computerized power pack which clipped onto a waist belt. On top of this went the brace. Philip was then given a walking frame with buttons on it, whereby he pressed first the right and then the left to power the computer system to activate his legs as he walked.

If this sounds cumbersome, it was the height of scientific sophistication compared to the crude system he had originally started out with where all the electrodes had to be placed individually and were sometimes in the wrong place or fell off. All you had to do with the hot pants were to pull them on and the electrodes would be in the right place.

Together with the brace, this was the combined system Philip was going to take home with him. It took time to get into, but was still a great advancement on the original system.

Of course, what had to be remembered was that Philip was still part of a research programme. Others were to use this system in the future. It had to be tested, as did the research subjects' reactions to any strains and stresses the new equipment might reveal.

Nor had Petrofsky by any means completed his research. The

electronics were capable of further refinement and Petrofsky was still working towards the master plan of an implant on the lines of a pacemaker.

As the often tiring and tedious daily attendance in the laboratory continued, it was only through having good friends in Dayton that the strain between Philip and me was kept within bounds.

Since our last trip, Skip and Donna had gone their separate ways and Skip was now remarried. His new wife, June, was a news reporter on the local television channel. We'd see her every night on TV and then go round to their house or to Bill and Debbie Elzholz's or some of the other police officers we had kept in touch with since our last visit.

One source of amusement was the excuses or explanations motorists tend to give in the confusion of a traffic accident. Our friends had a prize collection which appealed to Philip as a former traffic policeman.

Amongst the gems that actually appeared as statements on insurance forms are:

'My car was legally parked as it backed into the other vehicle.'

'A pedestrian hit me and went under my car.'

'The telephone pole was approaching fast and I was attempting to swerve out of its path when it struck my front end.'

'The indirect cause of this accident was a little guy in a small car with a big mouth.'

To add to the collection, Philip told a story about himself which happened one day when he was on motorcycle patrol in a north-west London suburb.

He was gaining ground on a motorcyclist who was travelling well in excess of the speed limit, when he entered a particularly long and nasty left-hand bend. Having parted company with his bike, Philip came round to find the errant rider hovering over him, deeply concerned for his welfare.

'I suppose you're definitely going to report me now,' he said, as Philip got to his feet.

Dazed, Philip replied, 'I don't think so, I seem to have broken my pencil.'

Philip was relaxed and happy, swapping a few tales with friends and this always helped to relax me as well.

My role out there was to make sure that everything ran as smoothly as possible, but sometimes I thought, why do I have to be little Miss Stuffed Shirt all the time? Philip could get out of order whenever he felt like it, so there were occasions when I'd step out of line and have a few drinks as well. I'm not saying I was always Miss Sensible or stone-cold sober for all of the time. A lot of the time it was pretty boring to sit round in bars, but with Philip drink played a major part in our social activities.

When we went out together in the evening, it worked out that I usually did the driving. This meant no drinking because I wasn't going to get done for DWI. Driving while intoxicated is what they call it out there and in the State of Ohio it means a custodial sentence: Do not Pass Go, Do not collect £200 – just go straight to gaol.

That would really have put the icing on the cake, so we were extremely sensible about driving. In any case, we'd both seen too many accidents to take risks.

When Ian phoned while we were in New Orleans, once again I was deeply involved in the project and Philip's part in it. I can't remember what I told Ian at the time, but I know I was sending out mixed messages. It probably sounded like yes and no. 'Yes, we will be together when we come home, but I'm not sure when that will be – no, I can't make any definite plans now.' Then I probably babbled on about Philip's progress. Later Ian was to tell me that I really only talked about Philip.

Hardly surprisingly, this wasn't what Ian most wanted to hear. He had parted from his previous girlfriend and had been looking for somewhere for us to live. Now he'd found somewhere that might be suitable and he wanted a plain answer to a plain question: should he go ahead? I wrote to him and he wrote to me, but even in my letters, he later told me, I avoided the issue of when I was going to leave Philip. I was finding betraying Philip more difficult than I had imagined.

It was when we got back to Dayton from New Orleans that Philip made the worst attack on me in the whole history of our time together.

We were in the apartment and although I can't remember what sparked off the row, at the back of it was the fact that without bringing Ian into it, I'd told Philip I was contemplating sorting out my own life when we got back to England. In theory, Philip didn't have an answer to this because every time I put a foot wrong he stormed at me to push off. He would later deny that he meant it, but I told him that whatever he meant or didn't mean, I felt in a permanently tenuous position.

It was a feature of the way Philip's anger worked that instead of just having an argument, he would turn it into an explosive confrontation. Grabbing hold of me from the back, he put his hands round my throat and started to strangle me.

He wasn't pretending. I was fighting to breathe, forced down onto the bed by sheer strength. I was frightened he was actually going to kill me.

Philip could be upset, or he could be dangerously upset. Had I been able to judge the dividing line, I could have put a locked door between us. As far as speed was concerned, he had the reactions of a tiger. Four years of heaving himself around using his arms and shoulders had given him the strength of an unusually powerful man. Once he had a hold on you there was no chance of getting free. He had a grip like a Scotsman on a five-pound note.

As I felt his hands tightening round my throat, I thought he wasn't going to let go. He did eventually, but not before I felt something giving inside my throat. A few seconds afterwards, he wheeled himself out of the bedroom and out onto the balcony of the flat. Not a word was said. As I lay there shocked and bruised, not wanting to move, Philip stared silently across the daylight bustle of the city.

It was the eerie silence of a nightmare when you want to scream but can't. When I got up to examine myself in the mirror, there were some very obvious bruises on my neck and I found I was unable to swallow properly. In squeezing my neck, Philip had damaged the cartilage in my throat. But it wasn't until two weeks later that I went for medical advice. I didn't want to provoke another upset with Philip by seeing a doctor. We were supposed to be able to sort these things out for ourselves without any outside intervention.

But the problem with my throat didn't sort itself out and I had to see a doctor. This really worried Philip because the fantasy was that we'd just had a row and nothing too bad had happened.

To cover the bruising I had been wearing high-necked sweaters and at the hospital I told the doctor that I had injured myself by slipping when I got out of the swimming pool.

She looked at me curiously. 'Whatever you did,' she said, 'you certainly didn't do it that way.'

So I said no, I had a row with my boyfriend. It was degrading, but doctors, like the police, see all these things. And the cover-ups.

It wasn't an injury that the doctor could do anything about. She told me it was just internal bruising and it would take time to heal up. It took months. Every time I swallowed I could feel it. It was as if I had a tablet stuck in my throat the whole time.

That incident scared me, I must admit. I think it scared Philip. He was sorry for what he'd done, but in a way he felt justified. He always found some justification. He could always turn things round. He was very convincing too. Then I'd feel guilty and think I'd provoked him. It was the typical battered wife syndrome: you end up feeling guilty for having provoked the person who assaults you into assaulting you.

After Philip's attack, the main thing I wanted to do was to go back home. But we were three-quarters through the project and I was in the same catch-22 situation as before. If I left Philip then, if I just said, well sod you, then jumped on a plane then ran off with Ian and lived happily ever after, Philip would have had to pack up and come home too.

I had to live with the guilt of loving two men at the same time and making neither of them happy. But to be responsible for wrecking the work of the walk project was something which would have haunted me forever.

I was there with Philip for nearly eight months in all and as time wore on, Ian felt he wasn't receiving much encouragement from me about getting our future together. He got lonely and dispirited and he began to feel in his heart of hearts that I would never leave Philip. At that point, he knew me better than I knew myself. In my divided state of mind, I wanted to be with Ian but I couldn't give him a positive answer.

I always missed the mental stimulation of the job when I was

184

away, so at this stage I wasn't sorry for an excuse to shut myself away with some homework to study the complexities of PACE, due to be implemented in 1986. One of my colleagues at work had been sending out the new legislation as it was distributed.

The Police and Criminal Evidence Act was to bring in a mass of new rules and regulations involving the police force in a heavy load of paperwork and at home my colleagues were taking week-long courses to familiarize themselves with the intricacies. Every arrest now involved much more writing and documentation than before, providing a complete record of what happened to each prisoner from the time they were taken into custody to the time they left. At first sight it appeared that every time someone coughed or blew his nose you were expected to take a note of it. The procedures were all quite different from the way I'd worked before but if the amount of paperwork created by PACE hasn't done the cause of the rainforests much good, it has worked for us in many respects. With everything down on record, there is now less room for allegations that a prisoner has been locked in a cell for hours and forgotten about and to a large extent, it has stopped malicious complaints about the way people are treated.

While the homework gave me some sense of objectivity, on a personal level I was trying to de-intensify the closeness between us to prepare the way for a possible break.

No matter the rows that went on or the traumas surrounding our relationship, I still continued to monitor Philip's health as carefully as before and still tried to smooth the path of daily routines. I hadn't stopped loving Philip but during all this time, I was in two minds about my tangled feelings and remained acutely conscious of the pain he suffered.

To replace the Pethidine, Philip drank more alcohol and com-bined with a liberal mixture of painkillers and tranquillizers, he regularly took a potent cocktail. So I'd still be lying awake at night listening out for the sound of regular breathing and trying to calculate how much of anything he'd taken.

Apart from one or two very close friends, not many people knew when Philip was in extreme pain. His eyes seemed to sink into darkened sockets, the colour of his skin would change to a tell-tale grey and there would be a tightness in his voice. He wouldn't complain or refer to the pain; he'd keep it inside and try not to let it rule his life.

The central core to Philip's anger and frustration lay deep in the maddening conundrum of his pain. He was paralysed from the chest downwards, so why should his big toe suddenly start to hurt? Why did he sometimes get such terrible pains in his legs or his side? I had watched at Northwick Park Hospital while the doctors had done a muscle biopsy, cutting a hole in his leg with a scalpel. No anaesthetic had been given and while I was breaking out in a muck sweat just looking on, Philip was lying on the table reading a paper.

The phantom or root pains which follow spinal injury are particularly frustrating to the person who suffers them. It didn't make sense. Yet sometimes the pain was almost visible. And not just the pain, but the emotional hurt as well.

It was October when we said goodbye to Dayton, to our friends, to Jerrold Petrofsky and the laboratory. We had a lot to thank people for, a lot to be glad about and something worthwhile to take home with us.

When we arrived at Gatwick the photographers were there. Waiting until the plane was empty, I got Philip's brace out of store, strapped him into it and got him into his uniform. Andrew McEwen was there to see the moment when at last Philip was on his feet and able to walk out of the aircraft and down the steps. Philip marked the occasion with a few words:

'It's great to be home,' he said. 'Let these first steps on British soil show the way for thousands of other paralysed people.'

His triumphant return was the climax of three years of efforts by scientists to restore some of his mobility. It had taken huge resources of money, time and effort to accomplish the mission but as Philip put it: 'If it can work for one man, it can work for a thousand.'

On Philip's return from America, these two experimental missions – the research in America and that at St Vincent's – were replaced by a registered charity called WALK, the initials standing for Walk Again Leg Kinetics. The WALK fund, initiated by the *Daily Mail*, could now extend the scope of the original charities, paving the way not just for the paralysed to be able to leave their wheelchairs, but for a wider range of patients including some with neuromuscular disorders. All the research that Philip and the other guinea pigs had taken part in was pooled as a joint effort with the UK project. Roy Douglas came over from New Orleans to take plaster casts to fit the first patients with braces and two physiotherapists from St Vincent's were sent to America to learn the techniques of the electronic exercising machines, which had been set up at Northwood, and the intricacies of the bracing system.

The first English guinea pigs were rapidly put on their feet with Roy Douglas's bracing system, having prepared themselves at St Vincent's and undergone the fitness tests from the Medical Research Council.

The launching of a national campaign by the *Daily Mail* to raise money for the WALK fund, followed by the screening of the second part of *The Visit*, brought in a substantial amount of further donations. Arrangements were made to manufacture the electronic power pack in Britain under licence and more patients applied for treatment as the scope of the charity widened.

The sad part of it all, was that after we got back, Philip didn't use the brace very much. A picture of him taken at St Vincent's with Frank, Shane, Rena and Adam, the English patients, shows Philip, the pioneer, sitting in his wheelchair. Later he was to put part of the blame for this on me. He said, 'The fact that you went a bit weird and lost interest in me meant I lost interest in the brace.'

But even before I left, the brace was often airborne; thrown through the air when Philip lost patience with the process of putting it on, with all the intricacies involved.

It took an age for him to get into it and unless there was some specific purpose like a public appearance, Philip would say it wasn't worthwhile undergoing all the contortions it involved just to look at the dust on top of the cupboard.

The first thing facing us was getting back to our jobs. The fundamental changes brought in by PACE meant extra work. This had to be adapted to along with all the other minor and major legislative changes which go through parliament.

Plunged into a new round of activity, I wasn't able to arrange a meeting with Ian immediately and the first time we saw each other, unfortunately, was at a social gathering with other people around.

Not unnaturally, he was upset by this and when later we met at our old haunt in the woods, I found that he had changed.

He had found a new girlfriend whom he subsequently married. He had come to the conclusion that the situation between us was hopeless and he'd decided to make a new life for himself. So whatever I'd thought about leaving Philip, my mind had been made up for me regarding my future with Ian.

Looking back, I think if I'd been more honest with myself and with Ian, I would have realized he was probably right. I hadn't meant to hurt him but I had. We parted friends, saying it was our timing that had been wrong. I felt I'd lost a precious friend and confidant, but the only person to blame for the mess which had come about, was myself.

The trouble was, I was a mess when we got back from America. I felt mentally and physically exhausted and confused; not able to cope as well as I had in the past.

For instance, Philip could make me cry when he couldn't before. It took a lot to make me cry. If I did, it would always be on my own; I couldn't bear anyone to see and I would choke back the tears or keep my emotions under control. Now I would break down on the spot in front of him.

It was the start of my 'going weird on him', as Philip put it. Going weird meant that I wanted to run away from everything. When it came, the break with Ian had hurt more than I had been able to foresee. In my state of mixed emotions it seemed to me that everything had changed. I had changed, Ian had changed; even the police force had changed since I'd been away.

Perhaps I was slow to notice the change in Philip. Other people saw a mellower, better adjusted side. In the second part of the documentary, Desmond Wilcox had made a point of saying that Philip had become a more mature person, able to overcome a lot of his frustrations.

The point is, I'd always known the good side in Philip. The generous and kind side. The romantic side as well.

He would phone me up at work to say he loved me. 'I Just Called to Say I Love You' was a favourite record of ours. How I would have loved to dance with him to that. He would often come home, not just with a bunch of flowers, but with a whole standfull. He took a lot of trouble buying me beautiful dresses. I've still got a real leather one in my wardrobe which is a stunner – the sort of thing I would never have bought for myself. 'Lady in Red' was another record he'd play for me.

Sometimes he'd come home from work and I'd be tired and he'd sweep me on to his lap and say he was taking me out to dinner. He could make an ordinary evening into a little celebration. We had some wonderful times together. He wasn't bad for me all the time.

Under strain in America, Philip had given me a hard time. Now he seemed to be concerned to show the softer side of his nature, the side which I knew was a part of him but which had so often been taken over by the darkness of his other self.

At home, we bought new things for the house and we'd plan the alterations that still needed to be made. We had been out of the country so much, the house was never really finished.

I felt remote from it all. I'd always been the strong one; fetching, carrying and organizing. Now, if something fell on the floor, instead of leaping to pick it up, I'd leave it until later. I'd go off with the dogs and forget the ironing. Dogs know when you're down – they are wonderful company that way. Deep down, something in me had changed and I didn't know what it was.

From time to time, disabled people would get in touch with Philip, wanting to know what the WALK system could do for them or their relatives.

One of these was the mother of Michael Beeforth, whose spine had been damaged in a car crash when he was only a baby. Philip was Michael's hero and he and his Mum and Gran stayed with us when they came up from Kent for Michael to be measured for his brace. At the age of seven, he was quite a character and became the youngest person at St Vincent's to be given a walking brace. He really was – and still is – a wonderful little boy. Full of high spirits and fun, he liked to tell the most appalling jokes. Philip used to be in stitches. He was excellent with children, never talking down to them.

Michael didn't want to be left out of anything. He seemed to make light of the fact he was paralysed, sometimes throwing himself out of the wheelchair and manoeuvring himself all over the floor on his elbows.

189

To see him hurtling round in his brace at St Vincent's a few weeks later and enjoying the new-found freedom of running around for the first time would bring a lump to the throat of the most hard-hearted person in this world.

Chapter 13

Philip had never forgotten what it was like to be told: you will spend
the rest of your life in a wheelchair. A grim sentence for anyone,
and for a child the restrictions are particularly hard when it comes
to school and sports and wanting to be like the others. We had seen
for ourselves how dramatically life's opportunities altered for so
many disabled people once they had access to the new technology
and in the case of the children it was amazing how quickly they
adapted. At St Vincent's it was like seeing a small army suddenly
enter the land of the living. You'd see the children getting into the
back of the car, Mum hoicking them out at the other end, locking
the knees of the braces for them, then they're off and away on their
walking frames or elbow crutches, with the braces keeping them
upright.

Philip used to get letters with drawings on them from Michael
about his progress. He gets in his brace, goes off to an ordinary
school and takes part in gym. Nothing special is done for Michael
at school but it would probably have been a different story without
the WALK fund.

Philip's hard-won effort of bringing the new technology over here
had been worth it, and the psychological advantage of knowing that
he could stand upright and walk if he wanted to had made a
difference to him. He was never altogether comfortable with the
brace, but it had lessened the rage he felt towards his wheelchair
and against life itself.

The pity of it was, that just as so many things were going right, I had begun to fall apart. And I was afraid that my depression would take Philip down with me. I thought it was stress. It's a word that can account for almost anything, so in my mind that's what I called it.

At the beginning of 1986, I felt I should do something positive. I thought: I have got to step out of this and assess what is really going on. So I left home.

For once, it wasn't after a big row. We reached a decision together. We agreed that I woud go away for a time to sort myself out and that while I was away, Philip would see how he felt about me – whether he really wanted me around. Before I left, he said it wasn't necessary for me to go away for him to come to that decision because he'd already made up his mind that he did want me around. But I insisted I needed to have a good think about things on my own, and I wanted *him* to do the same.

To be honest, I was feeling too desperate to do much constructive thinking. My emotions were like a bowl of spaghetti; I couldn't pick out a strand and say this is the right one to follow.

So I went back to live in the section house like I'd done before. I moved into a room with just a desk, a bed and a sink. You had shared baths and toilets and a canteen. It felt like No Hope Hotel. Choosy when you're desperate? Well, you can't be. But after our lovely home, it was depressing.

Philip and I were in contact all the time I was away. We'd be on the phone, or I'd go and see him when I came off duty and we went out for meals and all the rest of it.

If it looked like an argument, I'd just get up and go. But that didn't happen very often. Philip wanted me to come back. He'd say, 'This is your home, our home – when are you coming back?' And I'd say, 'Once I've got myself sorted I'll be back. I just want to get myself sorted out.' I loved Philip and I doubted it would take very long.

At 30 I had visualized myself as married with a couple of children. One of the problems I was finding hard to cope with was that Philip and I would never be able to have children of our own, a dismal fact that had finally been confirmed by the fertility clinic. As is often the case when denied something, it had produced a stronger longing, and of late I had become exceptionally broody. It seemed that everyone I knew was either pregnant, had just given birth or was planning to become pregnant. Just walking down the streets, every other person seemed to be pushing a pram or bulging fit to burst. I used to look at them and think: *I want a baby*. At the time, it seemed yet another way of going weird – a problem I had to come to terms with before going back to Philip.

I was only supposed to have stayed away for a few weeks, but as time wore on and I felt as big a mess as ever, Philip suggested I went along to have a chat with a psychotherapist he had met at a seminar.

It didn't work, because although I knew I had a problem, I felt I was going down the wrong path. The psychotherapist was leading me in the direction of leaving Philip for good. This was hardly surprising after what I'd told her about our relationship – the physical abuse and the emotional blackmail and all that stuff – but breaking off with Philip was not what I wanted to do.

One day, she produced a pillow and told me to punch it. I couldn't. I just felt stupid. I could see the reasoning behind it, but punching a pillow, which was supposed to represent all my frustrations and aggression, wasn't going to help.

I wanted to get myself on course and back to normal, and knew that was down to me. But I wanted Philip to be dealing with the problem of his aggression in his own way. That was at the heart of our bargain. Love is a very strange emotion. It seemed I could still love Philip, yet hate the way he often behaved. My intention was to go back to him. But obviously I had apprehensions because I knew what he was capable of and that really was the big thing: I didn't want to be hit any more.

In fact, the balance of our relationship had changed to the extent that it now resembled something of a courtship. We had dates. One evening, I changed at the section house and went out for a meal with Philip at a fish restaurant we both liked at Harrow-on-the-Hill. It had been a lovely summer's day and the rosy glow of evening spread a blanket of enchantment over us as we sat at the table. Like two young lovers who had just met, we revelled in each other's company and had a myriad things to talk about.

Then, as with all our finest moments, there came a problem. This time it was me, not Philip who was the cause of concern. Earlier in the day I'd been bitten by an insect and during the meal, Philip commented that my arm looked as if it was gradually being blown up by a pump. By the time the dessert came round, my fingers looked like a bunch of bananas and the lymph glands in my neck and under my arm were like a bunch of grapes. I must have looked like rather an alarming human fruit salad because despite my insistence that all would be well in the morning, Philip made a detour going back and took me into hospital. There I was made to stay, my arm connected to a drip, with Philip sitting by the bedside holding my hand until I slept. The next day, when everything had gone back to normal, I phoned the nick to get a lift back to the section house, then called Philip to let him know I was okay. He was so upset I hadn't asked him to pick me up, that his reaction surprised me. He'd wanted to show me love and care and I'd simply bypassed him without thinking. It was a piece of thoughtlessness I regret to this day because in caring for Philip, I hadn't been perceptive enough to see that he needed to care for me as well.

During the time I was away, a lot changed in our relationship. On occasion we saw Stef. Things had changed so far as that relationship was concerned as well. Everything had settled down and she was happier. She became a mutual friend and at the end of the day, it's silly really, but I found she was a very nice person. She had bought a dress shop and had some beautiful designer stuff. Philip would say, let's see what Stef's got in her shop, and she always had things which were original and different. I bought some lovely clothes there. Obviously, we both thought a lot of Philip and in her own right I found that Stef was an interesting person. Very clever and very shrewd and always strikingly well dressed. I could certainly have done worse than to take a few tips from her.

I went out with a couple of other chaps but found no one who could hold a torch to Philip. They were relationships with no inner fire or spark – nothing to make the heart go bumpity-bump. Nothing to make you wonder what made that person tick – the core of interest that makes you want to know them better.

It was one night in August when I woke up with the most horrendous pain – the worst I've ever had in my life. Twenty times worse than the worst period pain. I thought, stupidly, it must be trapped wind. It felt as if I wanted to expel something. So I staggered down the section house corridors into the toilets and ended up on the floor with my knees up to my chest. Every gland in my body was pouring sweat, saturating everything from my hair to my feet and soaking my dressing-gown. I lay there for an age, unable to move or call out and waiting for the pain to subside. When eventually it did, I got back to my room, put on some dry clothing and collapsed into sleep.

I was at work the next morning, looking deathly pale I was told, but I put off going to the doctor. There was never really time to be ill unless it was an emergency and the pain had eased off. Six weeks later, I still wasn't feeling brilliant and it was Philip who finally talked me into having a check-up. The doctor did various tests, including a smear test and said the results would come through in about a week.

By that time I had gone back to Philip. It was now five years since the shooting and there was enough hope in my heart to believe that we were over the worst part of the trauma and could look forward to a smoother path.

Various people had looked after Philip while I was away. One was his cousin Sarah, the nurse, someone whose company we both enjoyed. We'd watched her grow from a schoolgirl into a qualified nurse and spent many hours talking through the tough times of her training along the way. She was one of the few people who had shown hope and encouragement for our relationship and she had been helped and guided by Philip. But much as she loved him, the strain of her long working hours, travelling backwards and forwards from the hospital then doing all that needed to be done at home, was too much for her.

Then there was a young girl – little more than a schoolgirl really – who had fallen in love with Philip. She stayed for a while, but apart from anything else, she wasn't mature enough to cope and apparently Philip reduced her to tears on more than one occasion. A former girlfriend also came and went. She truly loved Philip but later told me that all he'd wanted to talk about was having me home.

One of my happiest memories of this time was when we were asked to be godparents to 'little Philip', baby son of Hugh and Leslie Connolly. Hugh was a Sergeant instructor at the Hendon

Police Training College and became a close friend of Philip. They wrote an epic poem together and planned to write a full-length play. Little Philip was very special to us both.

Philip's greatest support on the male side came from three stalwarts who couldn't have been more different in personality. Number one was David Griffiths from next door, whose practical help at any hour of the day or night was as reliable as his insight and sense of humour. Russ Dalton, a schoolfriend from the early days who had become a commodity broker in New York, returned to London around this time and was another regular caller who helped to buoy up Philip's spirits. A third was John Spinks who combined the jobs of an ordained clergyman, with police Inspector, and with whom Philip enjoyed long philosophical chats. As far as religion went, Philip was the sort of believer who couldn't bring himself to follow any particular faith. With John Spinks, Philip could debate freely, feeling that his spiritual inclinations were genuinely accepted.

After an evening together, before I went back to him, I'd sometimes stay with Philip. Snuggled up closely to him one night, I fell asleep, waking in the morning to find a poem sellotaped to the dressing-table. I was on early turn so left before Philip was awake, taking the poem to work with me. In it, he compared his life to the *Titanic* – a ship wrecked at sea. The analogy was that I was like a lifeboat disappearing in the distance and that if I passed him by, his ship would sink. I decided not to stay away any longer.

I felt pretty delicate about going home. Putting all my cards on the table and admitting that was where I really wanted to be, was a risk. We still hadn't dealt with the problem of Philip's violence, albeit that he did say he felt he had it under control. From the times we'd spent together while I was away I didn't find it hard to believe. I knew that our relationship would always have its ups and downs but I no longer had the feeling that I would have to watch my step all the time in order to avoid disaster.

It was at the end of September I went back. We were to have three glorious days together. We went shopping in Pinner High Street for the first time and bought a carpet for the living-room: a symbol of stability. We planned to redecorate the house. We did ordinary things like playing Trivial Pursuit, watching television and cooking favourite meals. Above all, we were going to get married and share a wonderful life together.

Philip wanted to offer me every assurance within his power. We talked with truth and honesty about all the subjects that had troubled us. We even discussed my having a type of security blanket in the form of my own flat. If the worst happened and things didn't work out, I'd at least have some kind of financial independence. In the meantime, we planned to rent it out. If, despite everything, there was a parting of the ways, Philip said he would make a cash settlement. Because of the way it had been converted to Philip's needs, we both knew there would be no question of selling the bungalow and halving the proceeds, so under the circumstances it seemed a sensible arrangement. We were talking in terms of a marriage and we felt that putting our future together on a positive, practical track would act as an insurance against disaster.

On the third day, we spent one of the happiest evenings we had ever had together. We went to a restaurant and over dinner talked about when and where we were going to get married. It was an occasion which couldn't be celebrated without a few drinks. We were on a high – at last we had finally come through despite all tribulations.

When we got back, Philip said he knew that we'd finally got it right, so with hearts fit to burst, we had another drink, just to keep the celebration going.

We were lying in bed together, relaxed and clasped in each other's arms when I must have said something wrong because suddenly Philip snapped.

As usual he had taken some painkillers and probably a sleeping pill and all at once his beautiful eyes darkened and he was over that edge where drugs and alcohol met.

He didn't actually hit me, but he made a grab. He raised his fist and if I hadn't seen it coming, I would have been punched in the face.

I dived out of bed, shocked and shaking. Out of arms' length, I shouted, 'You're never going to hit me again. That's the reason I left you, because I was fed up with being hit.'

And he said, 'I'm sorry. I'm sorry, Vessa.'

So I said, 'Well, I want you to think about it because I'm not staying here if you hit me. I'm not staying here any more. Can't you understand, I can't take it.'

I was thinking, I can't believe this is happening – I just can't believe it's happening all over again. Everything we'd talked about over the previous days; all the hopes and plans we'd shared turned into dust before my eyes.

Naked and feeling vulnerable, I grabbed some clothes, and stuffed my things into a bag. I said, 'If you loved me, you wouldn't hit me.'

He said, 'That's not true, unfortunately. Don't go, please let's talk about it.'

I was frightened. Not just about what he might do to me, but because I thought I was close to cracking up. In my head a mocking voice was repeating, 'You thought your dreams were coming true, you thought your dreams were coming true . . .'

As I got to the door he was shouting, 'Don't leave me, *don't leave me*. I'm sorry, Vessa. Vessa, don't leave me.'

For a moment, I paused at the door wanting to go back. I saw Philip lying on his belly, both arms outstretched towards me, screaming, '*Don't leave me like this.*' I closed the door.

I knew that his mood would remain volatile until he went to sleep and woke up in the morning – repentant.

When I got to the section house, he was on the line saying, 'Please, Vessa, please come back. I want to talk to you.'

I said, 'I'm not coming back now. I've had too much to drink. I'll come back tomorrow and we'll talk. In the meantime, think about it.'

The next morning I put on my uniform and went to work. I was expecting Philip to phone, but he didn't.

It was the afternoon when Jan, David Griffiths' mother, phoned me at the police station to say they'd called an ambulance. Jan and Les, her husband, had heard the dogs barking and when they went into the house with the key we'd given them, they found Philip lying on the floor.

Jan couldn't tell me on the phone, but I thought I knew the worst. I went to my Inspector who organized a car and a PC to take me home. Although in no fit state, I wished I'd been driving myself. The police car didn't travel fast enough. Throughout the journey I was saying to myself, 'Wait for me, Philip . . . Don't let it be true.'

As we pulled into the driveway, there was an all too familiar scene: police *and* ambulance – it usually meant one thing. I ran into the house and collided with a police officer I didn't know, who was coming from the bedroom. The dogs were jumping all over me.

The officer said, 'I'm sorry, it's too late,' and refused to let me pass.

I went into the kitchen and threw my handbag across the room. The PC who came with me was trying to comfort me.

I insisted on being allowed to see Philip and after a time, I was let into the bedroom. He lay there naked and undignified on the floor.

Scrawled on the sheets in felt pen were the words, 'Sorry, Vessa'.

I gave him one last kiss and knew he had been dead for some time. Then I went next door to Les and Jan and sat with the dogs huddled close to me in the front room. I don't remember, but David Griffiths was there and he said I kept repeating, 'He promised me he wouldn't do it – he promised me . . .'

I was still in full uniform. The police officer who took me to the house brought the car up to the door and I was smuggled out. By this time the press had started arriving. They were already at the top of the driveway as we went out, so I sat in the car trying to behave as if I was just one of the police officers who had been called to the house.

Chapter 14

When Philip died, it was assumed it was suicide. No one knew exactly what happened, but there was a lot of speculation. I knew one day I'd be asked to put the record straight. A reporter phoned me up at the school where I'm a teacher and I was asked a direct question: 'Do you think PC Olds committed suicide?' And I said, 'No, I don't believe it.'

For this reason: he didn't particularly care whether he lived or died, but he did not deliberately kill himself because he wouldn't have done it that way. He wouldn't have done it to Vanessa without reconciling their friendship. He wouldn't have left things in such a terrible mess. Vanessa was virtually turned out of the house immediately afterwards. Philip left no will or anything. He wouldn't have committed suicide suddenly, just like that, without sorting everything out.

Yes, he'd taken a lot of pills and drink, but he did that every so often. He never counted the risks. Why should he when whatever he took was worth it to be out of the pain and misery he was suffering? You can talk about pain in an abstract manner, but what we're talking about is constant agony. I'm surprised he hadn't gone over the top before. He was in trouble and perhaps he knew it. I think that's why he scrawled what he did on the sheets. I think then, he knew he was going to die.

I saw a lot of him when Vanessa was away. He'd phone

because his plumbing had gone wrong or he'd fallen out of bed or something. He didn't like being alone with the pain. So I'd go in and we'd talk. He'd say, 'I think I've lost Vanessa for good,' and he'd be very unhappy – 'I want her back.' He was usually quite self-protective about his feelings, but on our own together, he did open up a lot.

He said he loved her completely and absolutely and didn't want anyone else. There were other people who loved Philip very much but it wasn't reciprocated. He couldn't manage without Vanessa. He phoned me up to tell me when Vanessa was coming back. He was terribly happy and excited. He spent days getting things ready.

Philip wasn't an easy person, ever. But he could be very funny. The first time I met him he was coming down the drive in his car. It was a beautiful car – silver-blue with a long bonnet: all the gadgetry, a computer and electric windows – a Datsun, 2 plus 2 Targa. It was quite a sight. Then suddenly there was this terrible noise. He'd fallen on the horn trying to get out. His leg had gone into a spasm and he was half in and half out of the car with the horn going for about twenty seconds. I ran out and said, 'Can I help?' He looked at me with this wonderful smile and said 'No, it's all right, this bugger's got horns everywhere.' We were friends from the start.

He had a wicked sense of humour – quite outrageous. My phone went one night and it was Philip to say, 'David, what's the name of the snake in *The Jungle Book*? Think fast because Vanessa's in the loo at the moment and I've got a lot of money riding on the answer.' It was the year of Trivial Pursuit. I said, 'Can't remember, I think it was Khan.' So he said, 'Are you sure?' I said, 'No, I'm not sure. Why don't you look at the back of the card?' He said, 'Look at the back of the card? I couldn't do that. It would be cheating.'

Ten minutes later the phone went again and he said, 'You bloody fool, you got it wrong. It was Nag, not Khan. Don't you know your Kipling?'

So I said, 'Well, don't you . . . ?' He was good company. We liked him a lot.

There was always this tremendous feeling with Philip that you could talk to him about anything. He didn't have to say very much for you to feel he really understood what you were talking about. If I went in and I had a problem, he'd know before I spoke. I think if you went to Philip with a problem of your own, he didn't see it as being another on top of all the ones he had to cope with. He saw it as something where he could be of help. And he certainly was to a lot of people, which is why he is so sorely missed. Oddly enough, we hardly talked about any of his own problems. His main problem was the pain: how much of it he could stand and how to control it.

With the sort of pain he had, you don't say, 'is the pain bad again now?' because the pain's always liable to be bad. Suddenly it tweaks, or a nerve ending jangles. It hovered between tolerable, bad and very, very bad. So when it was very, very bad – intolerable from our point of view – then everything suddenly turned sour. It didn't matter how damn good everything else was, it cast the world into shadow.

Philip could control the pain for a bit, but then suddenly; hell, there it was again. And he'd think inside, 'You stupid idiot for letting yourself be lulled into this, knowing the pain is going to be back. Damn me for being so gullible as to actually feel relaxed and happy. It's all right for everyone else, but not for me, because I'm going to be tortured by this for the rest of my life and it doesn't matter how happy I am with Vanessa, how happy I am with friends; whatever I do, however wonderful life is and whatever beautiful things there are to be seen and done in this world this bloody pain is still going to be there.'

I don't know if it is true, but that is my theory about what happened. I think Philip did get angry with himself. He couldn't bear himself being gullible in any way, or vulnerable, which is what he felt happened if he became relaxed and contented for a brief space of time. On that last night, they'd had a wonderful evening. Vanessa was back home, everything was going to be great and suddenly the demon reappeared, jangling the nerves and giving a repeat performance: Oh you thought I'd left you alone, did you? Well I haven't. And Philip was saying to himself, 'Oh God, how stupid I was to let myself be so damn happy about all this.'

My theory is that when the guard came down he was much more vulnerable than when he kept fighting all the time. And that's when he snapped.

Vanessa is right about the personality change: it was like a Jekyll and Hyde switchover. Everything would be fine, until suddenly there'd be this snap and I'd think, I can't handle this. It was all right for me because I could walk out of the front door. I could say goodnight politely before things got rough. 'Goodnight buddy', he used to call out. When I saw that sudden snap, I was glad I could walk away. Although often I didn't.

It's no good telling Vanessa she shouldn't feel guilty. If I had left him on his own and that had happened, I would feel guilty. It's a natural emotion.

Vanessa did the only thing she could have done. The alternative was for her to have stayed and got bashed up. Then Philip might not have died that night. He would have died the next time, or the next time, or the time after that. She would have been so badly beaten up, she couldn't have walked out of the door. Philip was incredibly strong. Maybe he didn't realize how strong he was. Vanessa had to leave for her self-preservation. That's where the guilt comes in.

Philip died, but it wasn't an ordinary death. You see, he should have died five years ago, after the shooting. That's what he always said. The spinal cord is not designed for the type of abuse Philip's took. If it hadn't been for surgery or medicine, he would have died. Let's face it – that was what nature intended. So he was on extra time. He didn't die before because of Vanessa. She kept him alive.

David Griffiths, next-door neighbour

Coming back from the house, I wiped my face, got out of the car and went into Wembley Police Station. Obviously, everyone there knew what had happened. I was told to go upstairs to the Chief

Superintendent's office where John Spinks came to see me. He was very kind.

I couldn't stay where I was because the press had tracked me down and the police station was already besieged with reporters and phone calls.

My immediate reaction had been to phone my parents and Dad had got into his car at once and driven down to London. As I left with Dad, one of the police officers, I can't remember who, pressed a bottle of Scotch into my hands and said: 'You need this.' I thanked him and replied, 'I intend to make a very big dent in that when I get home.' Then I went off with Dad.

Philip had died sometime in the morning of 1 October. There couldn't be a funeral until the postmortem had been done.

I didn't think that Philip had deliberately ended his life. Part of me thought it was possible; the other part knew how reckless Philip had always been about mixing drugs and drink. Either way, Philip was dead. Either way, I blamed myself for having left him on his own when he had pleaded for me to stay.

After Philip died the days all rolled into one. I had forgotten about the medical tests I had undergone only a week ago. Soon after I arrived at Ross-on-Wye, I received a letter from my doctor saying that abnormal cells had been discovered in the smear test. I didn't give a damn really, but Mum persuaded me to see a specialist. She said he would probably arrange to give me some laser treatment.

The specialist, a top gynaecologist, gave me a pelvic examination and said that it wouldn't be possible for him to give me any laser treatment. According to him, I was pregnant – about three months on he thought.

A bizarre conversation then took place with me saying, 'Oh no I'm not,' and him saying, 'Oh yes you are.' So finally I ended it by saying, 'Not unless it's the immaculate conception, I'm not.'

I was sent for an ultrasound scan and returned to stay with Mum and Dad.

Philip's funeral took place on 9 October. Held at St Andrew's Church in Harrow, it was a service funeral. A magnificent show by public standards. The church was packed with over three hundred police officers of all ranks, led by the Police Commissioner, Sir Kenneth Newman. Outside, the route was lined by recruits and instructors from the Police College at Hendon.

Philip had an escort of motorcycle outriders and beforehand there had been an altercation about which unit should be chosen: the Special Escort Group, whose job this would normally be, or the Traffic Patrol motorcyclists; Philip's old unit. I can't remember who won the day, but I know he would have chuckled about it.

I travelled in the car immediately following Philip and was put at the front of the church with his family. After that, memory blurs the details except that I remember on the coffin were Philip's cap and the Queen's Gallantry Medal on a velvet cushion. A couple of hymns which had a special significance for us both were played at my request: 'Guide Me, O Thou Great Redeemer', and 'Jerusalem'. Philip loved the passion of this rousing hymn. As John Spinks gave the address and talked of Philip's courage in the face of pain and of my love for him, I tensed myself to hold back the tears. I knew it was important to be dignified and that if once I broke down, I might not be able to stop.

I remember wondering what had happened to all Philip's closest friends. Like Mum and Dad and Chris and Tracey, they'd had to jostle for places at the back of the church. Coming out, I saw Shane Colley, one of the guinea pigs at St Vincent's and gave him a big hug. He was standing strapped up in his brace at the back of the church and it meant a lot to see him there.

The service was followed by a private cremation at Ruislip Cemetery. Only close friends and family were there. I laid a single red rose on Philip's coffin, the last symbol of my love.

I'd managed to hold together until the end of the service and then the stiff upper lip wilted as I felt a curtain of grief fall around me – goodbye my love.

It was at the reception afterwards that Philip's mother crossed the room to tell me that I would have to leave our house because it wasn't mine. I would have to collect my personal belongings and hand over the key. Philip had died without making a will and I was told I had no claim to our home.

I was homeless. Not only had I lost Philip but I'd lost everything.

The dogs as well, because now there was nowhere to keep them.

The shockwaves seemed to come from miles away. I was a stranger to Philip's mother; she had been a stranger to her son as well. She knew nothing of our relationship, nothing of all that we'd meant to each other. There had been an unbridgeable gap between mother and son in life, but now blood was thicker than water – that's what they always say.

The state I was in, someone could have chopped off an arm and it wouldn't have hurt. So when I got the result of the scan and learned I had a tumour I thought: let it kill me. But Mum and Dad had other ideas and within four days of the funeral, I was operated on at the Clementine Churchill Hospital in Harrow. They removed a growth the size of a small football. The surgeon told me it had strangulated which accounted for the pain I'd had in the section house a couple of months before. He said it must have been growing for a long time and was amazed I'd managed to walk about as normal.

I'd only noticed that my jeans were getting tight. 'I'm getting fat,' I'd said to Philip, although I hadn't been eating much and I'd never had much of a tummy. I was always tired and felt as though I had perpetual flu. But I didn't pick up on the physical symptoms. All the time I stayed away from Philip, I thought I'd been suffering from stress.

Part of the reason I hadn't been able to think straight was that my hormones were so disrupted they had been whizzing round my body like a taskforce, sending out confused messages. I'd got to the stage where I thought I was having a nervous breakdown, but the really big problem was that my body had gone wrong. All the time I was putting the physical symptoms down to stress, the tumour had been destroying one of my ovaries, causing an emotional reaction.

The specialist had thought the tumour was malignant. I knew there was a query but I felt out of it all by then. I wasn't too bothered about living. If I was going to die, that was fine by me. But it wasn't malignant. It was ungracious not to care. But I didn't.

I was on BUPA so I had a private room, but there was another reason for my isolation: no one was supposed to know where I was.

At the hospital I was booked in under another name. Philip's death had made headline news and the inquest was still to come. The newspapers were linking Philip's death – or suicide as it was said to be – with my flight from the house. Some were saying it was all because I had broken off our engagement. They had that wrong, but the press had scented a sensational story and I couldn't have coped with the questions. There were enough unanswered questions going round and round in my mind as it was.

After I came round from the operation, I heard a familiar sound: the scraping of metal on wood. It was probably just someone else passing in a wheelchair, but I thought it was Philip coming to see me.

The only person I wanted to talk to was Philip. And I'd left that too late. It wasn't just the trauma of his death, I desperately wanted him to know what had happened, because if my illness had been discovered earlier, Philip would have known the reason for the way I behaved. He'd have understood why I was so mixed up and confused and why I let our separation drag on for so long. He'd wanted to show concern and sympathy, and he didn't have the opportunity. I'd always wanted to seem strong and able to cope.

In the last year of his life, Philip had mellowed considerably and I was optimistic that the suicidal impulses were fading. Inevitably I was left with a sense of guilt, but I couldn't harden my heart to thinking: well, I did my best and that's it. I had it on my conscience that if only I hadn't left him that night – if only I had gone back the next morning – Philip might still be here with me. I was filled with guilt.

At the inquest, the coroner returned an open verdict. The cause of death was down as multiple drug and alcohol poisoning, but to record a verdict of suicide, the coroner said he had to be sure that what Philip did was for the sole purpose of taking his own life and neither he nor anyone else could be certain of that. The evidence showed that the amount of alcohol he had consumed – nearly four times the legal limit for driving – could have confused him enough not to realize how many drugs he had taken, and that he had taken a last fatal drink within 30 minutes of his death.

Four drugs had been found in his stomach: Valium, prescribed as a muscle relaxant; Fortagesic, a powerful painkiller; Normisson, a sleeping tablet, and Piriton, an antihistamine which Philip took for aiding sleep.

These were the pills Philip took regularly, probably no more than he'd taken lots of times before. Although none of them agreed with alcohol, he had managed to combine them for years without fatal results. The mixture of drink and drugs Philip habitually took had always been a dangerous combination.

The number of times I had lain awake just to hear if he was breathing normally had been for good reason. I used to hide his pills and pretend he'd run out of Scotch, depending on what sort of state he was in. While I was away, he'd promised to be careful. Maybe the fact that he knew I would be coming back had helped him to keep that promise. On the other hand he might just suddenly have decided he'd had enough.

If I couldn't be sure whether it had been an accident or not, even a court of law wouldn't have had much chance of establishing the truth. In itself, the verdict was ambiguous. Even the 'sorry' note on the sheets had two interpretations: sorry for the row, or sorry for doing what he did?

I gave my evidence in a written statement. I was still convalescing and was spared having to appear in court in person.

I told the truth in as few words as possible: that on the night of Philip's death we had been planning happily for our future but that an argument had blown up and I had left him 'upset and angry'.

After this, I think a lot of people blamed me for Philip's death. No one could have blamed me more than I did myself for leaving him alone, but I still didn't think he had deliberately committed suicide. It was a subject we had discussed many times and I believed that if he had consciously decided to end his own life, he would have done it with dignity – immaculate in his uniform propped up on a cushion. Philip's death, sprawled out on the floor for someone to find him, had no dignity at all.

The pathologist's report had shown that when he died Philip didn't really have any major health problems apart from his disability. He always said that he had the constitution of a rocking horse and he must have been right. Despite the drug and alcohol abuse, there were no signs of liver damage. Apart from the bladder and kidney infections paralysed people are prone to, he had a good constitution and might have looked forward to a reasonably average lifespan.

Yet all along, Philip had constantly talked as though death was around the corner. He always said that if anything happened to him, I would have the house and that he wanted me to live there with the dogs and be happy. While we both knew the whys and wherefores of criminal law, civil law was initially a closed book to us. Philip's understanding of our legal situation was that as I had lived with him for over three years but had not married, I would be recognized as his common-law wife. According to him, I would be a wealthy woman if he died. But I didn't want him to die. I wanted him to live. And when you are trying to encourage somebody to go on living, taking him round to a solicitor's office to make his will, isn't something you're in a hurry to do.

He had said, 'There is only one person who has ever cared for me and that's you. If I die, this is your house. Don't leave it. Fight for it.'

It cost me £2,000 in solicitor's fees to discover that under the intestacy laws, there is no such thing as a common-law wife.

Everything belonged to Philip's next of kin, his mother. And as far as she was concerned, I didn't exist. I realized that at the funeral.

Philip had anticipated that his family might contest his wishes. But since his wishes were not down on paper, signed and sealed by a solicitor, they made little difference. The lack of a piece of paper, the lack of a wedding ring, cost me everything Philip had wanted me to have.

At the time, one of the most painful aspects about being turned out of the house was that I couldn't make a home for the dogs. Woody and Donny had been like children to us. The bungalow had been their home as well.

Now well-grown, Woody and Donny had been staying next door with the Griffiths family until I could find them a permanent home. Most other people either hadn't got the space, or like the Griffithses and my parents, had dogs of their own. In the end, they went to Gus in Norfolk, but my heart broke again when I said goodbye.

After Philip's death, everything seemed to have been taken out of my hands. I was desperate to get back to work, but I made a slow recovery and it was over six months before I was passed fit.

They were hard times, tough times, and when at last I returned to London, I was in a pretty negative frame of mind to go flat hunting. The section house felt like a trap and after the home I'd shared with Philip, nothing else seemed to compare.

On a Sergeant's salary of about £12,000 a year after tax, I had felt relatively well paid. It was 1987 and it wasn't until I found out what even the pokiest flat was going to cost, that I realized how drastically I was going to have to adjust my ideas.

But I didn't. I didn't adjust to anything. Coming back to the same part of the world where everything reminded me of Philip and yet where everything about it was so different, I hit the bottle instead.

While I looked round for somewhere to live I moved in with someone who offered me temporary digs. The offer of help came out of the blue. Ken was a local businessman whose girlfriend was a friend of mine. The four of us had gone to the theatre one evening to see *Mutiny!* shortly before Philip died. Ken's office had been an occasional 'coffee stop' when out at work, but apart from that I hardly knew him.

Ken was an extremely hard-working, self-made businessman who worked long hours and just came home to crash out. It was an immaculate house, which looked as if it was hardly lived in although he would sometimes entertain friends and business contacts there.

Ken had a constantly stocked cocktail cabinet and from the moment I arrived, I started to drink my way through it. During the time I was there, I must have cost him a fortune in Scotch. He was more than generous and I proceeded to drink him out of house and home.

He would come home from work, poor chap, and I'd be sitting there with a glass in my hand, half drunk in his favourite chair. We'd have something to eat and I'd finish the job by getting blind drunk. Then I'd stagger upstairs, blot-faced and fall into bed. On the nights he was out it was the same routine except I didn't eat so got drunk earlier.

I didn't stop to think what it was like for Ken, coming in each night to a virtual stranger who was as depressed and boring as I was. But he was marvellous – too marvellous for his own good. There was no reason for him to be so kind and tolerant. There was no emotional side to our relationship, no involvement of any kind. I just mopped up his drink and support while he tried to pick me up both physically and metaphorically.

I had a couple of flings with other people. But I was drunk when I went out with them, so it was pretty negative. I was probably still drunk when I went off to work in the morning. Not falling over drunk, but I had permanent hangovers and everything was a chore.

I still had to go to my doctor for check-ups and one day I told him how I was drinking so much and feeling quite desperate and that it had got to the stage where I was contemplating suicide.

In fact, it was more than just contemplation. I was planning my suicide down to the last detail. I'd decided to go out in style. I knew exactly what I was going to wear. Out of several ballgowns Philip had bought me, I had made the appropriate choice: a beautiful Frank Usher dress – black.

Oh yes, I was a bit dramatic. I was going to have my hair cut and styled, my nails were going to be painted; my legs and armpits newly shaved. I would make sure my skin was smooth, and I would wear my usual light make-up.

Because of being in the police force, I'd seen a lot of suicides and attempted suicides. Often people get it wrong, end up with brain damage or permanent kidney or stomach damage, so afterwards their lives are worse than if they had never attempted to kill themselves. I didn't want to finish up a vegetable. I would just have been a burden on my parents. I wanted to make sure I did it properly, so I'd collected the necessary pills – Valium and some others – from previous prescriptions. I already had the knowledge of what was a lethal dose. Mixed with plenty of alcohol, I knew the cocktail would work.

There was another point I had considered. When people die, they relax their bodily functions, so I was going to see that I wouldn't be in too much of a mess. First, I was going to use suppositories to make sure my bowels were empty and while I could still stand, I would go to the loo and empty my bladder. Suicide is a messy business and after what I'd seen, I didn't want to offend whoever had to deal with it.

I'd written letters to Mum and Dad. I wanted to explain the reason why I was committing suicide. I wrote them both long letters but, reduced to a few words I said that the reason I was so unhappy was because I'd lost Philip and I felt there was no purpose to my life any more.

Everything was planned except where I was going to do it, because I felt it would be too unkind to commit suicide in the house of this chap who had done nothing other than offer me help and support.

The thought of the perfect suicide kept me going for a while. At least, ironically, there was something positive about it. It was a time when every plan seemed to go wrong.

I had been negotiating for a flat, but there was a problem over the survey and the deal fell through. When I asked Ken if it was all right to stay on for a bit while I found another place, without too much hesitation he said, 'Well no, I honestly don't think it is.'

Because it came from someone who was okay – he wasn't being horrible – it was the biggest kick in the pants I could have had at the time. Originally, Ken had only invited me to stay for a few weeks while I found my feet. But it turned into four or five months in which I had taken over his home completely and disrupted his life.

It was a shock. It was a kick up the bum. But I thought no, he doesn't owe you anything. Why should he be landed with the drunken, miserable cow I had become? So I packed my bags and went.

By turning me out, Ken had done me a favour. It made me look at myself. It made me think: I'm not going to live like this – I'm not going to be that sort of person. But it wasn't an overnight change.

I went to live in some vacant police property over in Hanwell. It was really run down and grotty. Bare floorboards, wallpaper on some walls and not on others. It was damp, almost derelict, and on a main road with a pub across the way from which blasts of noise issued at night. There was no cooker so I made do with a toaster and an electric kettle.

The place was half furnished with some of the things I rescued from the bungalow. I had our old 1930s bedroom suite, which had now developed chronic woodworm, the TV Philip had bought me and the carpet we'd bought together as a symbol of stability, just before he died. I also had a dryer and a washing machine which packed up after a few weeks.

I couldn't grumble. The place matched my state of mind. I thought, this is what you deserve and this is what you've got. If ever there was an ideal setting for a suicide, this was it.

The place was due to be upgraded and as an emergency case, I was lucky to have been offered anything at all. The only thing that stopped me from doing what I wanted to do was that Jenny, a girl from the section house, had joined me. By now, nobody thought it was a good idea for me to be on my own. I was grateful to her for wanting to be there with me because, after all, I was a limited companion and I felt it was unfair on her to be landed with my problems. I stayed at Hanwell for about six months through autumn and winter, not bothering to improve the surroundings. At Christmas I put up a few bits of tinsel around the place in case anyone called.

There were friends I could talk to like Jenny and everyone at work was wonderfully supportive. Without their help and understanding, I probably wouldn't be here at all. But I couldn't really tell anyone the full story because I wouldn't have known where to begin. Also, I still felt that some people blamed me for Philip's death. I didn't want to talk about it. So I went into my shell.

For two years the world went dark. If I wasn't going to do anything dramatic, I was still badly bitten by the 'if only' syndrome.

If only I hadn't left Philip that night. That was the chief thing. I don't think I will ever be able to cast off the guilt. Not because I don't want to, but because to think I might have been responsible for someone's death is a bit difficult. If I knew positively whether Philip had intended to kill himself I might be able to come to terms with it. Not knowing is the hard thing.

Then, with hindsight, there was the matter of whether or not I did the right thing for Philip by being so accepting, so centred on him and his problems. Everything radiated from him and maybe in the end, that was an additional burden on him. It's true you can only do your best and be what you are, but I didn't do my best all of the time. There was the affair I had with Ian when I was thinking of leaving Philip. I judged myself on that.

I was still drinking in excess, but not as much as before. I knew that I needed to talk to somebody and when my doctor recommended a counsellor, I thought it was a good idea.

The counsellor said she could refer me to an alcoholic clinic, or I could work it through with her. I decided to stay with her because this wasn't another punch the pillow operation. She didn't judge or criticize; she just made me answer my own questions. I talked and talked and talked.

The self-destructive stage lasted longer than the drinking. It wasn't something I could talk about to friends because to tell someone other than a professional counsellor that you want to bump yourself off only frightens and embarrasses them.

At one point, I was driving up to Mum and Dad's and a stray urge came over me to drive my car into the central crash barrier on the motorway. The thought that I might involve an innocent person, let alone not be effective in killing me outright, put a stop to that one.

I came to realize that in wanting to commit suicide, I had been looking at a mirror image in which Philip's streak of reckless determination was not reflected in myself.

The job and life with Philip had never given me time to think. When I did, torrents of pain and guilt came pouring out.

Then I decided to stop feeling sorry for myself. The fact that I had a responsibility to get up and go to work proved to be the string round the parcel. Although going to the station and dealing with other people's problems didn't do anything to solve my own problems, it stopped me from falling apart.

The force Chief Medical Officer had restricted my duties to allow me time to recuperate from my operation and I had gone back to work on a nine-to-five basis. The trouble was, that as soon as work was finished I was lost again.

I went out with other people when they asked me and for a time I had a boyfriend. He was the tall, dark, handsome, rugby-playing type I once thought I would marry until I fell in love with someone who was dark and handsome, non-sporty and disabled. Doug was kind and gentle and considering I wasn't the most fun person to be with, he was remarkably patient.

I met his parents and he met mine but whenever we went anywhere all I'd do was talk about Philip and eventually he couldn't live with Philip's ghost any longer. In comparison with the bond I had with Philip, no relationship stood much of a chance.

Because the love between us hadn't been physical love in the usual sense, I'd felt it was based on a love for the real person, very special and unique.

When we were together at our best, in tune with each other and with life, we always said we were two halves of the same person. And perhaps because they were paid for in hours of darkness and pain, the shining hours we spent together had the vivid quality I thought I could never find again.

Because of the intensity of our relationship, we would always have had our ups and downs. I loved a man of fiery temperament, but who for much of the time could be soft, loving and gentle – a man of enormous excitement, danger and charm.

For Philip, pain had become a complex, living part of himself. It was the pain inside the pain I had wanted so much to heal.

I'm not discounting the fact that we had yet to solve the main problem of our relationship. The violence in it still troubles me. The nearest we came to identifying the reason for it was in Dayton. Post-trauma syndrome following the shooting, the unbearable frustration of living under the restrictions of constant pain, or the chemical reactions of pills and alcohol? Philip was never treated for it, so I'll never really know.

Every police officer sees violence in their everyday jobs and it's a problem which isn't easily answered. A lot of the domestic violence takes place under the influence of drink. But alcohol can't be the complete answer because, fortunately, it doesn't work that way on everyone.

Having been in violent situations myself, I feel I have gained a greater understanding of the victims – not by telling them what they ought to do, but by telling them what they can do; what is possible under the law. I think it's helped me to understand the type of

215

situation where a woman comes into the station having been badly assaulted by her husband or partner. Often you've seen that woman before. Every time she comes in she's in a worse state than the time before and eventually she reaches a breaking point where she decides to sue him for assault. Then a few days later, when her face doesn't hurt quite so much and the memory has faded a little bit, she withdraws the allegation. Her husband never goes to court and is never dealt with for the offences he has committed.

I would look at someone like her and think: you stupid woman. What on earth is the matter with you – how can you let anyone do that to you? And now I know, and knowing has helped with understanding and with asking the right questions, communicating effectively with the people involved.

I can tell the woman concerned about the support services and if she turns round and says, 'Right, I've had enough, I'm going to take him to court and see it through,' then she can be helped. Once it has all gone through the system, she can pick up the pieces and, with luck, make something of her life.

Soon after moving into a small flat in Harrow I went back to normal shift work. Once again I was doing earlies, lates and nights with its eight-hourly routine and the changeover system peculiar to the police force which means that you're finishing one shift at 10 p.m. and you're back on duty at 6 a.m. the next day.

Even when I was walking the beat in the city, I'd savoured those moments on the early shift when the sun came up over the empty streets, when a cat disturbed a piece of paper which rolled at your feet and you felt a stirring of the soul as the birds started up in the trees.

I'd lost all that. I'd often thought that terribly wrecked people don't notice their surroundings. It was a long time before I could drive into work and respond to the sun lighting up a magnificent sky, the shape and colour of a beautiful tree or the moonlight frosting the dew.

For me, the natural world has always been the great restorative. At first, after Philip died and I was staying with Mum and Dad at the cottage, I was haunted by a vision of walking with Philip through long-grassed meadows, hand in hand, or sheltering under the leaves of the trees – a dream of Philip walking with a spring in his step, able to feel the ground beneath his feet. A dream that was never to be.

But of the three healing forces – time, work and the natural world – work remained the best therapy.

We all moan about the bad things, but I wouldn't have another job. The work tests your ability to deal with people, the challenge that drew me in the first place.

Much of our work is not about crime at all and by no means all our time is spent going out on the streets and arresting people. We deal with the mentally ill found wandering the streets. We look after kids who are lost or missing and those who have been abused. We deal with accidents and people who simply need help. Some of the people we encounter are disturbed and aggressive; some are just old or confused. A lot of time and patience goes into finding the right place for them and seeing that they get the appropriate care.

Although the caring side of the profession attracted me, it would be wrong to give a diluted impression of the job. There is a certain amount of social work about it, but the type of active policing required today increasingly makes it a far tougher job.

I have stood alongside colleagues at scenes of public disorder while things are being thrown at the thin blue line. I have been assaulted, kicked and thumped by male and female alike. All types of threats are made. Once, a man who was wielding an axe announced his intention of chopping my head off my shoulders – I believed him too. In my time, I've received many bumps, cuts and bruises, scrambling over walls and fences chasing after suspects. Once, I arrested a man shortly after he'd murdered his wife with his bare hands.

The whole question of decision-making – of the few moments when you have to decide whether someone who may be a witness or suspected of a crime is willing to have a reasonable talk, or if he's out of control and going to deck you – is a matter of split-second thinking. Your decision may later have to be justified in a court of law where hours of questioning and pondering will go towards deciding whether what you did was right or wrong.

When the chips are down, I have no qualms about achieving my purpose which at times can seem like a very tall order: namely the keeping of law and order.

Assessing human nature is still the greatest fascination of the work. I could do this job for another fifteen years and still be surprised by the fact that a proven criminal, convicted of the darkest deeds, looks no different from anyone else. If anything, he may be more prepossessing than average. The human face can hide so much and appearances count for so little.

Protecting our democracy is just part of the job, but it is a job in which the riots and violent confrontations of recent years have put many of my colleagues in hospital. They are today's unsung heroes and heroines.

When Philip was shot, the public responded on a tide of support and goodwill, yet he was just one of the many to prove that despite the blue serge and silver buttons, we are human beings like anyone else.

My job, the broad communication with the outside world, kept me going through the dark days and it was that I missed most when Philip and I were in America. I am happy to be part of the police force and I think it gives more to the public than they realize.

Although in the Metropolitan Police Service, women only number about twelve and a half per cent of the force, it's a job in which nowadays they can reach a senior rank. Hopefully, with their femininity intact, their sensitivity alive and their experience of value. So there's no saying if I'll get through, but at some point I intend to pick up the challenge and take my exams for promotion to the rank of Inspector.

Philip would have had a good laugh because the senior officers were often the butt of his jokes. But I think if I ever get there, he would have been quite proud as well.

Colleagues in the police service have a habit of being blunt, and more than one person has told me that by now I should be meeting other people and getting myself fixed up and sorted out. I know what they're saying, but the answer is – hold on a second – I still don't feel like that. One day I will, I know I will, but I don't think it's something you can set out to plan.

In the span of a lifetime, the five and a half years I spent with Philip is not very long. But those years were so packed with vivid experiences, they were like a lifespan.

Although meant in the best possible way for the best possible reasons, the advice that time is the greatest healer, is probably the truest, though the least comforting. The worst thing about grief is the length of time it lasts. Shock gives way to agony, agony turns to grief and time goes on for ever and ever.

So I don't feel selfish in taking time, because there is no time limit on grief.

Epilogue

It has been said you should never go back. But in the spring of 1989, I did go back – to Dayton. With me I took a strange cargo. This was Philip's white motorcycle helmet bearing on the front the crest of the Metropolitan Police. Philip had strong and sentimental feelings about it. At home it had been kept in the sitting-room, a talisman of what he had been and what in moments of fantasy he imagined becoming again: a cop on a motorcycle, mobile and free.

I had taken it from the house before it was closed to me. Like a nomad with one treasured possession, I had kept it with me wherever I was staying. Now it was time to find an appropriate resting place.

After Philip's death, I had received a lot of wonderful letters from the public and the friends we had made in America. Among the condolences, there had been questions concerning the manner of Philip's death that I found hard to answer. Had it really been suicide? Where had I been? No one had been able to reach me.

I knew that what needed explaining ought to be done in person. Knowing it would be painful, I wrote back asking them to be patient. Being broke was one excuse for the delay. At the time my finances wouldn't have seen me to the Isle of Wight for a weekend, let alone the United States for a stay of ten days.

Getting myself together and saving enough money took nearly three years. On the plane, this time on my own, flying economy class instead of first class as I had with Philip and treated like a VIP, I began to have apprehensions. I wondered about the reception I would get from our American friends – those who had made our last visit feel like coming home. It was always Philip first and foremost. I was the afterthought, the invisible woman.

Perhaps this time the invisible woman would materialize as an embarrassment, a reminder of uncomfortable memories best forgotten.

Any doubts about American warmth and hospitality soon vanished when I landed in New York where Chuck Bennett was waiting to greet me with open arms and to guide me through customs and immigration. With him were two cheerful friends: John Mathews, a senator's aide, and David Attrill, ex-chief of the British Royalty and Diplomatic Protection Department. David was on his way back to the UK, so we waited in the airport bar until his flight was called. Swapping police stories with these men in business suits, I felt relaxed and at home.

I was staying in an apartment lent to me by Angie, the redoubtable owner of P.J. Reilly's, the most famous police bar in town. Talking into the small hours with Angie, I realized that she had made a place for Philip in her heart. Chuck seemed more reluctant to talk about Philip. Dearest Chuck, the picture of the big burly American cop with the heart of gold – perhaps he was afraid of the outcome – that I'd break down or something. Or maybe he felt uneasy about the manner of Philip's death. I could understand that for some people, the possibility that it might have been suicide made it a difficult subject to handle.

While in New York, I attended a Police Representatives' meeting – all about police officers' moans. In New York, the police have the press in the same building and on this occasion they were looking for possibilities of curbing the information given to the press without infringing their constitutional rights to freedom of information. Always a tricky problem.

This was all discussed over coffee and Danish and it became apparent that this could have been a Met meeting with similar problems and gripes.

Afterwards, I went over to the Drugs Enforcement Agency building for another meeting, this time about charitable fund-raising. Their latest drive was to send a group of disabled and terminally ill children on a holiday to Florida. All the arrangements had been made by these case–hardened chaps who were at pains to think of every detail the children would need on their holiday. Our police force also do a tremendous amount of fund-raising for all sorts of different charities. There is always some sort of sponsored activity on behalf of charity going on and every police station always has a collection box in the canteen.

Next day I went to the Police Academy Museum where Chuck was waiting, having given the place the usual recce – usual that is for anyone in the Diplomatic Protection Squad. It's second nature for them to flush out whoever is at the top. I saw crack for the first time, so now have a better idea of the drug; the way it's carried and used and its effects. In its original form it looks like a rather gritty marble chip – dirty white in colour. Bits are then chopped off, heated up and smoked. The effects are to give a very quick, incredible high, followed by an equally quick let-down. Cocaine-based, crack can also produce over the top and sometimes sexually violent behaviour. It's easy to make and process, relatively cheap and has become the fashion among young drug users. It is also very difficult to detect because when carried in a trouser pocket for instance, it can be mistaken for innocuous bits of grit.

The following day, Chuck took me to La Guardia Airport to see me off to Dayton. Skip and June were waiting to greet me together with Lew and Joyce Poe. Lew is an Airport Police Lieutenant so I was treated to a VIP welcome at the newly renovated airport. Philip and I had spent a lot of time with Lew and Joyce on our last trip to Dayton, enjoying barbecues at their house where the password was 'Wild Turkey', or as Philip had renamed it, 'Old Gobbler', in honour of the quantities of local bourbon he had consumed there.

Lew, a Vietnam War veteran had taken the news of Philip's death to heart. In a quiet evening set aside to take them through what had happened, I realized for the first time, that in shutting others out, there had been some selfishness in my grief.

A tough, immaculately dressed, long-serving cop, Lew gives the impression he's not easily messed with, but he still found it hard to talk about Philip without a crack in his voice. He 'really loved the guy', he said and it was evident that he had difficulty handling Philip's actions on the night he died.

As I was going home, he showed me a couple of marks made on the doorstep by Philip's wheelchair. Though everything in his house is normally kept immaculate, Lew told me he was going to leave them to honour Philip's memory.

Throughout the evening, I felt that Philip had been with us, sitting in his usual corner by the fireplace with a glass of Old Gobbler in his hand.

How much better he could have explained things.

I wished that more of Philip's art of communication had rubbed off on me. This came home to me again when I visited Skip and June. But by the time we had stayed up until the early hours of the morning, drink had loosened our tongues and allowed the emotions to flow. On the day Philip died, Interpol had tracked them down to a bowling alley and given them the news, and almost immediately they were pursued by the press for more details. Philip's sudden death had shattered them. They too, needed to share their grief and frustration and I found that they had almost as much to tell me as I had to tell them.

It appeared that after I had left home during our period of trial separation, Skip and June had been receiving two or three phone calls a week from Philip. These were usually late at night and sometimes lasted nearly two hours at a time. On occasion Philip had talked about suicide and, of course, such a threat had caused deep anxiety, not to mention the anger and frustration they had felt about being unable to do anything except just listen. I learned that not all the calls had been totally negative, but on occasion they had interrupted card or dinner-parties and like good friends, they had talked to him, trying to help as best they could.

One of Philip's plans had been that if things didn't work out between us, he was going to come out to the US to live. He hoped to teach at the Dayton Police Academy or otherwise find a useful job with the Police Department in Dayton. He told Skip and June that he was prepared to wait a year for me to come back and if I didn't he would put his plans into action.

As well as the close bond he had with Skip, Philip had also had a special relationship with June. He had plainly admired and adored her and it was great to hear that she had stood no nonsense from him, putting him in his place when necessary and not allowing his many tried-and-tested charms to sway her judgement when making some of his wilder statements. When he talked about suicide, how much did he mean it and was it just the pills and the alcohol talking? June could only tell him not to take any more.

I listened with admiration. June had been a nurse before her media career. Her behaviour and way of talking is very like my mother and she, too, could always get the best out of Philip.

This couple who had found such an affinity with Philip, spent several heartbreaking hours talking about him and putting the circumstances of his death into a different light. I was shocked as much by what I was learning about the telephone calls, as the intensity of Skip and June's emotions. I felt unhappy about the way I had treated them both, leaving them in the dark until then about what had really happened when Philip died. At the same time I began to realize what a tightly bound barcel of mixed grief and guilt sudden death leaves behind. Also the fact that guilt is probably the most useless of all the emotions.

If the time comes for me to grieve again, I hope I will not forget this lesson: unloose the ties with those who also grieve.

Before I went to bed that night, I cleaned Philip's helmet. Not having known of his plans to go to America, I realized my instincts had been right in bringing it back to Dayton.

A few days later, Dayton held its National Police Memorial Day. This is the day when once a year all across the US police departments and sheriffs' offices honour their dead. I learned that in the previous year, fifty-seven police officers had died in the line of duty, with many more injured every year.

James Newby, the Chief of Police gave an address in which the name of Philip Olds, QGM was added to their roll of honour and I felt proud to have been invited to the ceremony.

The American flag was lowered and the 'Last Post' played. In the emotionally heightened atmosphere of the service, I felt profoundly moved that these police officers so many miles from home saw fit to honour among their dead a British bobby whom they had regarded as a friend and colleague.

After the ceremony, I presented Philip's helmet together with the goggles and leather gloves he had worn in those far-off days when he rode free. Seeing his proud belongings on display at the Police

Academy in Dayton, I felt that I had laid Philip's ghost to rest at last.

Here in Britain, there is thankfully nothing like the same death toll among our police officers; some twenty-five in ten years according to official statistics. But nor do we do them the same honour. In the years since Philip died, much brave blood has been spilt on our streets and those who serve the public in the name of justice bear the scars mentally and physically.

When Philip and I were in Dayton, we had been shocked to hear the news about PC Keith Blakelock who had been stabbed to death in the Broadwater Farm riots of 1985. Unarmed, he had been escorting firemen when killed, yet there seemed to be less evidence of the public sympathy shown at the time of Philip's shooting only a few years before.

While in Dayton, I visited Wright State University. I'd met with several surprises on this return trip and none more so than to find the Petrofsky project disbanded and the laboratory closed down. The project work designed to keep bones and muscles in healthy condition was now part of the mainstream orthopaedics department, and for the time being at least, Petrofsky had abandoned further research on the electronic walking system.

I learned that Jerry had left the university after internal political wranglings. His grants had been cut and he was now in California where he had set up a private health clinic for paraplegics taking with him Jennifer Smith, one of his former patients.

Some of the research work initiated by Petrofsky continues at Dayton, but nothing further had come of his plans to develop the implant which was to have been the nucleus of the final stage of the combined walking system.

Nan Davies had been dancing in her brace when we left Dayton but I learned that none of the original guinea pigs was now using the electronic power pack which Philip had brought back with him to Britain. It had needed further development to turn it into a practical proposition and Philip, like the other guinea pigs, had abandoned it when he got home.

My appointment with John Gillen, Philip's former GP, at the university campus began with him warning me that according to medical ethics, he couldn't discuss Philip's medical record without written permission from his family. Had I been married to Philip, it would have been different, as with so many other things. However, I had the satisfaction of being able to tell Dr Gillen that after going cold turkey when his Pethidine supply from England ran out, Philip never again returned to hard drugs. The knock-on effect had been a redoubled intake of alcohol, a drug not on prescription.

Dr Gillen went on to explain that in the United States, it would not have been normal practice to take a patient off a hard drug without a gradual weaning process.

With that wonderful power called hindsight, I was beginning to realize how much of Philip's suffering had gone unrecognized.

Less evident than the physical suffering had been his psychological pain – the pain in his soul that had gone untreated and the secrets of which were now shrouded away under the seal of medical ethics, ironically enough at the Pain Clinic in Dayton. Whatever the psychological reasoning, Philip had simply been driven mad by pain and shock. Not clinically or permanently mad, but enough to be responsible for his Jekyll and Hyde behaviour.

Coming back to the Wright State University Medical Center again was a reminder of what a contrast this glamorous place was compared to the old-fashioned hospitals we have at home. Dayton was typical of all the up-to-date medical centres I'd seen in the US, usually of the standard of our private hospitals and clinics, and in some cases a lot better.

Without Philip, going round the familiar campus again was like taking part in a scene re-enacted many times before but with the main player missing. And without Petrofsky, the man who had provided the original driving force, the dynamics of the situation had changed irrevocably. Wright State University had become a ghost town to me.

My last quest was to find out what had become of the original guinea pigs who had shared that first wonderful surge of optimism with Philip. At the Marriott Hotel, now restaffed from top to bottom and a reminder of the transient nature of both hotel staff and guests, I had a small and rather forlorn re-union party. I met Debbie Hendershott and José Almeyda, the two main lab technicians from the original project. Both had come to England to help set up the WALK fund and together with the other technicians, had formed the nucleus of the Petrofsky team. With Jerry now in California and the project they had all been so closely involved with disbanded, they were a disappointed bunch.

They were genuinely sad to hear about Philip's death. To them he had been more than just another patient and how I wished I could have been the bearer of good news rather than having to deliver this final, crushing epitaph.

I heard that Nan Davies was now married with two children. If anyone had been marked out to take their rightful place in the world, it had been her. Another guinea pig made good was Gene Lieber who had continued to use the keep-fit technology and was looking, according to recent reports, as strong and muscled as a footballer.

I had also learned while I was there that Jerry Petrofsky was planning to open a clinic in Dayton, called the First Steps Foundation. Money was being raised for this Nautilus-type gym where patients suffering from a variety of disabilities could use the electronic technology to keep their bones and muscles fit so that they would be in good shape should the promised 'cure' come along. A strong hope for the future is the continuing research on a system which will enable the patient to stand and walk at the touch of a button. This work is, however, extremely expensive to develop and the mechanical method offered by the brace Philip brought back to Britain is still the current limit of expectation.

It seemed that the jungle drums had been working and on my last Sunday in Dayton, Sue Steele drove all the way down from Washington DC to see me. Quite something for a quadriplegic. While taking part in the Petrofsky project, Sue had been studying Communications at the University and was now with an international news channel, travelling the world as an independent person.

Sue's record since leaving the Petrofsky project had been impressive. After it closed down she graduated and went to England where she worked for a charity in London.

It was in England that she started to understand something of Philip's frustrations.

'There were times', she told me, 'when I got so depressed about the way people treated me. Don't get me wrong, I don't mean I was treated unkindly in any way – in fact the problem was more a sort of smothering. What I found there was a basic inability for people to accept my independence.'

Sue was only echoing what Philip and I had discovered for ourselves. In Britain there is plenty of sympathy and willing help for the disabled. But they would rather do things for themselves without having to ask for help. In America there seem to be more ramps and lowered kerbs, and planning and forethought have made life very much happier for many people in wheelchairs.

For Sue the aggravation had been increased when she came to London and found that the offices she was working in near Euston station were virtually inaccessible without help. As the offices were a charity for the disabled, she saw the situation as ironic. Doing what no one had apparently contemplated before, Sue went straight to the source of the problem and tried to persuade the Local Authority to install ramps. The fact that for years the disabled had gained access to the place only through the good offices of the able-bodied, had led to complacency. 'No one has complained before, so there can't be a problem', was the all too familiar attitude.

While in London, Sue won a small victory for the disabled: after she left ramps were fitted.

Reactions to a person in a wheelchair vary from pity, curiosity, to the desire to turn away. As I found from being with Philip, people can almost kill you trying to be helpful, but to a disabled person the big clue to friendliness is whether you acknowledge the person first or the disability. Most people, in trying to be helpful, would talk over Philip's head to me. It's a small thing, but every time a disabled person is talked down to or ignored as though incapable of rational conversation, it's bound to come as a put-down.

This didn't apply so much to Philip personally because he was usually the one everyone wanted to meet. With Philip no longer a symbol for the disabled, a lot had changed. What I hadn't quite realized was that although research and fund-raising still goes on, without the spotlight of publicity which focused on someone like Philip, public interest and support drifts off into other directions. Charities, like so many other things, go in fashions.

On the other hand, the everyday frustrations all disabled people experience have hardly changed at all. Philip would make light of these whenever possible, but sometimes we would come up against a problem of bureaucracy gone mad which was more or less intractable.

An example was Philip's annual appointment at Acton Town Hall. Although probably the best-known disabled person in the country at the time, he was required to report to the medical officers once a year in order to prove that he was disabled so that he could claim his disability pension. Philip had no objection to keeping this appointment provided he could get into the place, but with goodness knows how many steps up to the front door there was no way he could have got into the Town Hall for the medical examination unless two of the lads, usually Mick Rawson and another police colleague, carried him bodily up the steps.

What was a disabled person on their own expected to do – call out, 'I'm on the pavement, come and examine me'? Or, as Philip once suggested to the medical officers, come down the chimney?

The fact that Philip hated fuss and generally chose to make a joke of such situations, doesn't alter the fact that there are some stupid anomalies in attitudes towards the disabled that wouldn't really take an awful lot of thought to straighten out. Going to vote in Pinner was another example, with a flight of steps up to the polling station and the official pencil with which to mark your ballot paper hung frustratingly out of reach. I could cite a hundred and more other examples where the advertised 'facilities for the disabled' are often about as much use as a chocolate teapot.

In the US, Philip was generally more relaxed, due as much to the new-found freedom of access as to the fact that attitudes to the disabled were more frank and open. In America, he felt like a human being in society, not stared at because he had the cheek to go where only the able-bodied were usually seen.

To have dreamed of an American future, in his heart Philip must have felt the burdens lighten when he arrived on US soil. Only after talking to Sue Steele did I realize how much, as a disabled person, she appreciated her lifestyle in the States.

If I'd had any doubts about my quest – wondering why I had returned to the US and what I'd hoped to hear or find, I felt on my arrival home that the ghost I was laying to rest had led me along the right paths.

The satisfaction I have in telling this story is the hope that Philip's struggles will not be forgotten. As someone who shocked a nation by angrily labelling himself 'the Cripple of the Year', he showed the darker side of disablement. And by not disguising the frustrations, he showed the value of a fighting spirit.

Through no wish of his own, Philip became the acceptable face of disablement, the standard bearer who, in gaining the support of the media, led the disabled back into society to take their rightful place alongside the able-bodied. For five and a half years, everything that Philip said and did was news. By not self-consciously banging the drum or taking up a militant stance, he attracted enormous support for the cause of the disabled.

One other quality, initially recognized by Sir David English at that first fateful meeting in Buckingham Palace, was Philip's spirit of bloody-minded determination, which ultimately gained him his place on the Petrofsky project and acted as an inspiration to so many other people, not only the disabled.

Philip gained satisfaction from the feeling that the research he pioneered would eventually help others, if not himself. That research still has a long way to go. But it has not been abandoned. At St Anne's Ward at St Vincent's Hospital in Northwood Hills, the work of the WALK fund continues, enabling many disabled people to walk again.

Philip lost his own battle, but the struggle for practical solutions and a better understanding for people like him goes on.

Philip was fiery, multi-faceted and tough. Like the solitaire engagement ring he gave me, which I wear to this day.